For Sale
By Owner:
Sell Your House, Condo or Townhouse and Save

· · · · ·

By the Editors of Socrates

SOCRATES™
**KNOW HOW TO DO MORE
AND SAVE**

Socrates Media, LLC
227 West Monroe, Suite 500
Chicago, IL 60606
www.socrates.com

Special discounts on bulk quantities of Socrates books and products are available to corporations, professional associations and other organizations. For details, contact our Special Sales Department at 800.378.2659.

ISBN 1-59546-240-6

Printing number 10 9 8 7 6 5 4 3 2 1

For Sale By Owner:

Sell Your House, Condo or Townhouse and Save

· · · · ·

Special acknowledgment to the following:

Tracy Schutzman, Managing Editor; Steven Pincich, Associate Editor; Chip Butzko, Encouragement Press, Production; Jeannie Staats, Product Manager; Peri Hughes, Editor; Alison Somilleda, Copy Editor; Kristen Grant, Production Associate; Edgewater Editorial Services, Inc.

Get the most out of
For Sale By Owner:
Sell Your House, Condo or Townhouse and Save

The enclosed CD contains a read-only version of this book, the Socrates Real Estate dictionary as well as instructions to link to the dedicated resource section of Socrates.com:

www.socrates.com/books/ForSaleByOwner.aspx.

Use the seven-digit registration code provided on the CD to register your purchase at Socrates.com. Once registered, you will have access to more than $100 worth of FREE forms, checklists and additional material.

Your registration also provides you with special discounts on selected Socrates products, designed to save you time and money with your Personal, Business and Real Estate matters.

Table of Contents

· · · · ·

1
. . . . . .
Advice to
Sellers

Whether you are buying a larger home or downsizing, starting a new job out of state or just ready for a change, you have made the decision to sell, and you are ready to move. The decision to sell your home means you have many things to consider before putting your home up for sale.

Your home must be in ready-to-show condition at all times. Be prepared for the buyer or agent to give you only 5 minutes' notice to show your home. Also, be aware that you may be displaced several times each week for showings and during open houses. If you work from home, will the interruptions be a problem? Pets can also be a problem when trying to keep a home in ready-to-show condition. Prospective buyers may be allergic to dander or afraid of large pets. It is important to make arrangements for pets to be caged or removed from the home during showings.

There is also the possibility that your home may take longer to sell than you anticipated, which means you may face the unpleasant possibility of owning two homes at the same time.

The reality is that selling your home can be a stressful time for the entire family and an emotionally draining experience for the seller. Selling a home dedication, hard work, an objective view of the entire process and patience.

"My best advice to sellers is to first price your home right then stick with your price. Do not get impatient and repeatedly drop your price. Second, it is important to market your property. Marketing is what attracts buyers to your home. Third, be available to show the home. Finally, maintain your home. So often, sellers will stop all maintenance on a home hoping for a quick sale. If a sale does not happen quickly, the home may begin to look neglected."

Robert Picarellaro
Prello Realty
Flat Fee Realty Company

Before putting your home up for sale, consider these factors:

- What are your reasons for selling?
- Do you have a specific timeline you need to follow, such as school registration?

- Do you need to sell your home before you can move or buy another home?
- Is an illness or other health factor precipitating the move?
- Can you devote the time needed to market actively and show your home?
- Can you be objective enough to receive feedback from potential buyers?

There are as many good reasons to enlist the services of a real estate agent to sell your home as there are for you to try to sell it by owner. This chapter will cover the advantages and disadvantages of selling your home or investment property by owner versus listing with an agent. The next few pages will explore the reasons why it might be a good idea to enlist the help of an agent to sell your home.

Who Needs a Real Estate Agent?

Anyone who is remotely interested in and capable of doing so should try to sell their home by owner first. However, not everyone who has the capability of doing it can. The National Association of Realtors® (NAR) reports that on average, it takes a for sale by owner (FSBO) property twice as long to sell as it would for a real estate agent to sell a property.

Financial reversals, divorce, illness, the threat of foreclosure or losing a job may all precipitate a quick sale. Keep in mind, however, that there are no assurances that a real estate agent will guarantee a quick sale. He or she is facing the same market conditions and competition that you would be facing as a FSBO.

There are often mitigating factors for why a seller would enlist the help of a real estate agent, including:

In a Hurry to Sell

Perhaps you have stumbled across the perfect home in the perfect area at a perfect price. Not wanting to risk losing this opportunity, you submitted an offer to purchase and your offer was accepted. Now you must sell your current home quickly in order to complete the purchase of your new home. Other reasons you may need a quick sale include finalizing a divorce, concentrating on overcoming an illness or facing the loss of a job.

Regardless of the reasons, the clock is ticking. The entire deal hinges on the sale of your current home. Most real estate agents have a built-in support system that allows them to jump right in to list and begin marketing your home. They have the resources to quickly create a marketing brochure, get the home listed on the Multiple Listing Service® (MLS), advertise open houses and promote your property to other agents through their office network.

Job Transfer

Transferring employees from one location to another is common practice in corporate America. To help employees sell their homes quickly and become settled in the new area, companies who regularly transfer employees often have an existing relationship with a realty company that specializes in handling relocations. The realty company will continue to show the seller's home even after the seller has moved and will help with the purchase of a new home on the other end. Knowing that the job of selling the old home is being taken care of by someone else gives the employee peace of mind to concentrate on the new job.

Moving out of State

Out-of-state moves require long-term planning and a lot of coordination. If you have not sold your home before moving day, it will be very difficult to market the property, schedule showings and show the property from another state. Listing an empty property with a real estate agent ensures that the agent will continue to market the property and schedule showings. He or she also can work on your behalf at the closing.

Inability to Show Your Home

If you are a frequent traveler or work far from home, showing your home in the evening or only on weekends will limit the number of potential buyers viewing it. Out-of-town buyers may schedule only a short visit to an area to find their next home. In this instance, every minute counts. Buyers and real estate agents often will schedule appointments to view only the homes that will fit into their schedule during the day. If you are not available to show the home due to your travel or work schedule, you may be placed on the B list.

Making the B List

Homes that are placed on the B list are those that require an agent to make an appointment to show. Homes relegated to the B list miss the first few rounds of showings because scheduling appointments to see these homes takes more planning. If the buyer does not find a home that meets his or her needs in the first few days, the agent goes back to the backup list of properties and plans showings of the homes without lock boxes or whose instructions require an appointment by calling the listing agent. You want to avoid becoming the 10th, 15th or 20th home a buyer looks at during a weekend tour. The more homes a buyer sees the more tiring the process becomes. Your home will become indistinguishable from all the rest and may be forgotten altogether.

Why Use a Real Estate Agent?

We have already explored a number of reasons why listing with an agent to sell your home may be necessary. Other reasons for considering using an agent to help sell your home include:

Property That Is Unique

Unique homes need to attract unique buyers. Perhaps your property has an unconventional design or layout, or the home may appear smaller in size from the outside. Attracting the right buyer may be a challenge. A real estate agent with a network of agents will talk up your property to bring more buyers to see your home while communicating its uniqueness and eliminating surprise as a factor when potential buyers walk through the front door.

Property That Is Difficult to Find

Property that is located on a busier street will be seen more by potential buyers as well as friends of potential buyers. Secluded properties will not be easily seen by people driving by and will need more promotional efforts to reach the same amount of potential buyers as a home located on a busy street would.

Emotions Get in the Way

Your home is an extension of you. If you grew up in the home, you may find it difficult to hear candid comments about it, or you may not be able to negotiate objectively with a prospective buyer. An agent can filter these by removing personal comments about your property and sticking to reasonable and objective comments, which will prevent emotions from getting in the way of negotiations.

What Do Real Estate Agents Really Offer?

The typical real estate office may be a small office consisting of local agents, or it may be part of a national company and have 150 or more agents working from it. Agents work every day with buyers who are buying and selling properties. In many cases, real estate is their full-time profession. The typical agent provides knowledge and services that the average seller may not have.

Expertise of the Market

Agents have the experience of many transactions to draw from. They have data at their disposal that most sellers do not, such as the original listing price, the sold price as well as information on comparable homes that have sold in the area. They may have first-hand knowledge of the condition of recently sold homes in your area that may be different than yours. In addition, agents will learn what features of your home to highlight and the most effective way to present your home to prospective buyers.

Instant Support System

The combined efforts of many may be drawn upon to find prospective buyers for your home. Experience shows that if a home listed by the realty company is available, the agent from the office will show the properties listed with his or her office before other homes listed with competing offices. That is also true with FSBO properties. Very few real estate agents—perhaps as few as 1 percent—will take the time to call the owner of an FSBO property to inquire if the owner is cooperating with real estate agents. Most sellers are willing to give a 2 to 3 percent commission to buyers' agents to close a sale.

Marketing Commitment

An agent will outline a complete marketing plan to promote your property. The plan may include Internet exposure, including virtual or guided tours, weekly or monthly ads in a local paper, scheduling open houses and producing an informational sales brochure that provides key information and highlights the features of your home. With each listing, your home will automatically be included in the MLS, which may be viewed by anyone at **www.realtor.com**.

Maximum Exposure

An office of 150 agents may have 10 to 15 agents at any one time working with a prequalified buyer. These agents will happily recommend the properties listed by their agency before showing properties listed with other agencies or for sale by owner—giving your property first crack at being seen by their clients.

Negotiation of Deals

The agent verifies that the buyer is qualified to purchase the property and handles all price negotiations between the buyer and the seller. He or she also completes the paperwork and makes sure the property status is changed to reflect the acceptance of a contract.

Neutrality

A real estate agent views each property as a possible transaction and does not have the same emotional ties to the property as the seller.

The Multiple Listing Service

The MLS will post only those properties that are listed for sale with an agent or flat-fee listing service that is a member of the NAR. Individual sellers of a property cannot get their home information posted on the MLS without first signing with a flat-fee listing company or agent.

Disadvantages to Using an Agent

Ask a number of homeowners what they think of real estate agents and you will receive a variety of responses. They are either loved or just tolerated. One person may have great admiration and praise for real estate agents and their ability to sell property. This is likely someone who had a very good experience working with one. Another may harbor contempt for real estate agents and the profession as a whole. Obviously, this is someone who did not have a good experience working with one. Like any profession, some individuals are excellent representations of their industry while others are not.

Nobody Knows Your Home Like You Do

As a result, nobody will work as hard at selling your home as you will. Real estate agents who show your home during an open house for your listing agent may not be familiar with your area or may not be able to answer important questions about recent upgrades made to the home or about the schools serving the neighborhood.

High Commission Rates

Services offered and performed by the agent may not be worth the amount of commission paid to the agent upon sale of your home. A homeowner selling a $750,000 home listed through a real estate agent will pay between $37,500 and $52,500 in sales commission when the home sells. In a sellers' market, the home may sell quickly–perhaps as quickly as 3 weeks–and the seller may feel the agent did not have to do much to earn the commission.

The amount of commission paid to a real estate agent has remained the same for decades, even as home prices have climbed. A homeowner whose house sold for $35,000 in 1970 using the same 6 percent commission average paid $2,100 in commission, which is split between the listing agent and the buyer's agent. If the small home today sells for $250,000 the listing agent and buyer's agent split a $15,000 commission.

Agent Slow to Produce a Sale

On the flip side, if the home is slow to sell, the buyer may question how hard the real estate agent is working to secure a sale. To keep interest alive on a slower moving home, the agent may ask the seller to lower the sale price of the property. If your home is priced at $500,000, at a 6 percent commission rate, the real estate agent's commission will be $30,000. If the home is not selling quickly and the agent suggests that you drop the price of the home $25,000, you will be forfeiting $25,000 of profit whereas the agents will give up only $1,500 in commission.

Feedback May Be Difficult to Receive from Buyer

Your real estate agent will try to follow up with the real estate agents who showed the home to their clients and open house attendees to get their feedback. Many open house attendees will leave only an e-mail address, phone number or no contact information at all, making follow-up difficult. Following up with a showing agent can also prove to be a challenge. If your listing agent is able to make follow-up contact, he or she may be paraphrasing the contact's comments. Be on the lookout for repeated descriptive vocabulary such as quirky, odd or weird, which in fact may be your agent's words and not the buyer's actual comments.

Limited Number of Open Houses

An agent may be unwilling to hold an open house every weekend or on Saturdays, preferring instead to hold only one or two each month. Some realty companies have rules governing when a real estate agent can hold an open house or how many open houses can be scheduled for a property each month. For example, one local office of a national real estate agency will not allow agents to hold open houses during a holiday weekend. While everyone is entitled to enjoy a holiday weekend, real estate agents have reported that open houses conducted during Labor Day weekend have been heavily attended by out-of-town buyers who wanted to spend the long weekend looking at as many homes as possible.

Unfamiliarity with Your Neighborhood

Agents, other than the listing agent, who show your home during an open house may not be familiar with the features of the home or the surrounding neighborhood. The real estate agent may not know that the garbage is picked up twice a week, the village plows the sidewalk after each snow, the public library bookmobile visits your neighborhood each Friday between 4 and 6 p.m., summer camp programs and concerts are held at the park each summer or that there are little league and softball teams. Unless a buyer is familiar with the neighborhood, which many will not be, he or she may never learn about these programs during a showing.

Bad or Shady Reputation

A buyer may avoid looking at your home as a result of a bad experience with the listing agent or the agent's company. The same holds true with an agent who is difficult to work with or abrasive toward fellow real estate agents. The agent may alienate other agents and cause them to avoid showing homes listed with him or her.

"We live in a unique neighborhood in which our school district and mail delivery are provided by one city while all other services—police, fire, permits, etc—are provided by another. During a Sunday open house, our agent was unable to come, so she arranged to have an agent from her office show the house. When the agent arrived, we asked if he was familiar with our neighborhood. His response was that he had heard about the neighborhood but did not know much about it. We were disappointed by the agent's lack of familiarity with our area's uniqueness. Needless to say, we began to question how effectively the real estate company could sell our home if their agents were not knowledgeable about the uniqueness (and advantages) of our neighborhood."

Steven Michaels
FSBO Homeowner

A real estate agent may have killed a deal if he or she is hard to get along with or difficult to work with. That is something you would not know about in advance, but that kind of attitude can make other real estate agents not want to show your agent's listings. It is only natural to avoid working with someone who has a bad attitude or a condescending nature.

Agents who are rude, arrogant and difficult to work with will not have as many showings as agents who are cooperative and enthusiastic. A buyer's agent will see a certain listing agent's name on the multiple listing sheet and immediately take that home out of his or her showing schedule. Just because an agent is a top producer in your area does not guarantee that he or she has the respect of other agents in town. The only way to guard against this is to check out the reputation of the agent you are thinking about hiring or getting personal referrals.

Before signing with a real estate agent, always ask for references and do your homework. Inquire about how long on average it takes him or her to sell a home. What is the office policy about real estate agents attending agent open houses? Are they mandatory or optional?

> **Example**
>
> A property was listed with a real estate company for 4 months and only a handful of showings had been scheduled. The owners canceled the listing and signed with another local real estate company. The move paid off. The night the new sign went in the ground the seller heard a knock on the door. A couple was standing at the front door. They told the owner that they had been interested in looking at the house since the day it was listed but had such a bad experience with the first real estate company that they refused to look at any house listed by that company. As soon as the listing changed to another real estate company, the buyers were interested in seeing the house and wanted to know if they could make an appointment for a showing. They loved it and immediately put in an offer to buy. The home sold the next day.

Selling by Owner

Millions of homeowners have successfully sold their homes by owner and when asked will tell you they would do it again. Whatever your reasons for selling your home FSBO–the possibility of saving the 6 percent commission, a bad experience with a real estate agent during your last home sale or knowing you can do a better job selling your home than anyone else–selling your home by owner can be challenging and rewarding.

"About 50 percent of our customers have sold properties by owner in the past. The other half is new to the FSBO market and are selling their first house on their own. What we have experienced, however, is that newbies to the market are smarter and better informed sellers than ever before. They have done their research and know what to expect."

Professional Realtor
Flat Fee Realty Company

Advantages

Choosing to sell your property by owner takes dedication and commitment to secure a sale. It also provides you with a sense of control and accomplishment. Other advantages to selling by owner include:

Reaping Greater Profits

Selling without a real estate agent and saving a 5 to 7 percent commission adds up to bigger profits from the sale of the property.

You Know Your Home and Neighborhood Best

There are details about your home and neighborhood that you know but a real estate agent may not, such as how often the trash is collected, how the schools compare to surrounding districts, special events conducted in the neighborhood, the number of children living on the block, etc.

Knowledge of Updates and Key Features of Home

A real estate agent will not know all the details of the home, such as when a room addition was added, whether the pipes are copper or steel, when the electrical wiring was updated or the age of the roof.

Greater Price Flexibility during Negotiations

Working with real estate agents as go-betweens may take several days of back-and-forth negotiations before the details are all worked out. Talking directly with a buyer provides face-to-face negotiations and produces a faster outcome.

You Set the Schedule

You can arrange showings around your schedule. A potential buyer parked in front of your house may call you from a cell phone asking to see the house. If listed with a real estate agent, the buyer or previewing agent would first call the listing office and schedule the appointment, the listing office would contact you to relay the appointment time and then call the buyer or real estate agent back to confirm the appointment. On rare occurrences, the listing office may miscommunicate an appointment time and provide the seller with the wrong showing time or date, causing confusion for everyone.

Disadvantages

Selling by owner presents certain challenges that may require you to work harder to get a sale. Since you are only one individual and do not have a network of agents talking up your home, your marketing efforts may attract fewer qualified buyers, even if you are doing an excellent job of marketing and advertising your own home. Other disadvantages to selling by owner include:

Higher Costs

The cost of advertising to market your property may run into thousands of dollars and could cut into your profit from the sale. Typical advertising costs include creating a full-color brochure, placing classified and space ads, listing with a flat-fee MLS realty company, and postage and printing for postcards. There is no formula for how much money to spend on advertising in relation to the price of the home, but a good rule of thumb to follow is to estimate that you will spend $500 per month for marketing, ad placement, brochure creation and printing and classified advertising.

Attracting More Lookers than Buyers

Real estate agents often prequalify their clients and show only the homes clients are qualified to buy. FSBO sellers are not privy to the same privileged information as real estate agents and do not know if a potential buyer has been prequalified by a lender or if he or she is just a curious looker.

Holding Open Houses

Scheduling, advertising and showing your own open houses week after week is a big time commitment and can be emotionally unfulfilling. Some weeks you may have 18 groups through, and other weeks you may have only one person show during the entire 3 hours.

Placing ads in the local papers, preparing the home, making arrangements for the kids and pets to be somewhere else, conducting tours for the buyers that actually show up–or worst-case scenario, no one shows–then following up a few days later with each prospective buyer can be exhausting, not to mention time consuming.

FSBO-Phobic Buyers

Some buyers are uncomfortable buying homes directly from the seller and will only buy a home listed with a real estate agent.

Emotional Attachment Hinders Sale

Selling the home you grew up in or raised your children in or selling mom or dad's home can stir up many emotions that can unknowingly sabotage a sale.

Agents vs. Brokers

Real estate professionals go by many different titles: agent, broker, Realtor® and realtist. The different titles reflect the varying experience and certification levels of a sales associate. All real estate agents and sales agents are licensed and regulated by the state.

While the title distinction may not matter to you, it is important that agents who bring potential buyers to see your home are licensed real estate professionals. The various titles a real estate professional might include on a business card are defined below.

GRI Accreditation

The Graduate Realtor® Institute (GRI) symbol is the mark that indicates that a real estate professional has made the commitment to providing a high level of professional services by securing a strong educational foundation. Realtors with the GRI designation are highly trained in many areas of real estate to serve and protect their clients better. Agents with the GRI distinction have graduated from the GRI program, which includes 90 hours of coursework on topics from marketing and servicing listed properties to real estate law.

Broker

To become a real estate broker, an agent must take additional GRI accredited classes, have a specified amount of experience in the field and pass another exam. A real estate broker has the right to open, run and own a real estate office and to work independently of an office. Most brokers also have agents working for them and are entitled to a portion of their commissions.

Realtor®

A Realtor® is an agent or broker who is a member of the NAR and likely a member of his or her local real estate board. Members of NAR have access to the MLS and usually have more advanced training than agents.

Agent

A real estate agent is someone who started out as a sales agent, completed the required number of hours and classes and passed a written examination to become an agent. This person is licensed to negotiate and transact the sale of real estate on behalf of the property owner. A real estate agent must pass a certification course and state examination covering the legal aspects of real property and must pass a background check in order to become licensed. A real estate agent also must satisfy a certain number of hours of additional training each year in order to maintain this license.

Realtist

A realtist is the designation given to an agent or an agent who is a member of the National Association of Real Estate Brokers (NAREB). The NAREB is the oldest minority national trade association comprised primarily of African-American real estate agents, brokers, property managers, appraisers, developers, mortgage brokers and bankers dedicated to enhancing the economic advancement of its members and the minority and underserved communities it serves.

Nonrealtor Real Estate Agents

Real estate licenses are issued by the state; therefore, a real estate agent is not required to be a member of the local MLS board to become a licensed agent. An example of why a real estate agent may not need to belong to the local MLS is if he or she is a dominant agent in the sale and buying of property in a specific niche area such as condominium buildings or a specific neighborhood. As the most knowledgeable agent in the area, he or she may have such a stronghold that he or she represents almost every sale and purchase in the area.

Alternative Realty Companies

Alternative Agents

While traditional real estate agents may offer full service to clients, there are more options available today to a real estate savvy seller. Alternative agents offer similar services to traditional agents but with fewer frills. While a traditional agent may offer marketing services and conduct open houses, alternative agents may provide sellers with only the tools to market their own home and conduct their own showings and open houses, thus saving the seller thousands in real estate commissions.

Discount Real Estate Agents

An alternative to listing with a traditional real estate company is the discount real estate agent. A discount agent is a licensed real estate agent who may agree to sell your home at a reduced commission rate—well below the standard 5 to 7 percent. The amount of marketing produced to sell your home is minimal. It is usually limited to a listing sheet description and a listing on the MLS.

A discount agent may provide minimal services to the seller, essentially leaving it up to the seller to make follow-up calls, to show the home, to negotiate a contract and to counter offers. The discount agent may charge up to 5 percent of the sale price, half of which is paid to the buyer's agent. Then the discount agent will split the remaining amount–minus any extra fees–with the seller. This is where the seller must be careful in tracking the extra charges the agent may charge back. The discount agent will put a price tag on every service he or she provides. Usually a minimum number of services are included in the deal, but if the agent performs any services outside the scope of the agreement, you will be charged a pay-as-you-go fee that will be deducted from your portion of the commission.

For example, a discount brokerage firm charges between 1 and 4 percent off the commission refund for each service it performs for the client. If you ask an agent to place a follow-up call to a prospective buyer, the company may charge you 1 percent for each call, which will be deducted from your portion of the commission after the home sells. If a seller is not careful, the a la carte fees charged by a discount agent may add up to almost as much as a full-service realty company.

The disadvantages to listing with a discount agent include the fact that other agents may avoid showing your home because of a reduced commission rate. The buyer's agent will receive a 1.5 percent earned commission check compared to the standard 2.5 to 3 percent commission amount he or she would receive from the sale of the property.

A discount agent offers similar services as a flat-fee listing company, but that is where the similarity ends. A flat-fee listing service offers limited services to the seller without any frills or additional services built in.

Flat-Fee Listing Services

The most recent nontraditional listing option available to sellers is the flat-fee listing company. This option offers sellers a listing on the MLS for a specified time period or until the property is sold, a For Sale sign with the realty's name and a place to put the seller's phone number, and online promotions with three or four local and national real estate services.

Whereas a discount agent will charge the seller the discounted commission upon sale of the home and then give back to the seller one-half of his or her share of the sale, the flat-fee listing service does not charge a commission. At the time of signing, the seller must declare how much commission he or she is willing to

"Sellers must be aware that not all flat-fee listing agencies are created equal. Remember, this is a segment of the industry that is still in its infancy. Each flat-fee listing agency is trying to carve out its niche. Case in point, some flat-fee services advertise that they will list your home on the MLS for free. The catch is that they require the seller to purchase a new title insurance policy (usually from them) before they will list the home on the MLS. In many instances, the flat-fee listing agency makes more money from the commission of the insurance policy than they would have if they charged the seller the standard $399 fee."

Professional Realtor
Flat Fee Realty Company

give to a buyer's agent if the agent presents an offer to purchase the property on behalf of the buyer. The flat-fee listing company gets only their one-time fee.

Since the flat-fee listing company is a licensed real estate company, any offer received from the buyer's agent is first presented to the listing company, who will then present it to the seller. Depending on the comfort level of the seller, the listing office may conduct all negotiations with the buyer's agent, or the seller may conduct his or her own negotiations once the initial offer has been received. However, if a buyer who is not working with a real estate agent presents an offer to buy, the seller may accept the offer directly and negotiate the sale price with the buyer and the sale will be commission free.

Each state has enacted its own laws. Recently, the NAR has teamed up with several states to prevent Realtors from offering clients a limited service fee. States with a minimum service requirement are: Missouri, Texas, Illinois, Oklahoma, Iowa, Utah, Florida and Alabama. Check your state laws before signing an agreement.

An example of a flat-fee listing agreement might read as follows:

Marketing Agreement

Flat Fee Realty Group, LLC (Listing Agent) and _____ (Seller), by their signatures below, agree to the following terms and conditions with regard to Seller's efforts to list for sale the property at: _____ _____ (the Property) together with its undivided interest in any common elements and accumulated reserves of the building (if applicable).

1. Agent's Listing

Seller does hereby give Listing Agent a right to list the Property for a period of 1 year commencing _____, 20_____ and terminating at midnight of _____, 20_____ ("the Listing Period") and the authority to promote and advertise the Property for a list price of _____ Dollars ($_____) and to offer a buyer's agent commission of _____ Dollars ($_____) to be paid by Seller directly to buyer's agent (if one exists). Buyer's agent shall receive the entire commission noted above at closing less a $150 transaction processing fee. Seller reserves the right to sell the property him or herself and will pay no commission (or transaction processing fee) if Seller's sole efforts procure a bona fide offer without the assistance of a buyer's agent.

2. Agent's Services

In consideration of a flat-fee payment of $499 payable upon activation of the listing within the MLS, Listing Agent hereby agrees to provide Seller the following for the period noted above:

a. a listing on the MLS for the listing period noted above;

b. a showcased listing on **www.realtor.com** (includes up to six photos to be supplied by Seller);

c. a listing on real estate Web sites linked to the MLS;

d. free changes to the listing during the listing period;

e. free and unlimited open house notifications on the MLS and **www.realtor.com**;

f. access to selling documents such as a state's disclosure forms and sales contracts;

g. a professional yard sign with space for your phone number (provided upon request);

     _____ Check here to receive your free yard sign

h. one free exterior photo to be included on the MLS and Web sites (provided upon request);

     _____ Check here to request a photo be taken of your property

i. if an agent represents the buyer, the Listing Agent will: accept delivery of and present to Seller offers and counteroffers within 24 hours of receipt, assist Seller in developing, communicating and presenting counteroffers and answer Seller's questions relating to offers and/or counteroffers.

3. Additional Products

The following items are available for purchase at an additional cost. Please indicate which products (if any) you wish to purchase by placing a check mark in the appropriate box:

_____ Virtual Tour Package $129
(Includes five different 360-degree views and five still photos. The tour will be posted to the MLS Web site as well as **www.realtor.com** and **www.chicagotribune.com**.)

_____ Combination Lock Box $39

_____ Enhanced Internet Listing $29
(Includes up to five additional photos, up to 2,500 characters of expanded text description and unlimited open house advertising on **www.chicagotribune.com**. Photos to be provided by Seller.)

4. Seller's Option to Terminate Agent's Listing

At any time during the Listing Period and at no cost, Seller may request that Agent's right to list the Property be terminated. To be valid, such request must be submitted to Listing Agent via fax or e-mail. Once validly requested, such termination shall be effective within 48 hours.

5. Agent's Option to Terminate Listing

At any time during the Listing Period, Agent may terminate this Listing Agreement for nonpayment or if Seller has caused Agent to incur any MLS fines (see paragraph 6(a)) or legal fees due to claims arising out of Seller's misrepresentations or negligence.

6. Seller's Duties and Obligations

Seller hereby agrees that during the Listing Period, Seller shall:

a. Communicate to Listing Agent via fax or e-mail acceptance of any offer on said property within 24 hours of acceptance. Seller must provide information on any contingencies, buyer's agent name and firm (if applicable), purchase price and closing date. Failure to fully comply with above notification requirements may result in MLS related fines (currently $100 per occurrence).

b. Reimburse Agent, within 10 business days of Agent's written notice, for any MLS-related fines incurred due to Seller's failure to timely communicate to Listing Agent all events and actions noted above.

c. Pay cooperating agent the commission noted in Paragraph 1 of this agreement if the property is sold to any purchaser represented by a licensed real estate agent during the term of this agreement or within 90 days of its cancellation or expiration. However, Seller shall not be obligated to pay cooperating agent commission if Seller has entered into a valid written listing agreement with another licensed real estate agent.

d. Schedule and perform all showings of the Property and open houses without agent's assistance.

e. Make all legally required disclosures to any prospective buyer or buyer's agent, including but not limited to disclosing all known information on lead-based paint hazards to any prospective buyer and/or buyer's agent.

f. Not violate any fair housing laws, including but not limited to refusing to sell to any person because of race, color, religion, national origin, sex, ancestry, age, marital status, familial status, handicap, military status or sexual orientation.

g. Not execute a sales contract that requires Agent to hold earnest money.

7. Seller's Warranty of Authority to Sell the Property

Seller warrants that Seller is authorized to execute this Agreement and to deal with and on behalf of the Property as herein provided.

8. Indemnification

Seller hereby indemnifies and holds Agent and Agent's agents harmless from any and all disputes, litigation, judgments, costs and legal fees incurred in the defense of same, arising from Seller's negligence, Seller's failure to timely supply Agent with required changes to MLS as detailed in paragraph 6(a) of this Agreement, misrepresentations by Seller or incorrect information supplied by Seller to Agent or any third party.

9. Resolution of Disputes Arising out of This Agreement

The parties agree that any dispute, controversy or claim arising out of or relating to this Listing Agreement or any breach thereof by either party shall be resolved by arbitration in accordance with the Code of Ethics and Arbitration Manual of the NAR.

10. Agent's Limitation of Liability

In the event that a dispute arises between Seller and Agent or any purchaser of the Property or said purchaser's agent regarding any acts or omissions, negligence or other liability, Seller agrees to hold Agent harmless from said liability. Should any court, mediator, arbitrator or alternative dispute resolution tribunal find Agent liable, Agent hereby expressly limits its liability under this Agreement to _____ _____ Dollars ($_____) as liquidated damages with respect to liability in the listing and sale of the Property.

11. Nature of Agent's Services to Be Provided to Seller

Seller understands that Agent is solely in the business of providing real estate brokerage services and does not provide its clients, including Seller, legal advice of any kind. For all legal advice pertaining to the Property, this Agreement, execution of a sales contract and/or closing of the Property, Seller hereby agrees to consult an attorney or attorneys, who shall not be Agent's employee or agent, and provide all necessary documents and disclosures to said attorney(s).

Agreed to by Seller(s):

_____   _____
Print Name   Print Name

_____   _____
Signature   Signature

_____   _____
Date   Date

Agreed to by Agent:

_____
Signature

Credit Card Information

(Please complete information below if paying by credit card. Your information is received by a secured fax and will remain confidential.)

Card Type: Visa® MasterCard® American Express® Discover®

Card No.: _____

Name on Card: _____

Billing Address (include city, state and zip code):

_____

_____

_____

Card Expiration Date: _____ Total Charge: $_____

Can You Negotiate with Agents for a Better Deal?

Traditional agents charge between 5 and 7 percent of the sale price of the listed property. In some parts of the country, the standard commission is 5 percent where in others it is no less than 7 percent. Negotiating the best deal with your real estate agent could save you thousands.

Commission Rate	Listing Price	Commission Amount
5 percent	$500,000	$25,000
6 percent	$500,000	$30,000
7 percent	$500,000	$35,000

The commission rate is calculated based on the recorded sale price of the property. If the listing price is $500,000, but the agreed upon sale price is $475,000, the real estate agent earns a 6 percent commission of $28,500. If the seller gives the buyer a painting or roofing allowance of $5,000 at closing, the commission paid will not change since the commission amount is based on the recorded sale price of the property.

You may be able to negotiate a better commission rate if there is a current shortage of listings often referred to as a sellers' market. In a buyers' market, real estate agents may not be as willing to negotiate a lesser rate because they know that it may take more time and advertising to sell your home.

Discount agents may provide limited sales assistance such as providing For Sale signs. The seller is required to show the home, run open houses and agent's open houses, and create and place advertising to attract buyers. Depending on the agreement structure, the flat-fee listing service may provide buyer follow-up, advertising and/or cooperative advertising opportunities, and handle the negotiations and contract signing. A flat-fee listing company is usually a member of the NAR and has the opportunity to list your home on the MLS.

Keep in mind that if you negotiate a lower commission rate with your listing agent, the buyer's agent may be reluctant to show a prospective buyer a home that has a lower than standard commission rate or is being offered for sale by owner without a commission paid to the buyer's agent.

It is to the homeowner's benefit to pay a 2.5 or 3 percent commission to the buyer's agent as an incentive to show your home to prospective buyers. Include commission information on your brochure and advertisements.

Be Aware
Absent of any written notice of a commission rate, courts in some states have held the homeowner liable for the full (5 to 6 percent) commission even though no listing agreement was signed or terms discussed.

Advantages of Working with a Discount Agent

The advantages of working with a discount agent include:

- You save at least half of the commission you would be spending if listed with a full-service real estate company. You only pay between 2.5 and 3 percent. You decide how much to pay the buyer's agent for bringing you the offer. If you sell the home on your own to a buyer who is not represented by an agent, there is no commission to pay.

- Even if a buyer not represented by a real estate agent presents an offer, the discount agent may still handle all price negotiations the same as your listing agent would. They handle all the paperwork and simply present you with a contract to sign at no extra charge.

- You gain MLS exposure that would not be possible if selling as an FSBO. In fact, you will gain more national exposure with a discount agent than you would with a full-service agency. Most discount agents will list your home on up to five Internet sites popular with buyers. A full-service listing agency will only post one picture of your home and promote the property through the MLS, **www.realtor.com** and periodically through local publications.

- Like a full-service real estate agent, the discount agent will provide all disclosure forms you will need to present to the buyers, such as the Lead-Based Paint Disclosure form or a standardized Real Estate Full Disclosure form.

Disadvantages of Working with a Discount Agent

- Traditional full-service agents may not show homes listed by a discount agent. Especially if the discount agent is located outside your area, traditional agents will avoid showing your home because you are not represented by a local real estate agent.

- Read the fine print carefully. Hidden fees, due at the time of closing, may be embedded deep within the contract. Be particularly wary of any flat rate fees tacked onto the sale of the home. Make sure that the contract reads that any commissions are due at the time of closing, not at the time of receipt of a signed contract. This protects you in the event that a purchase agreement falls apart before settlement.

Interview agents before you decide to sell a home yourself. Interviewing a minimum of three agents from competing agencies will provide you with information about the amount of marketing each agent will coordinate.

Selecting the right agent to list your home requires time and thorough investigating. The right agent is not necessarily your friend, neighbor or a relative. The right agent is someone you are comfortable with and can trust. Inquire with neighbors and friends in the neighborhood if there is a preferred neighborhood real estate agent—someone who has sold a number of homes in your area and has a good reputation.

Check References

During the real estate agent interview session, request a list of references from satisfied home sellers in your neighborhood. Contact each reference and ask them what he or she thought of the agent who listed his or her home. Inquire how long the home was for sale and how negotiations were handled. Were they satisfied with the amount of advertising the real estate agent coordinated? Were there any communication problems or disagreements? How thorough was the comparative marketing analysis (CMA), and how quickly did the agent ask the seller to lower the price?

Create a list of at least a dozen questions and compare answers before selecting a real estate agent.

Different Types of Listing Agreements

There are as many types of listing agreements as there are situations in which each agreement is used. From the flexible open listing agreement, which favors the seller, to the more standard exclusive right to sell agreement, you need to understand each type of agreement before signing on the dotted line.

Exclusive Right to Sell

This is the most common type of agreement and the most favorable to your agent. During the term of the agreement, the listing agent is entitled to a commission no matter who sells the property—even if you, the homeowner, find your own buyer. For example, if you know of a buyer that is interested in buying your home, some agents may allow you to include a clause that will exempt you from paying the commission if the named individual purchases the home while listed with the agent. The agent may limit the exclusion to up to five names. Often, this type of contract will also have a clause included. The clause states that the agent is entitled to the full commission between 6 months and up to 1 year after the listing expires, if a buyer who looked at the home during the period the home was listed with the agent comes back to purchase the home.

Some contracts take it a step further. They state that the real estate agent is entitled to the full commission between 6 months and up to 1 year after the listing expires, if a buyer who looked at the home during the period the home was listed with the agent comes back to purchase the home, even if the seller signs with another agent in the meantime. Read all fine print carefully.

Some contracts go even further and prohibit a seller from signing with another agency for a full year after the expiration of the original listing contract. A restrictive contract like this will stop you from trying to list your home with another agent for a full year even if the original listing agreement contract expired before a buyer was found.

A typical right to sell agreement may look like the following:

Exclusive Agreement
To Sell Real Estate

For and in consideration of your services to be rendered in listing for sale and in undertaking to sell or find a purchaser for the property hereinafter described, the parties understand and agree that this is an exclusive listing to sell the real estate located at:_____

_____, together with

the following improvements and fixtures:_____

_____

_____

_____.

The minimum selling price of the property shall be_____Dollars ($_____),
to be payable on the following terms:_____

_____

_____

_____.

You are authorized to accept and hold a deposit in the amount of_____Dollars
($_____) as a deposit and to apply such deposit on the purchase price.

If said property is sold, traded or in any other way disposed of either by us or by anyone else within the time specified in this listing, it is agreed to and understood that you shall receive from the sale or trade of said property as your commission _____ percent (_____%) of the purchase price. Should said property be sold or traded within _____ days after expiration of this listing agreement to a purchaser with whom you have been negotiating for the sale or trade of the property, the said commission shall be due and payable on demand.

We agree to furnish a certificate of title showing a good and merchantable title of record, and further agree to convey by good and sufficient warranty deed or guaranteed title on payment in full.

This listing contract shall continue until midnight of _____, 20____.

Date: _____

_____
Owner

_____
Owner

I accept this listing and agree to act promptly and diligently to procure a buyer for said property.

Date: _____

_____
Agent

Exclusive Agency

An exclusive agency agreement is similar to an exclusive listing except you may sell the property yourself without paying the commission. Only one agent is assigned as the exclusive listing agent. You only pay the agent if the agent or agent's subagent brings in the buyer. You can retain the right to sell the property yourself without paying commission. Most agents will be less likely to agree to this type of arrangement unless, again, you have a specific individual in mind who may be willing to purchase your home.

Open Listing

In this type of listing any agent can act as your agent in soliciting buyers, but at closing you have to pay a commission only to the agent who brings a ready, willing and able buyer to the transaction. You can give an open listing to as many agents as you wish. This arrangement is not popular with agents and your home will not get the same market exposure as other homes.

Net Listing

The least common type of listing agreement is a net listing. The net listing specifies that the commission paid to the agent will be the difference between the net amount you want from the sale and the amount the agent or agent can get for the home. Most agents will not agree to this type of listing unless the home is priced below market or they believe the home will sell quickly and still yield a normal commission. It can be a great incentive, but it also can pit the agent's duty to you against his or her own interests. Many states have banned net listings for residential sales.

One-Time Show Listing

In a one-time show listing, the agent can show the home to one potential buyer listed by name and is guaranteed a commission if the home sells to that buyer.

Option Listing

In an option listing, the listing agent has the option to purchase your home and then sell it for a profit. There is no reason for you to go this route. If your agent wants the property at that price, someone else will too, probably for a bit more. Some real estate companies may promise to purchase your home if it does not sell within a specific time period. Check the fine print. The sale may be quite a bit below market price, and there may be additional fees and obligations.

Dedicated Agents—Always in Your Best Interest

Dual Agent

The real estate agent can act as both the listing agent representing the seller and as the representative for the buyer. Because the agent can act as both the buyer's and seller's representative at the same time, a conflict of interest may arise if the listing agent represents a prospective buyer for one of his or her own listings.

Many states now mandate that if an agent operates as a dual agent, he or she must disclose that information in writing to both the buyer and the seller before negotiations on the property begin.

Many sellers and buyers feel that neither the buyer nor the seller may be represented to their fullest if the agent represents both parties during the sale. From that belief sprang the concept of an exclusive buyer's agent.

Buyer's Agent

This is the designation for the real estate agent who represents the buyer. More and more buyers are enlisting buyers' agents to avoid conflicts between sellers' agents. Buyers' agents often require buyers to sign an exclusivity agreement saying the buyer will work with the buyer's agent for a certain period of time and will pay a flat-fee, an hourly rate or a commission to the agent based on the sales price of the home.

In some instances, the contract stipulates that the buyer will pay the agent a prespecified commission amount, even if the buyer decides to purchase a property by owner. This is protection for the buyer's agent who may have spent several days showing the buyer properties, only to have the buyer decide to purchase a home for sale by owner, thus eliminating the commission. The buyer agrees in advance to pay a commission to the agent to compensate for the time spent looking for property.

Under this type of agreement, the agent will provide the buyer with information regarding comparable home sale prices, help determine an offer price, work with the buyer during the negotiations and help the buyer find inspectors, lenders and attorneys.

The Real Estate Attorney

There is no law that requires you to hire a real estate attorney to complete the sale of your home. Whether you hire an attorney to help you sell your home is a matter of local custom. Home sales in areas such as Chicago, New York and Boston routinely include the services of an attorney. The attorney reviews the contract for language that may be disadvantageous to his or her client, and handles all the legal paperwork, transfer taxes, utility bills, the ordering of surveys, title insurance and deeds. In some instances, the attorney will also handle all negotiations for the seller. Other areas rely on the real estate agent to handle the same legal paperwork as the attorney. If selling FSBO, always consult a real estate attorney to ensure you are following your state's procedures and requirements, or you may learn at the last minute–at settlement–that you forgot to obtain an important legal document, without which you cannot complete the closing.

Other areas utilize the services of a closing agent rather than an attorney. The closing agent handles all the paperwork at the closing, leaving you, the seller, the daunting task of reading and signing it all. The closing agent does not represent the buyer or the seller—his or her only interest is to ensure the sale is completed. The closing agent may be hired by the escrow company to make sure that the proper paperwork is completed and the closing goes smoothly.

Why Hire an Attorney?

If you are selling by owner, you will need someone to prepare the documents, help arrange the details of the closing, tell you what disclosures the law requires and handle negotiations if asked by the seller to do so. The services of an attorney are recommended:

- if your deal is complicated; and
- if there is a chance that the buyer will not satisfy the terms of the contract.

Attorneys can help:

- remove emotion from the deal by maintaining an objective view;
- negotiate the contract for you;
- protect you from getting a bad deal if negotiations turn nasty; and
- obtain the necessary approvals, certifications and transfer documentation for the closing.

"One of the best pieces of advice I received before putting my home up for sale by owner was to hire a good real estate attorney and everything will fall into place. I heeded that advice and hired an experienced real estate attorney and the sale went off without a hitch."

Steven Michael
FSBO Seller

In a state where attorneys draft and negotiate the closing documents, the attorney is your advocate.

A good real estate attorney will guide you from purchase negotiations to providing the correct documentation at closing, eliminating the chance for pitfalls. A real estate attorney normally works on a flat-fee basis, which is dependent on the type of property you are selling, how complex the closing will be and how much negotiations he or she will be required to perform.

Your attorney will be able to inform you of the local and state laws you must comply with prior to selling your home. He or she will provide you with and help you execute the offer to purchase, contract to purchase, purchase agreement or purchase and sale agreement forms. The attorney will advise you of disclosures the law requires you to make to a buyer, order the title search and survey or any other state or locally required forms and deal with any problems or issues that come up with a title search or inspection. The attorney will also accompany you to the closing appointment.

During your initial meeting with the attorney, discuss your preference as to who should be the negotiator. Typically, when a seller uses a real estate agent, the agent will present the offer to the owner or seller's agent. When the home is FSBO, the attorney can substitute for the agent in this role. The attorney serves as a buffer between the buyer and the seller.

In a society of increasing litigation, an attorney can take a difficult situation, where anything can go wrong, and utilize his or her experience to successfully navigate all the variables associated with the purchase of property.

Multiunit Structures

For the most part, discussion has focused on the sale of single family homes and town homes. Condos and co-ops are making their first big comeback since the 1970s and have high appeal to young singles, newlyweds, retirees and empty nesters, and divorced or widowed individuals. The primary appeal to a condo, co-op or multiunit structure is that it typically costs less to purchase than a comparable single family home and upkeep is easier. When selling a condo or co-op, there are special considerations to be aware of that do not apply to single family home sales. Each consideration is touched on briefly. You should consult your condo or co-op board for your requirements as a seller before putting your unit up for sale.

Condo

A condominium, also referred to as a condo, is a building with multiple residential units. Each resident owns his or her own unit. Common areas of the building, including the lobby, courtyard, pool or exercise area, ballroom or party room and parking garage are owned jointly by all owners of the association.

Condo owners automatically become members of the condominium association, a group that controls and manages the building. Major decisions are made by the condo board. The condo board is made up of a panel of representative owners, selected by vote by the association members. Some associations require a unit seller to give the condo board the first right of refusal if they think the sale is to someone who will be detrimental to the entire building. A condo seller should obtain a copy of the building's bylaws before putting the unit up for sale to make sure the seller is following procedures as outlined in the bylaws. Failure to follow board guidelines can result in expensive litigation down the road, delays in closing or a voided sales contract.

Co-Op

A co-op, also known as a cooperative apartment is similar to a condominium as it is a building with multiple residential units. The big difference is that the residents of a co-op do not actually own the apartments or units they live in. Instead, they own stock in the corporation that owns the building or complex. Purchase of that stock provides the tenant with a proprietary lease giving them the right to occupy a particular unit. This small but technical distinction can make it difficult for buyers to obtain mortgage financing due to the fact that there is no individual ownership of the units. Buyers of co-op units must submit detailed applications to the board and be approved by the board before the property transfer can take place. Most co-op sales are cash deals because banks are reluctant to provide financing on stock collateral versus real property.

Association Fees

Buyers of a condo or co-op will want to know about association fees, including monthly maintenance fees, reserve funds, subletting practices or restrictions, special assessments that may be in effect or planned and other important financial considerations. Sellers must provide receipts showing association fees paid by the seller are up-to-date before the transfer of property can be made.

Maintenance Fees

In a co-op or condo, owners are charged a fixed monthly maintenance fee that can be raised to cover special assessments or building repairs. The fee is set by a vote of the board of directors within the guidelines set by the association bylaws. Items typically covered by the association or maintenance fee include doorman service, air conditioning, electric and heat, sports and recreational facilities, outdoor lighting, cable TV or Internet service, landscape services, pool maintenance and lifeguard personnel, exterior maintenance, water, sewers, and snow and trash removal. If the building has an attached parking garage with parking attendants, those costs also will be included in monthly fees. Real estate taxes and insurance fees are included in the monthly fee as well. The unit owner must disclose all maintenance and monthly assessment fees associated with the unit. If you are selling a condo or co-op, prepare a breakout of monthly fees and special assessments for buyers. This will help them compare fees charged to your unit with other units in the area.

Reserve Funds

A reserve fund is an amount of money set aside by the co-op or condo board to pay for capital improvements, routine maintenance, unexpected repairs and other maintenance expenses that may occur. Similar to a forced savings plan, a portion of your monthly maintenance payment is set aside into an escrow-like account. Maintaining an adequate reserve fund is an important selling feature. Without enough funds in reserve for repair or improvements, the board has to decide if the improvements can be delayed or if they will be forced to assess a levy, or special assessment, on each unit owner to cover the costs of the repairs. Newly converted condominiums do not have established reserve funds and may require the first owners to contribute several thousand dollars to establish a fund. Buyers of new units may be required to contribute money to build up the fund quickly.

Subletting and Renting

Most condos allow owners to sublet or rent their units when they are not occupied by the owner. Some associations, however, may limit the total number of units available for rental at any one time to keep the owner occupied/renter occupied ratio stable. If there is no rule in the bylaws stating that the unit cannot be sublet or rented, then the owner is probably free to sublet. If a building is more than 60 percent rental units, banks may not agree to loan mortgage money to a buyer. A lower owner-occupancy rate may increase insurance rates and reduce the resale value of the units in the building.

If there is a lack of specific verbiage in the condo bylaws, this means the board can vote at any time to ban subletting without the vote being subject to approval by the shareholders. If the right to sublet is granted to original buyers in a new condo or co-op building and this right is spelled out in the prospectus and bylaws, the board cannot later decide to suspend the subletting privilege.

Co-op rules may be more restrictive than a condo's rules. If the right to sublet is granted to a co-op owner, the board may have the right to screen all applicants. Be prepared to share a portion of your rent receipts with the co-op. In times of economic hardship or when sales are sluggish, co-op boards frequently allow owners to rent their units for a period of 2 years.

Co-Op Boards

Co-op owners own shares in a co-op corporation that, in turn, owns the building. When you sell your co-op shares, you transfer your share ownership back to the corporation, which then issues new shares to the new owner upon closing. Usually, the transfer of shares is not direct from seller to buyer. The co-op board has complete control over the sale with the degree of control mandated by the terms of your co-op agreement.

The co-op board may have strong control in screening potential residents and may accept or reject potential buyers at its sole discretion without stating the reason for the decision. The potential screening is done to ensure that only unit owners who are desirable and financially stable tenants are allowed to buy into the building. The law prohibits discrimination based on race, religion, national origin or ethnic background. However, the board may reject a buyer based on income, financial status, occupation or credit history, all indicators of a potential buyer's ability to keep up with monthly maintenance payments. The board may exercise its right to refuse acceptance of a prospective tenant based solely on financial reasons.

Making the Decision to Sell by Owner

Planning the sale of your property requires due diligence and a thorough understanding of your options and requirements. Have you made up your mind to sell by owner? The following chapter prepares you for the work ahead to help make your FSBO experience fun, stress-free and positive.

2

· · · · · · ·

Are You Prepared to Do the Work?

Selling your home is hard work and requires planning, tenacity and patience. If you just stick a For Sale sign in the ground, buyers will not necessarily line up to buy your home. The most successful sellers plan 6 months ahead to prepare for the sale of their homes. They know that taking time to understand the market thoroughly and spending a few dollars wisely will increase the chances that their homes will sell quickly.

Estimate Time and Money Needed for Improvements

If your home is in poor condition, improvements can increase the sale price. Before you choose which projects to tackle prior to putting your home on the market, make a list of the improvements you want to make and then rank them in order of importance. Your priorities will depend on your budget and whether you hope to enhance your home's market value to increase your profits or to sell your home more quickly.

Start your list by surveying open houses and model homes in your area. Take special note of current designs, styles and features such as pantries, bonus rooms, home offices and kitchen layouts. You may decide to replace the kitchen counters with granite or a trendier surface, convert a den to an office or remove or paint dated paneling.

"A successful FSBO seller understands the dedication and time commitment required to sell a property without realtor assistance. The seller is available to show the home at any time. If they are not able to show the property for any reason, they make arrangements to have a neighbor show the home in their absence. A successful seller is also responsive and checks his or her messages frequently throughout the day then promptly returns calls from Realtors or buyers."

Robert Picarellaro
Prello Realty
Flat Fee Realty Company

Prepare Your Home for Sale

Make sure the home is as clean, clutter-free and inviting as possible. The hardest part about selling will be keeping up appearances as long as your home is for sale. Review this checklist at least every other day to make sure your home is show-ready at a moment's notice.

Seller's Daily Checklist

Front yard
Pick up toys in yard and store out of sight
Keep lawn and shrubs trimmed and neat
Entryway
Clean doors and windows
Mop floor, shake out rug, vacuum carpeting
Water flowers or plants
Dust shelves and/or entry table
Keep windows washed
Put away shoes, coats and backpacks
Living Room/Family Room
Put away newspapers, magazines, books, games, toys and videos
Straighten coffee table, bookshelves and other areas
Mop floor or vacuum rugs
Vacuum upholstered furniture; wipe down leather or vinyl
Dust surfaces, including TV screen
Sweep fireplace and remove excess ash
Wipe down ceiling fan blades
Water houseplants
Kitchen
Mop or vacuum floor
Clean appliances
Wipe countertops and cabinets
Clean sink
Put away kitchen sponge and dish towels
Open windows or run fan to remove cooking odors

Bathrooms
Wipe wet shower stalls and bathtubs
Mop floors
Put out fresh towels
Empty wastebaskets
Clean sinks, mirrors and faucets
Put away laundry

Bedrooms
Make beds
Mop floors or vacuum rugs
Put away shoes, laundry, clothes, books or toys
Open curtains or shades
Tidy up closet

Home Office
Straighten desk and bookshelves
Put away files
Mop floor or vacuum rugs
Dust surfaces, including computer screen
Polish cabinets and woodwork

Basement
Clear clutter blocking access to furnace, electrical box or laundry room
Sweep stairs
Sweep or vacuum rug
Dust surfaces
Organize toys and games
Clean doors and windows

Garage
Remove unused tools from shelves or wall
Organize tools on shelves

Remove the Clutter

To make your home appear larger, remove all clutter. When buyers walk through the front of your home, they want to see a clean, spacious area that affords them plenty of living space. Clean out closets, basements, children's rooms, playrooms, attics and garages. Clutter makes the home look smaller and buyers will think the home is too small. Walk through every room in your home and identify areas of clutter.

To achieve the uncluttered look, remove almost everything from tabletops and shelves. You do not want to make the room look stark and unlived in, but you do want the key features of the room to attract the buyer's attention.

Remove coats that are not being worn and half your clothes from closets to make them appear larger.

Tip
Remove as many family pictures or memorabilia from shelves or tables as possible. While looking at a home, buyers can be attracted easily to family photos or knickknacks, thus distracting them from the features of the home.

In the kitchen, remove children's art hanging on the refrigerator and pack away or remove old, worn cookbooks. Reduce the amount of junk in junk drawers— buyers like to peek in drawers. Clear off kitchen countertops as much as possible by removing any small appliances. Reduce the number of items stored in the cabinets.

Give away games, videos and toys that your kids have outgrown. You may be tempted to pack everything away and just put the boxes in the basement. This will accomplish little more than moving clutter from one room to another. Instead, have a garage sale to eliminate unnecessary items. Use the money you earn to store larger, bulkier items.

Consider renting a storage unit. Many storage companies now deliver storage containers right to your door. You simply fill the pod/container with boxes or furniture. The storage company will pick up the container when it is filled, take it back to their facility and store it for you until you are ready to retrieve it again.

Organize

People buy homes that appear spacious, clean and solid. Look through every closet in the home. Remove old shoes, pack away coats that may be out of season and organize the shelves and racks to give an orderly appearance. Arrange clothing neatly in each closet and reduce the number of items stored on shelves and on the floor. However, now is not the time to consider installing closet organizers. Built-in systems seldom return the investment. Instead, purchase a shoe organizer or sweater shelves.

Clean

Clean everything, including carpets. Clean and organize your basement, attic and garage. Ask a friend to assess your efforts, especially sensitive issues such as pet, mold or mildew odors. Wash windows and mirrors so they sparkle. Clean the oven and all appliances. Remove grease spatters from walls and polish chrome fixtures and surfaces. Polish stainless steel appliances and porcelain fixtures. Clean smudges, especially around doorknobs and light switches.

Paint

Repaint dark walls with a lighter color to make the rooms appear larger and cleaner. Repaint rooms that may look worn or dingy. Use white or off-white paint. Bright lights and white walls make rooms look bigger. Remove old or dated wallpaper and replace heavy draperies with sheers. Use higher wattage light bulbs. If you cannot repaint the entire home, pick the rooms that have the loudest color or look the dingiest.

Polish It Up

If you have hardwood floors under old carpeting, pull up the carpeting and get the floors refinished. If the floors are in good shape but just need a buffing, purchase a can of hardwood cleaner. Buffing older floors will minimize any scratches or nicks and will save you the time and cost of refinishing.

Tighten It Down

Rattles, squeaks and leaks leave the impression that the home needs a lot of work. Repair squeaking steps and wobbly banisters. Repair the leaking roof and remove all signs of water damage by covering first with a stain kill and then painting. Repair leaky faucets and pipes. Prevent mold from appearing by putting down a clean bead of caulk around tubs and sinks. Clean tiles with a lime or hard water deposit remover. This will remove the dull film on tiles and make them look shiny and new. Tighten loose doorknobs, light switch plates and cabinet hinges. Oil any hinges that may squeak. Sand or shave down sticking doors and then repaint them. Tack down all loose molding or loose wallpaper.

Repair or Replace

Make sure everything is in good working order, including all heating and air conditioning systems. Make sure that outlets work, toilets flush, and windows and doors open and shut smoothly before putting your home up for sale. All heating, air conditioning, ceiling fans, heaters and appliances that stay with the home should be in good working order.

> "The heating system and hot water heater both worked fine when we decided to sell our home. We wanted a quick sale for top dollar, so we opted to replace both units to attract more buyers. Our strategy paid off. Our home sold in 3 weeks. The buyer told us the new heating and hot water systems are what sealed the deal. Not having to worry about putting in new systems for the next 10 years helped him decide to buy our house."
>
> Judy Fitzgell
> FSBO Seller

Choose Which Repairs and Improvements to Make

There are two types of buyers: the type that is willing to make some repairs to a home if everything about it is right and the type that does not want to do any work to the home at all. As the seller, you need to determine how much work you will put into the home before you put it up for sale. In homes that are described as being in mint condition, the walls are painted white or neutral and electrical, plumbing and heating systems have been upgraded or are new. Carpeting has been replaced and the home is immaculate.

Homes sold in as-is condition or described as needing a little TLC may be broken down and in need of repair. They usually need a lot of work. These homes also may be advertised as handyman specials.

Mint condition homes will sell for more money than homes that are sold as-is because most buyers do not want to do any work on a home. They may not have any time to devote to repairs, or they may simply not have the money to make them. While it is not necessary for you to renovate your home completely before putting it up for sale, there are some projects that will improve the salability of your home immediately.

Plan Your Projects Room by Room

Once you have removed the clutter, assess each room with a critical eye. Make a list of improvements for each room that will likely make your home sell. Look for outdated color schemes, faded draperies and worn carpets. For example, do your bedrooms look dark or dingy? How do the walls look when posters or pictures are removed? A fresh coat of paint may be all that is necessary to lighten and brighten the room and give it a whole new appearance. Is the carpet worn, dirty or torn or can it just be cleaned?

In the bathrooms, remove any rust stains and fix faded or water-stained wallpaper, cracked tiles or cracked grout. What shape are the bath towels in? Do they match, or are they all different colors? Are the edges frayed? An inexpensive fix is to purchase all new bath towels and a new rug. The kitchen should look fresh and have plenty of storage and counter space. Once you make your list of room improvements, you need to set a budget.

Set a Budget

Organize your budget according to what you can afford, what is necessary– replacing a heating system or repairing cracks in the garage floor, for example–and what is optional. Time constraints might make you consider giving a repair or redecorating allowance to the buyers to spend on repairs that are most important to them rather than make the repairs yourself. When setting your budget, determine how much time you have to devote to each project.

Determine Your Time

Review your room-by-room project plan. Estimate how much time will be required to finish each project. Some projects may be quick and will take only a few hours.

Other projects may require 1 or 2 days to complete. How much time do you have, and how much time and money are you willing to devote to repairs? Choose the projects you can do by yourself quickly and hire a professional to complete the rest.

Add Value to Your Home before Selling

Recouping your remodeling investment when you sell your home may be your goal, but when it comes to resale value, not all home improvement dollars spent will be recovered. Minor redecorating projects, such as painting a room or updating carpeting, typically will generate 100 percent payback. You may be considering remodeling an out-of-date bathroom or putting in a new kitchen to make your home more attractive to buyers. As a rule, kitchen remodeling projects and bathroom additions almost always pay back 90 percent or more of their costs. Finishing a basement, however, usually pays back only a fraction of the cost to improve. The return on investment for other improvements generally falls somewhere in between.

Before spending major investment dollars to improve your home, consider the following inexpensive tips to make the interior of your home show-ready and the payback estimates based on a compilation of surveys for the most typical home improvement projects:

Payback Estimator		
Project	**Estimated Cost**	**Payback Amount**
New heating system	$2,000-$7,500	100%
New air conditioning system	$2,000-$7,500	75%
Minor kitchen remodeling	$2,000-$10,000	94%-110%
Major kitchen remodeling	$9,000-$100,000	90%
Add a bathroom	$5,000-$25,000	94%
Add a family room	$30,000-$50,000	85%
Remodel a bathroom	$8,500-$25,000	75%
Add a fireplace	$1,300-$5,000	75%
Build a deck	$6,000-$20,000	70%
Remodel a home office	$8,000-$10,000	65%
Replace windows	$5,000-$20,000	65%-75%
Build a pool	$10,000+	45%
Install or upgrade landscaping	$1,500-$15,000	30%-60%
Finish basement	$5,000-$20,000	25%

Tips for the Interior of Your Home

Give Your Home an Instant Face-Lift

A few key changes in your decor can make a dramatic difference.

- **Brighten rooms:** Shades of white account for half of all paint sales. It is clean, restful, and all furnishings look good with white. Also, consider painting the walls, ceiling and windowsills in each room with the same color. This strategy works best when the windowsills are small or molding is unremarkable—it will make the room appear larger.

- **Rearrange living room furniture:** Create a focal point by pulling the sofa into the center of the room facing a fireplace or picture window and then building the rest of the room around that one piece. Remember to shampoo rugs to remove the old traffic patterns.

- **Re-evaluate room use:** A rarely used guest bedroom or dining room can be converted into a den or home office.

- **Use standing screens to mask problem areas:** Tri-fold screens are one way to hide eyesores like home office equipment. Get creative with the screen you select. Several stores offer very attractive screens made from cloth, paper, bamboo or picture frames.

- **Fill an empty corner:** Place a large potted tree in the corner. Lighten up the corner by positioning a canister light on the floor behind the plant, pointing upwards into the plant or toward the ceiling.

- **Refurbish cabinets:** Strip and refinish old, dark wood. Paint cabinets to brighten up a dark room and add new handles or knobs. You can also cut out the center panels and replace them with glass fronts. Replace wood shelves with glass shelves. Install lighting inside the cabinets to showcase distinctive pieces. Add new hardware to give it a new look.

- **Regrout and reseal the tub.** If the tile or tub are from a different era and look dated, reglazing them can be an inexpensive way to give the room a new look. Add new towels and hang a new shower curtain. Remove soap scum or hard water stains with a tile cleaner to give the tile new life.

- **Let the light in:** Replace interior and exterior wood doors with french doors that have glass fronts.

- **Get rid of heavy drapes:** Replace with fabrics that blend with the surrounding walls. Add tiebacks on each side. Replace heavy fabric drapes with sheers.

- **Apply self-adhesive wallpaper borders:** Use borders to brighten up a child's room or a bathroom.

- **Cover a wall with mirrors:** Covering a wall with mirrors is ideal for bathrooms, entries, dining rooms and other small, dark rooms that lack impact.

- **Replace worn out bedspreads:** New, crisp linens or a comforter with matching pillows will liven up any bedroom.

> **Tip**
>
> Successful agents will often advise their clients not to do everything to the home. Even if your home is completely done, the new buyer will want to make it theirs by repainting, decorating, etc. If you have an area that is obviously not finished or could use some updating, point that one item out to the buyer. It will give them the feeling that there is potential to improve the home and immediately increase its value.

Look Objectively at the Exterior

Walk around the outside of your home. Remember what initially attracted you to it. Your home's curb appeal must impress a prospective buyer. Step back and look objectively at the condition of your home. Is the paint peeling? Is the lawn full of weeds or edged? Are there patches of dead grass or overgrown bushes? Fix screens that may be torn. Add a fresh coat of paint to worn shutters or faded doors and restain the deck. Your home should have a neat, trim appearance that is open and inviting.

Spruce up the exterior of your home to improve curb appeal and make buyers want to see the inside. Power wash the dirt off aluminum or vinyl siding. If your home looks drab, consider painting it white. Real estate agents report that white homes sell faster than any other color home. To add color to the exterior, paint trim, doors or shutters.

The following scenario plays out every day: A real estate agent makes an appointment to show a home to his or her buyer. The home has everything the buyer is looking for, but there is one problem. The owner has not had the time to keep the outside trimmed and neat, and the home has an almost deserted look. The real estate agent brings the buyer to the home at the scheduled time. The buyer looks in dismay at the unkempt lawn and overgrown shrubs and tells the agent he or she does not want to go inside. No amount of convincing will persuade the buyer to get out of the car. The agent and buyer go on to the next appointment.

Regardless of whether buyers are being overly sensitive or irrational, keep in mind your home has only one chance to make a favorable first impression.

Lawn and Yard

A well-kept lawn implies a well-maintained home and creates curb appeal. Cut the lawn weekly while showing your home. Rake leaves and sweep sidewalks on weekends. Remove dead limbs and debris from shrubs and trees where possible. Clean the gutters to give the home a well-maintained appearance. Edge the driveway and sidewalks. If you have a front porch, consider adding chairs or a hanging swing to create a cozy outside sitting room. Place potted plants or flowers to soften the space. Add window boxes to make the front of a home look more inviting and friendly.

Add Color

Plant extra flowers for more color or spruce up landscaping with potted flowers. A splash of color on the front porch or back patio is inviting and nice to look at.

Repair fences and touch up with paint or stain. Repaint or replace the mailbox. Touch up garage doors, front doors and gutters. A white picket or stained fence looks neat and trim. Peeling or faded paint makes the buyer look harder for signs of rotting or weathered wood.

Clean the Garage

Too much clutter in the garage can make it look small. Keep the insides of the garage free of clutter. Invest in a garage caddy that will organize your garden tools, shovels and rakes and sports equipment. Hang seldom-used bicycles from ceiling hooks positioned over the hood of the car. When showing the home, keep one or two cars parked in the garage to show that a two-car garage really does hold two cars.

Board Pets

Board dogs or other large pets while showing the home. Buyers may be allergic to cat or dog hair and may spend more time controlling their allergies than focusing on the features of the home. There are buyers who will not even consider looking at a home that has a family pet. They will leave as soon as they sense or smell that a pet lives in the home.

Front Entrance

The front entrance is a key part of the first impression. Here are a few simple ideas to make your home inviting:

- Hang a wreath or basket filled with welcoming flowers on the front door. Change the basket to reflect the seasons, e.g., a basket of tulips or daffodils in the spring, a basket of chrysanthemums in the fall or a wreath of red berries in the winter.
- Replace burned out light bulbs. Keep lights on and draperies open at night so interested buyers will see how nice the home looks lit up. Make sure the entry light and doorbell are in working order.
- Paint, clean or stain the front door.
- Remove old screens if they do not fit or operate properly.
- Replace missing address numbers and make sure the number is visible from the street in the early evening. If door hardware looks old or flimsy, replace it.
- Plant colorful flowers in pots or around trees or in the garden.
- During the winter, shovel snow from the sidewalks and driveway.

Keep outdoor lights lit during the day. This will give the home a brighter look. Put out a nice welcome mat and a potted plant if you have room on the steps or entryway. Avoid political, holiday or religious decorations or yard signs—now is not the time to take a stance. The goal is to attract buyers inside your home not to make political or religious statements.

Roof, Windows and Siding

Look closely at the exterior of your home. Experienced homeowners often gloss over misaligned shutters, bent gutters and loose shingles unless there is a leak, but these things jump out at first-time buyers. Paint and repair gutters. Replace loose shingles and flashing in the roof, especially where it is visible from the ground. Give a fresh coat of paint to window sashes, trim and shutters. Replace cracked window panes and broken thermal seal windows. Wash all windows, including storm windows and screens. If your aluminum or vinyl siding looks old and dirty, power wash it or repaint it with a color that matches the original color. For brick or mason homes, tuck-point loose or chipped bricks or stone and paint. Examine wood siding for signs of nails popping or split siding. Hammer any popped nails back into place.

Nine Ways to Attract Buyers

The sign is up and advertising has been placed in the local paper. You have a beautiful home for sale. How else can you attract buyers to come and see it? Consider trying the following nine ideas to attract buyers to your home:

1. Print promotional fliers highlighting the features of your home, the price and how to reach you to see the property. Include a brochure holder on the For Sale sign.

2. Send or deliver fliers or postcards to 100 neighbors, 100 business associates and 100 relatives and friends. Post fliers on church, temple, synagogue and community center bulletin boards.

3. Post a flier with tear-offs at 10 local supermarkets, train stations, athletic clubs, etc. Find out what day of the week the bulletin board is normally cleared and replace the flier each week until the home is sold.

4. Place a flier on 100 cars at the supermarket or train station.

5. Place a flier on 100 cars in local apartment complexes.

6. Include your cell phone number as the contact number on all of your signs and fliers so people can always reach you to inquire about the home or to schedule an appointment.

7. Rent a toll-free number for a talking ad describing the home. Prepare a script highlighting the features of the home, the price and local points of interest—close to a park, near good schools, etc.

8. Include your cell phone or toll-free number on your For Sale sign. Call 555.555.5555 to hear a talking ad.

9. Create a dedicated Web page that includes pictures of the home. Include the URL on your sign and fliers.

Selling the Hard-to-Sell Home

Some homes sell quickly, others do not. What can you do as a seller to offer incentives to buyers to purchase your property? There are a number of incentive options available, such as offering attractive financing, renting the property until the market heats up or evoking divine intervention.

Offering Seller Financing

Seller financing is a popular incentive to provide to buyers who may not qualify for conventional financing. This option works best for the seller who does not have a mortgage on the property. The seller may take back a portion of the amount of the sales price for 1 to 5 years. At the end of the pre-determined period, the buyer will pay the seller the remainder of the amount owed.

Lease to Buy Option

If a buyer does not have enough of a down payment to purchase the home, consider offering a lease to buy option. In this option, the buyer rents the property from the seller. The seller puts away a portion of the rent into an escrow account for the buyer. The renter and the seller agree on the length of time and a rental amount.

To make the offer more attractive to the buyer, move 30 percent of each month's rent into the escrow account for the renter. Put the other 70 percent toward paying the mortgage and maintaining the home. At the end of the lease to buy term, if the renter decides not to purchase the home, the accumulating escrow payments stay with the seller. A lease to buy option term may be 1 year or as long as 3 years.

The advantage to the buyer is that he or she is able to lock in a price for the home. The amount agreed upon will remain constant regardless of how much the home increases in value during the rental period, and each month, a predetermined amount of the rent paid goes into a forced savings plan.

The disadvantage to the buyer is that if he or she does not exercise the option to buy at the end of the lease term, the extra 30 percent the seller was putting aside stays with the seller.

Advantages to the seller include:

- The home is occupied by a buyer who has the incentive to help maintain it.
- The home is no longer empty.
- If there is a mortgage, the home is no longer a cash drain and may generate additional income.
- If the buyer chooses not to exercise the purchase option the escrow money reverts to the seller.

Disadvantages to the seller include:

- The agreed upon sales price is locked in during the leased period. If a cold market becomes hot, the sales price of the home cannot increase.
- The lease to buy option may be as long as 3 years, thus tying up any equity in the property for that length of time.
- The current occupants may cause damage to the home during their stay, resulting in large repair costs if they decide not to purchase the home.

Renting Until the Market Heats Up

In instances where the market cools down, the homeowner has the option to pull the home off the market and rent it until the market heats up again.

Picking the Right Season

Every season offers new opportunities and challenges for selling your home. Traditionally, spring and fall are the strongest selling seasons because they corresponded with the beginning and end of the school year and rental leases. However, times have changed, and the real estate business is now year-round. While timing is important, the changing seasons enable sellers to feature their home's best attributes.

The Spring Market

The spring market generally begins in late February or early March. It is strong for buyers who want to move as soon as school is finished for the year as well as buyers who may have had a big tax bill and are looking to reduce their taxes with a mortgage. If your home does not have air conditioning, this is an ideal time to show the home before the hot summer months.

The disadvantages to selling in a spring market are weather-related. Spring may bring plenty of rain and the possibility of flooding. Also, spring brings with it mud and slush. Buyers may track it in on their shoes and may mark a rug or hardwood floor.

The Summer Market

The summer market usually begins in June and ends in August. If your home has a garden or the lawn as a selling point, summer is an ideal time to show it. If you have kids who attend summer camps, it will be easier to keep the home clean for showings. Homes that have central air conditioning provide a welcome refuge from summer heat. If you live near or on a lake, be sure to point out the beach or dock.

The disadvantages to selling in the summer months include trying to keep the home picked up while the kids are home. Also, summer is a great time for family vacations, short getaways and a wide variety of weekend distractions that may keep buyers from seriously shopping for a new home. Real estate agents will tell you that August and December are typically the slowest months in real estate. In fact, many of them will take the entire month of August off because it is such a slow sales period.

The Fall Market

The fall market runs from after Labor Day until November. It is most active from the end of September until the middle of October and is strong with buyers who want their children to finish out the semester before moving. Be aware that if you list in fall, you will have the changing seasons to contend with. While you will have the turning of the leaves and fall flowers to enhance the outside of your home, you also soon will lose the colors of annuals or perennials in your landscaping plants.

The disadvantage to selling during the fall months is that fall is a very short selling season. Many buyers and sellers put off selling or buying homes until after the holidays. Any home not sold during the fall market and held over into the winter market may give buyers the misleading impression that there is something wrong with it. In many areas, snow covers the ground and obscures gardens and patios from view.

The Winter Market

The winter market has always been referred to as the slowest market. The big misperception is that home sales drop significantly during November and December. In reality, they drop only slightly. Sellers who remain on the market or put their homes up for sale in the winter months are truly motivated sellers. Buyers who are looking for a home during these months are serious buyers. Selling a home during the holidays can send an inviting signal to buyers or turn them off. Keep your holiday decorations low key.

The disadvantage to selling in the winter months is the loss of green foliage and inviting flowers, potentially making a home look stark. If you plan to sell your home in the winter, take plenty of outdoor shots showing your gardens or yard in full bloom. This will help buyers see what the yard will look like in the height of summer.

If you decide to put your home up for sale during the winter, you may want to make it available in January to get a jump on other homes in the neighborhood that may come up for sale in February. January is as strong a sales month as March. You also may wish to put the home up for sale in January to generate additional interest from buyers who are hungry for something new.

3

· · · · · ·

Key Factors to Consider

Is the Market Right for FSBO?

How quickly will I sell? In every market, there are homes that sell within hours and homes that sit on the market for years. Knowing the average number of days a home in your neighborhood spends on the market is important because it tells you the type of market you will be entering. If homes in your neighborhood are sitting rather than selling, there are likely more homes on the market than there are buyers—this is known as a buyers' market. The heavy competition in a buyers' market sends prices spiraling downward. If homes in your neighborhood are selling within days, there are likely more buyers than there are homes available—this is called a sellers' market. The demand for homes in a sellers' market may result in inflated prices or sellers getting their full asking price.

Sellers' Market

If the average number of days on the market is less than 30, it is considered a strong sellers' market. The typical sellers' market includes homes that have been on the market anywhere from a few days to perhaps 45 or 60 days. Keeping in mind that a newly available home will see most of its activity within the first 3 weeks on the market, a neighborhood with an average marketing time of 30 days indicates a strong market. In this type of market, you can price your home one of two ways: You can price it right with the market and sell it quickly, or you can price it just slightly above market and hope that homes are selling fast enough to justify the price increase.

Tip
Even in a hot sellers' market, buyers will avoid homes that are grossly overpriced. The hotter the market the more overpricing buyers will tolerate, but they will not touch homes that they consider to be out of the ballpark.

Much of a home's selling success is tied to pricing. If you price your home in line with a fair market value, it will sell. Maybe not tomorrow or the next day or even in a month, but it will sell. There is a buyer for every home.

Balanced Market

If the average length of time on the market is between 40 and 75 days, it is considered a balanced market. A balanced market means there is a similar number of buyers and sellers. It also means that prices may continue to climb at a healthy rate each year. A balanced market will not tolerate overpricing. In a hot market, buyers have little time to react before they must make an offer, or they risk losing the home to another bidder. In a balanced market, buyers have time to see and compare many homes before making a decision. If buyers believe your home is overpriced, they will move on to the next one.

Buyers' Market

If the average number of days a home sits on the market is more than 75, you are in a buyers' market. In this type of market, buyers may take a long time deciding whether or not to make an offer. Sellers who are most successful in this market do not test it by overpricing their homes. If your home is priced right but is taking a long time to sell in a buyers' market, do not despair. Other homes in the neighborhood are probably facing the same conditions. If you are serious about selling, cut your price as close to your bottom price as possible and just wait until the market improves.

> **Tip**
>
> Talk with neighbors and other sellers in the area to find out the average market time in your neighborhood. An average market time of 90 to 120 days may be perfectly acceptable depending on economic conditions and mortgage interest rates.

Other Market Indicators

Another indication of how strong or weak your local market may be is how the list price and the sales prices of homes in your neighborhood compare. According to the NAR, homes sell for an average of 94 percent of their list price. If a home sells for 98 percent of its list price, the market may be a sellers' market. If a home sells for only 90 percent of its list price, then you may be in a buyers' market. The condition of the home and how well it was priced are factors to consider. The law of averages, however, should give you a good indication of the type of market you will be facing.

> **Tip**
>
> If you keep track of the list prices and sales prices of homes in your area, it should be easy to calculate how closely to their list price they sold.

Determining the Value of Your Home

Factors that determine the value of your home include total square footage, upgrades you have made and whether the home is brick versus wood or a manufactured home. What kind of home do you have? Is your home in mint condition or will considerable work be required to make it habitable? Determining the type of home you have will help you set your price.

The Tear-Down

This type of home needs to be knocked down and built again from either a new foundation or the existing foundation. A tear-down is a home that has a weak foundation or is on a slab, or the structure may be sitting on a brick foundation or on concrete blocks. Any home is a candidate for tear-down status, from century-old farmhouses to relatively new construction. The quality of construction is a factor as is the layout of the home. Homes that are considered tear-downs are generally priced for the land value only. Sellers will indicate an as-is condition or may note the home is priced to reflect the value of the land.

> **Example**
>
> A home in an established neighborhood was built from a catalog kit and sat on a brick foundation. There had been several hodgepodge additions put on the home over the course of 50 years. Local building codes would not allow any more additions to the home due to the brick foundation, so the seller priced the home to reflect the value of the land only. The home sold and was torn down to make room for a new one. The home had little value—all the value was in the property.

Total Rehab

This type of home needs complete gutting down to the bare walls and studs. In some cases, the exterior brick or wood is also replaced and the home is essentially rebuilt from the inside out. While it may seem to make more sense just to knock it down and start all over again, there are reasons why buyers will purchase a home that needs complete rehabbing. The structure itself may be old, but it is solid and exudes charm. The home may be relatively new, but it needs a complete electrical and plumbing upgrade, new floors and other improvements. These improvements may include cable or security systems, which makes it cheaper to rip out the floors and walls rather than try to work around existing materials.

Fixer-Upper

This type of home is structurally sound but just needs some tender loving care. Major construction will not be needed in a fixer-upper. The general layout of the home may be adequate for the buyer and the structure itself may be sound. The buyer will most likely need to install a new kitchen or bath(s), remove dated wallpaper and appliances, sand floors, replace carpeting, draperies and older windows and make other cosmetic improvements. A fixer-upper may still require thousands of dollars and several months' work.

> **Tip**
>
> Fixer-uppers sell for 24 percent less than other properties, on average, according to an NAR report.

Mint Condition

A home in mint condition is clean and has fresh, neutral decorating, refinished floors, and upgraded kitchen and baths. Upon moving in, the buyers will not be required to perform any work on the home, including painting or landscaping. Generally, homes in mint condition have brand new heating and air conditioning systems, newer septic systems, updated plumbing and electrical systems, new roof, etc. A home in mint condition will fetch top dollar since all the work has been done by the seller, and the buyers know they will not have to do any upgrading or redecorating for the next few years.

Check Your Curb Appeal

Does your home make a good first impression? Check out your curb appeal. A home that is visually appealing and in good condition will attract potential buyers driving down the street and get them emotionally connected to your home. Use the following checklist to view your property through an outsider's eyes:

- Are the lawn and shrubs well-maintained?
- Are cracks visible in the foundation or walkways?
- Does the driveway need resurfacing?
- Are the gutters, chimney and walls in good condition?
- Do the window casings, shutters, siding or doors need painting?
- Is garbage and debris stored out of sight?
- Are lawn mowers and hoses properly stored?
- Is the garage door closed?

When buyers pull up to your home, what is their reaction? You have only one chance to make a good first impression. A good-looking house will move them out of the car and into the house.

On the Inside

Strong curb appeal will lure potential buyers inside, but it has to live up to their expectations. The same rule about first impressions applies to the inside. If the interior of your home is old, dated and needs a little help, there are plenty of easy and inexpensive improvements you can make to your home's interior.

Cleaning is your number one priority. Your windows, floors and bathroom tiles should sparkle. Make sure you have clean heating and air conditioning filters. The dust from dirty filters will blow through vents and may make the home smell dirty. Shampoo dirty carpets, clean tubs and showers, repair dripping faucets and lubricate squeaky doors. Empty garbage bags each day. Keep your home neat and clean at all times. It may not seem fair, but a peek in the oven may be the hallmark by which a buyer judges how well you have kept up your home.

Remove unnecessary clutter from the garage, basement, attic and closets and straighten stored items. Also, remove any items that might make a statement that would be offensive to others who may not share your views, beliefs or sense of humor. If your home is crowded with too much furniture, consider putting some things into storage. If a room needs a fresh coat of paint, use a neutral off-white. The goal is to create a feeling of openness and spaciousness.

Home Sweet Home

Set a mood for the buyer. Freshen up your home with flowers and new guest towels in the bathroom. Think about how your home smells. You may have grown accustomed to the smell of a pet or cigarettes, but such odors can be a strong turnoff to others. Buyers form their first impression of your home when they cross the threshold. The smell of freshly baked cookies or bread will make the buyer feel at home as he or she walks through the house. You can quickly bake cookies without the mess by buying cookie dough in tubs or cut-and-bake rolls. In warmer weather, a pot of potpourri will give off a nice fragrance as buyers walk around your home. If you cannot be home to bake before a showing, plug in heat activated or continuous fragrance air fresheners. Avoid spray fragrances, as they only mask odors and may activate a buyer's allergies.

Remember, cosmetic changes need not be expensive. In fact, costly home improvements do not necessarily offer a good return on your investment when you sell. It is attention to the basics–anything that says this home has been maintained carefully–that will help you get the price you want.

Setting a Fair Price

Naturally, you want to get top dollar for your home. However, you do not want to scare off potential buyers by setting the price of your home too high. Setting an artificially high price may cause your property to sit on the market for months. Reducing your asking price later may lead buyers to wonder if there is something wrong with your home. To help you determine the fair market value of your home, you need to find out the value of other recently sold homes currently on the market in your area and create a comparative market analysis (CMA).

A CMA is the best tool to use in determining the correct price for your home. The most accurate CMAs compare your home to other homes that are similar in size, shape, condition and location. The CMA should include the number and sizes of rooms, number of bathrooms, amount of living space–actual square footage–lot size, garage size–attached or detached–location, number of fireplaces, etc. Additional comparative information includes upgrades to the home—whether the kitchen or bathrooms are newer or older, whether the basement is finished or unfinished, the age of the roof and heating and cooling systems, etc.

A Seven-Step Approach to Building Your CMA

A properly created CMA is a road map to setting your price and selling your home successfully. To build your CMA, take into consideration the following factors:

1. **Your location**—A good location is one that is close to public transportation, has a good school system, is close to parks and is situated in a neighborhood with well-maintained homes and tree-lined streets.

2. **Economic conditions**—A community with low unemployment rates plays a positive role in the pricing of a home.

3. **Supply and demand in the local housing market**—Do homes in your neighborhood sell quickly or linger on the market for a long time? Pricing is affected by the type of market you are trying to sell in. You may have to adjust your pricing down in a buyers' market. In a sellers' market, you have more flexibility to test the waters with a slightly higher price.

4. **Seasonal influences**—Selling during the holiday season and winter months when fewer buyers are looking for homes may cause a home to stay on the market longer or be priced lower.

5. **School district**—A good school district adds value to every property. If your school district's report cards reflect high test scores, a positive learning environment and a diverse curriculum, be sure to include that information in your home packet.

6. **Average home prices in the neighborhood**—Track sale prices of homes during the past 12 months and how long each property took to sell. Then take a look at asking prices of homes currently for sale and how long those properties have been on the market. Determine the average price of homes that are similar to yours and the average time on the market to help set your sales price.

7. **Extras**—Do homes in your neighborhood have pools, fireplaces, central air conditioning, etc.? List the amenities included in each home sold and how they compare to what your home has to offer.

The Internet provides unlimited research outlets. Visit sites such as **www.housevalues.com**, **www.domania.com** and **www.homescape.com** for information on sale prices of comparable homes. Review your local paper for monthly property sale recordings or visit your county recorder. A property sale transfer is public information and is available to anyone who inquires.

"Buyers have more information available through the Internet and have become much more knowledgeable about the communities and schools in areas where they may be looking to buy a home. It is always good to arm a prospective buyer with more information about the home, property, community and schools. This will help the buyer make a faster buying decision."

Robert Picarellaro
Prello Realty, Flat Fee Realty Company

Enter all of the information you gather into a spreadsheet. Having all of the information in one location will help you determine how much you can ask for your home. There is nothing scientific about setting the sales price of a home. There are so many variables–location, age and condition of the home, the current market conditions coupled with the uniqueness of every home–that it becomes difficult for sellers to be sure their pricing is right. During the first few weeks, buyers will let the seller know if the price is right.

Sample Worksheet for Comparing Home Values

Address	1234 Main	4567 Grey	890 Green	9008 Brook
No. of Bedrooms	4	4	4	5
No. of Bathrooms	2.5	3.0	2.0	3.0
No. of Stories	2	2	2	2
Lot Size (ft.)	60 x 130	66 x 133	70 x 128	75 x 135
Garage	1—attached	2—attached	1—detached	2.5—detached
No. of Fireplaces	1	2	2	2
Sq. ft of Living Space	2,509	2,489	2,987	2,989
Asking Price	$499,000	$515,000	$525,000	$535,000
Selling Price	$475,000	$499,000	$510,000	$535,000
Time on Market	**Sold** 3 months	**Active** 1 month	**Active** 6 months	**Sold** 10 days
Agent or FSBO?	FSBO	Agent	Agent	FSBO
Finished Basement?	Yes	Yes	No	Yes
Notes:	MBB; fireplace in LR; no FR; brick house; professional landscaping; dead end street; built in 1940; original everything.	MBB; fireplace in LR and FR; 2 full baths, 2 half baths, MBB; 50/50 brick and siding; professional landscaping; patio; sits on busier street; built in 1949.	No MBB; large sized rooms; unfinished basement; wide lot; original kitchen and bath; fenced yard with deck; built in 1955; needs a lot of updating.	MBB; medium sized rooms; finished basement with fireplace; large, fenced lot; new kitchen and baths; refinished floors; professional landscaping; patio; built in 1988—newer home.

Collect data only on homes that are in your immediate area. Once you have collected this data, compare the features, room sizes, etc. to come up with a comparable price.

Prepare Comparable Sales Information for Buyers

Real estate agents prepare comparable sales information for their buyers before an offer to purchase is presented to the seller. Be aware that agents limit their comparable search to homes listed on the MLS only and do not include sales completed by owner. This may be an acceptable practice in areas in which almost all homes are sold by a real estate agent. However, in an area where many homes are listed and sold by owner, this limited comparable exercise will work against you if a real estate agent provides you or the buyer with a CMA of your area.

To help buyers and real estate agents feel confident that your home is priced correctly, provide a list of homes that have sold in your surrounding neighborhood within the past 12 months. Include the address, number of bedrooms, baths, selling price, date sold, or if sold via a real estate agent or FSBO. Also, note any distinguishing features of the homes, such as a new kitchen, finished basement, all brick exterior, number of fireplaces, square footage of home, or that the home was sold in as-is condition or as a tear-down, etc.

Visit Open Houses and Take Literature

Begin attending open houses in your neighborhood a few months before putting your home up for sale to get a firsthand look at similar homes, their condition and what amenities they offer. Be familiar with the features that the other homes offer compared to yours and be prepared to talk about how your home's features compare to theirs. Being able to talk with potential buyers and real estate agents knowledgeably shows you researched carefully before setting your asking price.

Exclusions

Once you have put together a list of comparable home sales and active listings, it is time to decide what will be included or excluded in the sale of your home. Inclusions with the sale may be draperies, lawn items, benches, pot racks or a second refrigerator or freezer. Exclusions are most commonly dining room chandeliers or a specific fixture. A list of excluded items always should be provided to the buyer before negotiations begin.

The Appraisal

When the buyer applies for a loan to purchase your home, his or her lender will send a certified appraiser to appraise the value of your property and verify that the home that will serve as collateral for the loan is not overpriced. An appraiser is a professional who is trained to assess the value of commercial or residential property.

An appraisal is an estimate of the value of a property on a certain date after both an inspection of the property and comparisons of that property with other comparable properties that have recently sold have been performed. Appraisers look at several factors as they work to establish the value of your home, including amenities common to homes in your local market. The appraiser then compares the sales prices of homes in your neighborhood to determine the value of your home.

Factors that a qualified appraiser will consider include the value of comparable properties as determined by recent sales, the appraised property's location, the level of competition in the current sales market, the current supply of comparable properties and current market interest in such properties, i.e., supply and demand. In a particular market, appraisers try to use the same appraisal principles to ensure consistency and accuracy.

Once the research is complete, the appraiser will issue an appraisal report to the buyer that documents the factors the appraiser used to arrive at the appraisal amount. Photos of the property–front and back–and photos of comparable properties may be included in the report. The report highlights the positive and negative aspects of a property so that the client can understand the appraiser's evaluation process. Finally, it presents the appraiser's valuation.

The entire appraisal process is very similar to the initial CMA you created to help you determine the best price for your home before listing it for sale. The appraiser looks for comparable sales information the same way you did to determine the fair market value of your home.

The ideal appraiser is familiar with your neighborhood and has performed several appraisals in your area. Once the appraisal is ordered, the appraiser will call to make an appointment to examine your home inside and out. The appraiser may spend up to an hour examining the interior and exterior of your home. The appraiser, like the home inspector, will ask many questions about the age of the mechanicals of your home, how old the roof is and the number of bedrooms and bathrooms. He or she may ask for a copy of the survey, what types of renovations have been completed lately and what appliances have been replaced. The seller should answer all questions honestly. Take time to talk with the appraiser and provide a list of all improvements done recently.

To help your home appraiser out, provide a list of comparable homes that have sold in your area recently. The appraiser will use the list as a foundation and will also add a few newer comparables of his or her own.

Most appraisers are well-trained, experienced and do a thorough job researching homes sold in a neighborhood. Be wary, however, of the appraiser that does not do a thorough job looking through the home or does not ask many questions. Appraisers that are not familiar with a neighborhood will often take the easy route and just use the comparable sales data you provide. Appraisers have been known to sit and do appraisals from their cars and never inspect the property or enter the home.

If an appraiser determines that your home's value is less than the contract sales price, you will most likely be notified immediately by the buyer. Since the buyer is the person who orders the appraisal, the buyer will receive a copy of the report, not the seller. Not appraising at sale value means it is not likely that the bank will loan the buyer the full amount of the requested mortgage and may require the buyer to make up the difference between the sales price and the amount the bank will lend them.

> **Example**
>
> If the sales price is $100,000, and the appraisal comes back at $96,000, the buyer's lender may provide only 80 percent of the appraised value. On $100,000, 80 percent is $80,000. On an appraisal of $96,000, 80 percent is only $76,800, and the lender may be willing to loan only $76,800. That leaves the buyer with a $3,200 gap that the buyer must close to complete the purchase of your home.

The buyer may ask the seller to lower the sale price to meet the appraised value or to take back a second mortgage to cover the difference. If the seller refuses to lower the sale price or to hold a second mortgage for the buyer, the buyer has the right to cancel the deal based on an inability to meet the financing contingency.

Before lowering your price, ask to see a copy of the appraisal report. The buyer may allow the seller to review the appraisal report to ensure that other homes in the neighborhood were properly compared against the property. If the properties included in the report are not comparable to the seller's home, the seller may compile better comparable sales data and ask the buyer to present the new data to the appraiser.

> **Example**
>
> A home went up for sale by owner in a neighborhood with a few homes that were comparable to the seller's and that sold during the past 18 months. A contract was accepted, and an appraisal was ordered. The appraisal came back below the sale price. One home was located more than a mile away, another was located in a different zip code and a third was significantly smaller in size than the home being appraised. Seeing the report, the seller immediately provided the buyer with a list of a few homes that had sold by owner in the area that were closer in size and featured similar amenities. The buyer called the appraisal company and asked the appraiser why the homes provided by the seller were not included in the report.
>
> The appraiser replied that he had included comparable sales data only on homes that were listed on the MLS. In an area where more than 50 percent of the homes were sold by owner, the appraiser was overlooking several comparable homes. The buyer forwarded the seller's list to the appraiser and the report was amended. The amended report gave the home a higher appraisal and the sale went through.

Not all appraisers are willing to amend their reports. The buyer or seller must present compelling facts and information to get an appraiser to re-evaluate a property. Most agents report that appraisers often rely on the agent or the homeowner to provide comparable data from their initial CMA to use in an appraisal. It is a good idea to provide buyers with a list of homes in the neighborhood that are similar to yours and that have sold during the past 12 to 18 months.

Time Is Money

It is a good idea to place your home on the market as far in advance of purchasing a new one as possible. If you wait until you are ready to close on a new home, you may wind up making payments on two mortgages at the same time. If this does happen, ask your banker about a bridge loan to help you make the double payments. Lenders use the same criteria for offering bridge loans as they use for mortgages. Should you qualify for a bridge loan, beware of the expense; during the term of the loan, you must continue to pay both mortgages. Shop around for the best terms.

Keep in mind that when people move, sell and buy, there usually is a domino effect. Closing and moving dates have to be coordinated, and the move firmly commits everyone to a window of dates. Everyone meeting their deadlines is better for all involved. Put all agreements about dates in writing and protect yourself by negotiating financial penalties for failure to comply.

Showing Your Home

When a home is listed with a real estate agent, it is best to stay away when an agent is showing your home to give the buyer and agent a chance to talk candidly. The situation is quite different, however, if you are selling by owner. As the seller, you have no choice but to show the home to prospective buyers yourself. The best showings are the ones in which you have time to point out all the amenities of your property and the buyer has time to appreciate them.

Turn on all of the lights in every room, even the closets. Let natural light in by opening draperies and shades. Buyers like well-lit homes. Make sure your home is as clean as possible.

While preparing her home for a showing, one seller cleaned every room in the house but forgot to wipe down the black stove. As the sun set and the sunshine streamed into the western kitchen window, the dust and fingerprints on the stove stood out like a neon sign. Do not take shortcuts. Dust, vacuum and sweep every part of the house before a showing.

Start the showing by greeting visitors at the front door. During the winter, offer to take visitors' coats and place them in a room near the front door for easy retrieval.

Depending on the flow of the home, begin the tour in the living room. Move to the kitchen, dining room, family room and then the porch or patio. Point out the main attractions along the way, such as a wood-burning fireplace, hardwood floors, crown molding and built-in bookcases. If the home has a water view, talk about the changing view as the tide goes in or out or the weekend activity on the lake. During the winter months when activity on the lake has ceased or the garden is no longer in full bloom, have pictures showing the view during the summer months.

List the items that will be excluded from the sale, such as light fixtures or appliances. These items should already be listed on your information sheet. Practice your presentation until it flows easily.

The best showings take longer than 20 minutes unless the property is very large or unique. A showing of 5 minutes usually signals that the buyer has already made up his or her mind to move on to the next showing.

> **Tip**
>
> If a buyer comments during a showing on where he or she would place their furniture, the buyer is already picturing the home as his or her own. Consider this buyer to be a hot prospect.

As a FSBO, it is perfectly acceptable for you to call back buyers who have gone through your home. Call buyers directly to gain their feedback. If an agent has shown the home, contact the agent 1 or 2 days later to get the client's feedback about your home. After two calls without a return call, consider the prospect uninterested in your home.

> **Tip**
>
> When showing your home, avoid talking too much. Give the buyer time to let the information you provide sink in. Stick to the room amenities and attributes. If a room has a great view or large windows, stop and point these features out to the buyer. Do not rush the showing by moving too quickly from room to room. As you show each room, you can present alternative uses for it to fit the buyer's current living needs.

Lock Box and Ease of Showing

Lock boxes are an important selling tool. If you do not allow your agent to put a lock box on your door, you will miss out on a huge part of the showing market. A lock box is a rectangular metal or plastic box that attaches to a doorknob, gas pipe, water spigot, etc. and holds a key to your home. In the past, they were always located on the front doorknob. Homeowners today are more cautious about placing the lock box in an inconspicuous place, making it less visible from the street. It is not uncommon to find the lock box attached to the gas or electric meter, an outdoor water faucet or hanging from a railing or a tree limb.

The older lock boxes were combination locks, while the newer ones require an electronic key to open them. The older boxes were much less efficient and presented a number of security issues for homeowners. Sometimes a real estate agent would not lock the box properly after showing the home and anyone could access the key to the home. The combination locks were also easier to pick and agents would sometimes forget to replace the key. If an agent wanted to show a home, he or she first had to contact the listing office to obtain the combination for the lock box. If the agent mixed up the numbers, he or she could not get it open and the buyers would move on to the next appointment without seeing the home.

The vast majority of real estate agents today prefer the electronic type of lock box. The electronic key will open any lock box, making it easier and faster to show a house that has one.

Current technology even allows agents to unlock the lock box using their cell phones. In addition, a detailed history of who has entered your home is recorded and can be accessed by the listing agent at any time. The computerized key cards record which agent is seeing the property and at what time. The report can be accessed by the agent or the FSBO seller for follow-up. This is important if an agent who is in the area decides to make a last-minute decision to show your home.

Most real estate agents love the concept of a lock box. It is a convenience for agents who do not have to drive all over town to pick up and return keys to the listing companies. An agent can schedule five or six showings within a certain time period and will not have to wait for the sellers to let him or her in. Plus, if an agent drives by a home with a lock box that was not included on the buyer's A list, the agent can conduct an impromptu showing without wasting time tracking down a key.

"The majority of my listings are homes selling in the upper bracket or have sellers who prefer to be present or have the selling agent present during all showings. The reason is the homes are occupied and are furnished with valuable antique furniture or have expensive art collections throughout the home. The sellers are not comfortable allowing anyone access to their homes at any time of the day or night. The decision to not have a lock box may have slightly reduced showings. It has also reduced the number of unqualified home buyers who just wanted to see the inside of the home for curiosity's sake."

John Tilique
Real Estate Agent

Example

An agent who has a buyer coming in from out-of-town searches the MLS and prepares a list of possible properties based on the buyer's parameters. The agent checks the showing instructions, and separates the properties into two piles—properties with lock boxes and properties for which the agent must make an appointment or pick up a key. Because most agents and buyers are on a very tight timetable, the agent will place the properties that fit the buyer's needs and are easy to show on the A list and give a 30- to 45-minute travel and showing time for each. Properties that require the agent to pick up a key will not make it on that day's showing schedule and will be placed on the B list. They will be shown only if time allows or if none of the homes on the A list works for the buyer.

Tip

Sellers have the ability to rent lock boxes, even if not using the services of an agent. There are companies that will rent lock boxes to sellers for a monthly charge.

When a Lock Box is Not a Good Idea

For every reason to use a lock box, there are an equal number of reasons not to, and some agents disagree with their use. While they may be fine for homes that are unfurnished, homeowners with homes that are priced in the upper bracket feel that they lose total control over who is showing the property.

Homes with pets are also not good candidates for lock boxes, unless the animal is confined to a cage during the day.

Safeguard Your Valuables

Opening your home to strangers carries with it certain risks. Be careful to remove valuables such as jewelry and other items from view. Consider taking these precautions:

- Put away jewelry, guns, billfolds, checks, purses or bills or lock them in a home safe or safe-deposit box.

- Never leave money, credit cards or loose change lying around. If you have a change jar, put it in your dresser drawer and cover it with socks or underwear.

- Pack away coin or stamp collections.

- Do not leave extra keys on hooks in the kitchen or by the front door. If you are holding neighbors' keys, make sure to place them away in a safe area. Extra sets of car or house keys have been known to disappear during an open house or showing.

- Do not leave personal calendars or an address book open on a desk. If you have a planner, do not leave it open showing your personal schedule. Do not leave PDAs or cell phones out in the open; they are too easily hidden in a purse or pocket.

- Place some lights on a timer. Not only will a well-lit home look more inviting to people driving by, but it will deter thieves who may think you are home during the day.

- Pack away any valuables or items that you would hate to lose, including paintings, crystal vases, silver picture frames, etc. You would be amazed at the number of people who want a souvenir of a home they looked at or who just cannot help themselves.

- Do not make it easy for robbers. Pack away any silver serving pieces or dishes. Potential buyers will look in all closets, and a closet full of silver may be the jackpot a pretend buyer was looking for.

- Pack away medications. It has been reported by agents that after an open house or showing, sellers have reported medications stolen by supposed buyers. Keep nosy neighbors from snooping around your medicine cabinets and drug thieves from stealing your medications. Lock them away in a place that is inaccessible to people who visit your home.

It might be wise to put these items in a safe-deposit box or home safe before showing your home. The old adage—out of sight, out of mind—applies here. Remove the temptation. What a potential thief does not see, he or she cannot take.

Open Houses—Are You Ready to Give Up Your Weekends?

In an open house, you open your home to the public for the express purpose of having potential buyers walk through and look at every inch of it. For sellers trying to sell their homes by owner, it is the best way to attract attention.

When you list your home with a real estate agent, the agent is available to show your home at each open house. In addition to trying to find a buyer for your home, an agent may be looking for new clients. When you sell your home by owner, you are responsible for showing your own home during an open house.

Hosting the Open House

People are trusting by nature. So trusting, in fact, that they will open the doors and show their homes to just about anyone who claims to be a buyer. You would be well-advised to enlist the help of another person to show prospective buyers around. An open house is the ideal time for skilled thieves to take advantage of your trust. Thieves target open houses because they know that they can easily distract the seller while an accomplice looks for valuables. It is an ideal time for thieves to find out exactly what you have that can eventually be theirs.

As difficult as it may be to control, try to keep couples who attend a showing or open house from separating. Enlisting the help of a family member or friend to keep an eye on everyone that walks through your home will help safeguard your valuables. When you conduct an open house, it is not possible to prescreen or prequalify everyone who walks through the door. Unless you take precautions to protect your home, you may find valuable items missing.

Example
A prospective buyer signed the sign-in sheet with almost illegible handwriting, made a quick tour through the house and told the homeowner he liked the house and wanted to bring his wife back to take a look. The buyer never returned. A few months later, he appeared again during an open house. This time, the seller recognized the man and kept an eye on him as he walked through the house. Again, after a quick look, he told the seller he wanted to bring his wife back to look at the house, and again, he did not return. After the buyer left, the homeowner walked through the home and noticed that clothes in the master bedroom closet had been moved, indicating that the buyer was looking for valuables or other items. A month later the buyer showed up again at an open house. This time, the seller took no chances and escorted the buyer around the house. Again, the buyer left saying he wanted to bring his wife back for a look. Is there a wife? There may be, but most likely there is not.

As this example illustrates, there are people who drive around attending open houses each week even though they are not serious buyers or buyers at all. They have no intention of purchasing a home but still visit every open house in the neighborhood, again and again.

Hosting an Agents' Open House

Weekdays are still the best time to attract agents to come through your home and preview it for their clients. Every community has a designated agents' open house day. This day–usually a Tuesday, Wednesday or Thursday–is set up for agents to visit newly listed homes. They receive notices of all open houses on their weekly hot sheet. Often agents will caravan from property to property, staying long enough for a quick walk-through. An agents' open house usually is held between

9 a.m. and 11 a.m. and takes place the first or second week a home comes on the market. It may be extended to serve lunch to attendees if the home is new or priced in a higher price bracket.

Agents may see 10 to 15 properties during morning or afternoon open houses. They try to see as many homes as possible. Agents often comment that depending on how many new listings are on the market, they will attend an agents' open house only if they have a client looking to buy a home. If attendance is light during the first agents' open house, a second may be scheduled a few weeks later. Additional open houses may be scheduled if the home has been on the market a while or if there has been cosmetic work done to the home to make it more saleable.

An agents' open house may sound exclusive and imply that only agents may tour the home, but the reality is that anyone may do so. Some agents may direct their clients to visit the open house to get a first look at the new listing. Agents' open houses are friendly, social affairs where agents get together to discuss the market and share industry gossip.

Despite its name, you do not need to be an agent to schedule an agents' open house. Sellers who have listed their homes through a flat-fee listing company and whose homes appear on the MLS have the opportunity to schedule an agents' open house, because these homes are offering a buyer's agent's commission. Agents with clients who may be looking for a home in your neighborhood will attend the open house to preview it for their clients. Do not be disappointed if only a handful of agents and buyers attend the open house. Depending on the strength of the real estate market, the number of new listings and the time of year, only a few agents or buyers may show or several dozen may attend. To increase attendance at any agents' open house, extend the hours until 1 p.m. and offer lunch.

Saturday and Sunday Open Houses

Traditionally, the Sunday open house is a general open house and is scheduled for 2-hour periods between 12 p.m. and 2 p.m., 2 p.m. and 4 p.m. or 1:30 p.m. and 3:30 p.m. These 2-hour shifts enable a real estate agent with multiple clients to hold more than one open house on Sunday. Statistics show that only 5 to 15 percent of all sales are a result of an open house. That may be true with homes listed through a real estate agent; however, when a home is for sale by owner, the buyer may get his or her first look at the home during an open house.

A FSBO seller has only one property to worry about and has greater flexibility to schedule open houses than a real estate agent. By owner sellers are scheduling longer open houses and most often select a time between 12 p.m. and 4 p.m. or 1 p.m. and 4 p.m. on Sundays. This provides buyers with ample time to schedule and visit more open houses.

The number of open houses that sellers typically hold each month is increasing. Historically, open houses have been held once or twice a month. Sellers now are opting to hold open houses every Sunday in an attempt to gain additional exposure. This approach is similar to a viral marketing theory, i.e., the more people who view a home the greater the number of potential buyers who will hear about it. More interest will be generated, and the odds of an interested buyer being among the visitors are increased. Buyers like open houses because they can visit them on their own without their agent, and unlike a private showing, seller expectations from the buyer are lower.

Hosting a Saturday open house is another marketing tool utilized by sellers and is most effective during the first few weeks a home is on the market. Holding an open house on Saturday from 1 p.m. to 4 p.m. may attract people who are running errands or dropping their kids off at a sporting event. A husband or wife who has time to stop and walk through your home and likes it may bring his or her spouse back the next day.

Evening Open Houses

If your home shows well at night, consider hosting an evening open house. The buyer who is busy driving kids to practices, attending games or running errands may be too busy to attend a Saturday or Sunday open house. An evening open house may be held after work from 5 p.m. to 8 p.m. An advantage of an evening open house is that it gives working couples the opportunity to see your home together. Consider offering sandwiches or snack foods to attract more traffic. If you are selling in late spring, summer or early autumn, you will have additional daylight hours for buyers to see the front and back yards, patio or other key landscaping features.

Choose Your Date Carefully

When scheduling your open houses, review personal, business and school calendars. Avoid holidays such as Mother's Day and Father's Day, 4-day weekends, religious holidays, Memorial Day, Fourth of July, Labor Day, Christmas and New Year's and national sporting events. Some real estate companies have banned agents from holding open houses during holiday weekends or on holidays. Their reasoning is that the number of people who attend open houses during family celebrations or holiday weekends drops significantly and the time spent hosting an open house is not constructive.

Advertise Your Open House

Advertising an open house is essential to attracting interested buyers. Placing a rider sign on your For Sale sign announcing the date and time of the open house provides the best advertising exposure. Make sure the sign can be seen easily by people driving by.

Placing an ad in a local paper or major city paper is still one of the most effective ways to advertise your open house to buyers who may not live in your immediate neighborhood or town. When placing an ad, include the following information:

- **Your street address and city**—It is always a good idea to include a phone number in the event that a buyer who is unfamiliar with your area gets lost and may need to call for directions. The ad should also list major intersections near where you live.

- **The time of the open house**—Select a time period no longer than 4 hours. An open house longer than 4 hours makes you look desperate. Also, remember that you must be ready to receive buyers the entire time, which can be exhausting.

- **The price**—Some agents will not include the price of the home in their ads because they believe it will turn off potential buyers. Buyers do not want to waste their time looking at a home they cannot afford. If they are motivated enough, they may call the owner or real estate agent to inquire about the price, or they may avoid the open house completely and instead view homes that they know are in their price range.

- **A description**—Provide a short description of your home to help buyers select the homes they want to visit. Use adjectives to distinguish your property from all the other ads. Include:

  - number of bedrooms
  - number of baths
  - square footage of living space
  - garage size—1-, 2-, 4- or 5-car
  - number of fireplaces
  - family room
  - finished basement
  - library
  - sunroom
  - enclosed porch
  - eat-in kitchen
  - lot size

Most newspapers charge by the word. In order to keep costs down, use abbreviations. Some of the most common abbreviations include:

- 2-CAR ATT.—2-car attached garage
- 4BR/2BA—Four bedrooms/two bathrooms
- 3/4 BA—Sink, commode, shower
- AC—Acres
- A/C—Air conditioning
- BA—Bath
- BR—Bedroom
- DBL—Double
- DR—Dining room
- FLRS—Floors
- FP—Fireplace
- FSBO—For sale by owner

- FB—Full bath (sink, commode, tub with shower)
- FR—Family room
- GLFP—Gas log fireplace
- HB—Half bath
- HDWD FLRS—Hardwood floors
- HSF—Heated square feet
- HVAC—Heating, ventilation and air conditioning
- KIT—Kitchen
- LR—Living room
- MBB—Master bedroom bath
- MBR—Master bedroom
- RM—Room
- SF—Square feet
- W/D—Washer/Dryer
- W/W CPT—Wall to wall carpet
- WBFP—Wood burning fireplace
- WD FLR—Wood floor

Examples of good ads include:

> 3200 W. Ottawamac
> Open Sunday 1-4
> Anytown. Ready to occupy 5BR/3.5BA. LR, DR, island kit w/FR, granite counter
> hdwd flrs. Finished basement 2 car gar. $279,000 555.555.5555.

> 6023 W. Sunny Lane
> Open Sunday 12-3
> New Price
> Yourtown. Brick bi-level with subbasement. 3BR/2BA, eat-in kitchen, Lg. FR.
> Beautiful hdwd flrs in LR/DR kitchen & bedrooms. Oversized city lot with side drive
> leading to 2.5-car gar. Close to restaurants and train $469K 555.555.5555.

> 9503 Yellowleaf
> Open Sunday 1-3
> Mytown. Spectacular 2 yr. old mansion w/gorgeous Napa-style garden, yard & deck.
> 7,000 sf. Perfect for entertaining! Dramatic European entryway w/high ceilings &
> hand-scraped walnut floors. Enormous chef's kitchen w/subzero, etc. 3 huge spa-like
> BAs w/xtra lrg Jacuzzis, steam shower & rainheads! Lawn has b/i sprinkler system. 3
> plasmas incl. $1,095,000 555.555.5555.

Preparing for the Open House

Preparing for an open house means making sure your home is spotless. It is
important that the home be clean, with everything put away. Buyers will look into

closets, so make sure linens are folded and clothes are neatly hanging or folded. Do not cram items into closets just to get them out of sight. How your home smells is also important. Simmering potpourri or lightly scented candles make a home smell fresh and clean.

Sign-in Sheet

Create a sign-in sheet and ask visitors to sign it before they tour your home. Ask them to write down their name, address and phone number or e-mail along with the name of any agent they may be working with. To track the effectiveness of your advertising, also ask how they heard about the open house.

An example of an open house sign-in sheet follows:

Name	Address	Phone No.	Agent's name	How did you hear about the open house?	E-mail

Many buyers are wary of giving away too much personal information and may provide only a first name, the city instead of a complete address and e-mail instead of phone number. Be aware that a buyer may provide false information or an office number to avoid being contacted by the seller.

Follow-Up

A day or two after the open house, contact each person who attended and offer to answer any additional questions they may have about the home or neighborhood, especially if you did not have the opportunity to talk with them during the open house. Learning more about their interests and plans will help you determine whether the buyer is serious or just casually looking.

Condos and Co-Ops

Condominiums and co-op buildings often have strict regulations about open houses and when and how units may be shown. Condo regulations may require you to have two people in the unit plus an additional person in the lobby directing traffic to the correct set of elevator banks. Rules may also be in effect requiring that the sign-in sheet be located at the doorman's station. Advance notice of your intent to host an open house may be required, and the number of open houses you can hold each month may also be restricted.

Discounts on Other Socrates Products

In addition to a variety of free forms and checklists, you will find special offers on a variety of Socrates products. Visit **www.socrates. com/books/ForSaleByOwner.aspx** for more information.

4

· · · · · ·

Advertising

Advertising Your Home

You cannot sell FSBO without advertising to find prospective buyers. Begin by creating an advertising plan. Write down all your advertising ideas, who you want to target and your estimated cost to promote.

An informational packet to hand out to the best prospects might include the following:

- full-color listing sheet
- completed disclosure forms—lead paint and seller's disclosure form
- condo or co-op disclosure form
- demographics or interesting facts about the location and town and a newspaper article about the schools or community for the out-of-towners

The Cost of Advertising

Create an advertising plan that includes all costs associated with classified and display ads, fliers, postcards, Internet advertising, listing on the MLS, etc. Next, determine how often you intend to advertise or if each cost will be a one-time expense. Then, add up all costs to determine your overall budget. If homes in your neighborhood are taking an average of 3 months to sell, budget your advertising costs accordingly.

	Frequency	Cost	Size of ad/No. of pieces	Name of publication
Freebies				
Postcards				
Open Houses				
Signs				
Internet Advertising				
Discount Agent				
Totals		$		

If your home takes longer than 3 months to sell, you must decide if you want to continue paying for ads or if there are other less expensive ways to promote your home.

> **Tip**
>
> Spread your advertising out so that each week you are getting some type of promotion on your home out to potential buyers. The key is to get the attention of potential buyers and stay visible.

Successful FSBO sellers know in advance how much they are willing to spend to promote their homes. By putting together an advertising plan schedule, you will know how much money you will need to spend to market your property. Once you determine your advertising budget, stick to it.

Classified vs. Display Ads

The main difference between a classified ad and a display ad is that the cost of a classified ad is determined by word count, whereas the cost of a display ad is determined by size. Classified ads are printed in the classified section of the paper under a designated headline such as Open Houses or Homes for Sale. Display ads are larger and usually are sold in one-eighth, one-fourth, one-half, two-thirds or full-page increments. In the case of display ads, the advertiser is responsible for providing camera ready art to the publication. Display ads may be black and white or for an additional fee, color. The larger ad provides more room for a picture or a detailed description and may be placed on any page in the publication. An effective ad includes a catchy headline and a description of the property with lots of adjectives.

Best Display Ads

Expensive homes are typically promoted to the executive market through display ads in prominent local or national newspapers or national magazines.

The best display ads include an attention grabbing headline, a picture of the property, a detailed description of the amenities, the asking price and contact information. Below is an example of an effective display ad:

Larger than It Looks!   **Open Sunday 1-4**

Unbelievably spacious! 4 BR, 2.5 BA full-of-charm English Tudor home in Anytown near Central Park. A new cook's kitchen with granite counters and stainless features tons of storage and a breakfast room w/dining island that opens to sunny FR. Spacious LR with built-in bookcases, French doors & large WB fpl. Sep. DR overlooks front garden. Large MBR with full bath and walk-in closet The 2nd full bath & 3 more large BRs are all located on the 2nd floor. 2-car att garage w/ storage. Fabulous perennial gardens & huge Lannon stone patio makes for perfect outdoor entertaining. Move right in. Too many updates to list. Hurry, this one will go fast!

XXX Central Park, Anytown   **$799,000**   **555.555.5555**

Other Tips for Writing Ads

Follow these guidelines when writing your ads:

- Describe features of the property that appeal to your targeted group of buyers rather than the general market.
- Include features that translate into a benefit to the buyer: assumable mortgage, seller financing, etc.
- Always give the location of the property and the phone number in case the buyer gets lost on the way to see your home. Buyers are interested in specific areas and will pass over your listing if the location is omitted.
- Always include the price. A missing price suggests that the property is too expensive, and buyers are reluctant to call to find out what it is.
- Conclude the ad by giving the reader a call to action, such as:
  - Hurry, do not let this one get away!
  - There is nothing like it at this price!

Headlines That Sell

Good headlines grab a buyer's attention. When writing headlines, try to imagine what type of audience you are targeting and tailor the headline to that group. A Park-Like Setting! will grab the attention of a family. A Cook's Kitchen will interest someone who likes to cook. Move-in Condition! is perfect for the homeowner who does not like to paint. Bring Your Water Toys! lets a buyer know the home is located on new water. Solid as a Rock! and Built to Last! indicate a well-built home. These are all examples of catchy headlines.

Suggestions for other good headlines include:

- One Floor Living!
- Not Just a Home, It's a Lifestyle!
- Stop Staring
- Swing on Over
- Nestled in the Woods
- Beachcomber's Delight!
- Antique Lover's Delight!
- Quality from the Past
- One of a Kind!
- Charming Cottage
- Look No Further!
- Paint Brush Special!
- Walk Right in!

- Refreshed and Rejuvenated!
- Move Right In!
- Tennis Anyone?
- Golfer's Paradise
- Steps to the Beach!
- Hilltop Delight!
- A Golden Oldie
- Timeless Beauty
- Petite Retreat
- Dynamic Duo: Price & Value
- Spectacular Views!
- Privacy Plus

The Internet

Statistics show that more than 70 percent of home buyers shop online before making a purchase offer. That is up from 41 percent just 4 years earlier. Internet ads enable a seller to display multiple photos and provide a detailed description of the property.

The following are two examples of Internet ads:

1. Orchard, VA
    $259,000
    Single Family Property
    Year Built: 1977
    Approximately 2,442 sq. ft.
    3 total bedroom(s), 3 total bath(s)

    Type: Tri-level, Handicap features
    Fireplace(s)
    Spa/hot tub(s)
    2-car garage, Attached parking, RV/boat parking

    Heating features: electric fuel, wood fuel, forced air

    Interior features: dishwasher, disposal, range and oven, dining area, master bathroom, storm window(s), vaulted ceiling(s), walk-in closet(s), vinyl flooring, wall-to-wall carpeting

    Exterior features: territorial view, septic sewer system, dog run, partially fenced, tv cable available

    Exterior construction: wood siding

    Community recreation facilities

    Community security features

    Water view, mountain view, waterfront, high bank

    Lot is 62,291 sq. ft

    Located on a cul-de-sac

    Approximately 1.43 acre(s)

    School district: Buyer to verify

2. **Property Details: 4569 Winterberry Drive, Salem, OR**

    REMODELED BRICK HOME/UPDATED/LARGE FENCED YARD!
    Price: $599,000
    Type: Single Family Home
    Floors: 3
    No. of bedrooms: 3
    No. of bathrooms: 2.00
    Lot size/acres: 9,000 sq. ft.

ALS Sq. footage: 2,489

Garage size: 2.5

Year built: 1965

School district: Brier Township

Amenities: alarm, central ac, fitness center, gas range, patio, playground/ park, wood floors

Move-in condition! Lovely brick home with newer roof on wide 68 x 135 property with roomy 2.5 car attached garage. Beautiful hardwood floors. Cathedral ceilings on main floor living room and dining room. Remodeled eat-in kitchen with granite countertops, light wood cabinets, large double sink and newer whirlpool appliances, including dishwasher and disposal. Also featuring separate dining area, living room and beautiful year-round sunroom with baseboard heat and air conditioner–addition to the home– windows everywhere! Lower level large family room has built-ins and brand new carpeting. Lower level laundry room/second kitchen—with second refrigerator, cabinets and exhaust fan. Large patio and lovely fenced backyard with beautiful landscaping. 9,000 square feet lot. Brier School District.

Total 8 rooms/BR 3/Baths 2/2.5 garage

Living: 19 x 13/hdwd flrs and windows

Master: 15 x 14/hdwd flrs and windows

2nd br: 10 x 9/hdwd flrs and windows

3rd br: 13 x 11/hdwd flrs and windows

Dining: 13 x 10/hdwd flrs and windows

Kitchen: 13 x 10/ceramic tile

Family: 18 x 13/new carpet and windows

Sun/Florida: 17 x 13/hdwd flrs and windows

Utility: 13 x 8

Laundry: 12 x 8

CALL FOR AN APPOINTMENT!!!

Internet ads do not have the same space restrictions as print ads, so more information may be provided for a longer period of time for less money. A benefit of Internet advertisements is that out-of-town buyers may preview properties from anywhere in the country.

Mailings

Postcards are a great way to get the word out quickly that your home is for sale. A small postcard–four inches by six inches–may include a photo of the home, the number of bedrooms, baths and other features, the asking price, an Internet address, if one is available and contact information. The card alerts everyone in the neighborhood that your home is up for sale. In addition, the postcard can be passed along easily to neighbors' friends or relatives who are looking for a home in your area.

Door-to-Door Canvassing

If you live in an area where residents seem to move from one home to another without ever leaving the neighborhood, hiring a canvasser to attach fliers to front doorknobs is a great way to let prospective buyers know your home is for sale. The advantage of a flier over a postcard is that a flier allows more room for larger photos and longer descriptions. The flier can be black and white or color. There are companies that offer an insert program where you pay to have your flier–along with other company's fliers–inserted into a clear plastic bag and hung on the front doorknob. You also can do it yourself by hiring neighborhood students looking to make a little extra money. Equip them with fliers and rubber bands and pay them by the hour or based on the number of fliers they deliver.

> "Utilizing the services of a realtor to get their home listed on the Multiple Listing Service provides for sale by owner sellers with the comfort of knowing their property will be seen online by thousands. That increases the odds that their home will sell quickly."
>
> Robert Picarellaro
> Prello Realty
> Flat Fee Realty Company

Tip
Fliers can be attached to the front door but may not be placed in residents' mailboxes. It is a violation of postal regulations if letters, fliers, etc. are placed in the mailbox without proper postage.

Freebie Promotions

While marketing your home is key to getting the word out to potential buyers, marketing does not need to be expensive to be effective. Here are other inexpensive suggestions for promoting your home:

- Hang fliers on a community or library bulletin board or post office.
- Hand out fliers to morning commuters at the train station—get approval first.
- Advertise in a church bulletin.
- Post fliers at local day care centers, preschools or community centers.
- Send an e-mail to all your friends announcing that your home is for sale.
- Advertise a agents' open house if you are listed on the local MLS database.
- Place fliers or business-size cards with information on windshields or door handles of cars parked at the local grocery store or mall.
- Hold weekly open houses.

Talking Up Amenities

An amenity is something that contributes to physical or material comfort. It is a feature that increases attractiveness or value, especially for a piece of real estate or a geographic location.

Examples of amenities include improvements made to the home or unique features.

Always create excitement with your promotion copy. Descriptive copy is the only way to get across all the amenities a home has to offer and to distinguish your home from competitors. Good descriptive copy highlights the best features of the home and prompts buyers to go take a look.

For Sale Signs

A sign on your property is the single most effective advertising tool you have. It informs everyone in the area and anyone driving down the street that your home is for sale. Sellers who prefer not to place a For Sale sign on their property will not be able to reach out-of-area buyers who drive through a neighborhood looking for a new home.

Choosing a Sign

Two types of signs are commonly used—custom, professionally painted signs or the common red and white signs available at your local hardware store. A professionally designed and painted sign may cost between $50 and $150. A generic red and white sign costs between $10 and $20.

A hand-painted sign looks more professional and shows that you are committed to selling. The generic sign looks cheap. Surprisingly, however, the cheap sign will get more attention. The reason is that buyers are familiar with the design. It is quickly spotted and easily recognized as a For Sale sign. The hand-painted professional looking sign, on the other hand, may attract only one glance from prospective buyers, who assume the sign belongs to a builder, remodeling company or contractor. It is common for remodeling companies and builders to post a nicely designed sign featuring their company name and phone number in front of the home they are working on. In some neighborhoods, there are so many construction projects going on that it is difficult to determine who is selling and who is remodeling.

Examples of choosing the correct sign are:

- A million dollar home was put up for sale by owner. The seller started out with a cheap red and white For Sale sign purchased from the hardware store down the street. After 2 months, the seller decided to have a sign painted and hang it from a post in the front yard to make it higher and to make it look more like a real estate agent's sign. The hand-painted sign had little effect attracting additional buyers. The home sat unsold for many more months before it finally sold. The majority of the people who attended the open house commented that they thought the home was listed with a real estate agent since the sign looked so professional and did not realize that it was being offered by owner. In this case, the hand-painted sign had little effect in increasing buyer traffic.

- A seller posted a hand-painted For Sale sign on the front lawn. The sign looked great. It included all the important information, the words For Sale, Spacious 4 br, 2.5 ba, the phone number and the words Shown by Appointment. The sellers were getting few calls. As a test, they decided to place the generic red and white For Sale sign from the hardware store next to the nicer sign to see what would happen. The result was that the number of phone inquiries and appointments doubled. Potential buyers remarked that they recognized the red and white sign as a For Sale sign and thought the hand-painted sign was a contractor's or window installer's sign advertising that they were working on the home.

- A practicing real estate agent decided to sell her own home by owner. She put a red and white For Sale sign with her phone number on the bottom in her front yard. The first day she received 75 inquiries about the home. The response was so overwhelming that she had to remove the sign to stop the phone calls. The asking price of the home was just under $1 million!

- A seller decided to test how many people would call about his house if he put a For Sale sign in front of it. The seller decided that if the offer was right, he would move. If no offers came in, there was nothing to lose, so he decided there was no reason yet to spend money on a sign. The sign was a cheap red and white For Sale sign with just his phone number and no brochure. The home sold in 3 weeks for $1.2 million.

As these stories demonstrate, it is important that the words For Sale be very big—they should take up two-thirds of the sign—bold and not fade into the background or get lost behind cars.

Also, choose bright colors that will not get lost in the rain or darkness, blend into the snow or be camouflaged by green grass and bushes during the summer.

Price Changes

Regardless of the type of sign you select, decide in advance where you will post a new price rider if you lower your asking price. It is important to advertise the price change. Prospective buyers who looked at the home at the original listing price may find it more attractive at the reduced price.

Sign Placement

A key consideration in announcing to prospective buyers that your property is for sale is the placement of the sign. If the sign is low, cars parked in the street in front of the sign can block it from being seen from the street. If possible, position the sign so it is very visible from the street and may be seen by passing motorists from one-half to one block away.

Sign Wording

Information to include on the For Sale sign include the words For Sale, a contact phone number and Shown by Appointment—otherwise people will be knocking on your door unannounced. If the home is large but looks small from the outside, include wording to attract a larger-sized family. Never include the asking price on the sign.

Sign Size

The sign should be approximately 20 inches by 30 inches or larger. The stand should be sturdy enough to withstand wind, rain and snowstorms and be capable of holding an information box.

Open House Signs

Directional open house signs are very important to attracting lookers. Place them at busy intersections and then post more along the way to give buyers a path to follow. Put your address and phone number on them as well. Your address on the sign provides prospects with a destination in the event that directional signs fall down. Signs should also include directional arrows pointing toward the property. Putting your phone number on the sign will enable buyers to inquire about specific features of your home and determine if the home meets their needs before coming over.

After the open house is over, look at your sign-in sheet. You may be surprised to learn that more prospective buyers attended your open house as a result of the signs than in response to the ad you placed in the paper.

Information Box

Attach an information box to your open house sign. Fill the box with pamphlets describing the key features of the home and keep it filled. Providing a descriptive brochure helps bring in prospective buyers.

Information Flier or Brochure

In some areas, the home seller puts together a book and leaves it in a common area of the home. Prospective buyers and real estate agents will refer to the book upon entering the home to learn about special features, lot size and other relevant information. This binder includes copies of all disclosures and reports, such as well, structural, septic, etc., a copy of the plat of survey, a list of schools in the area and information about them, if available, and demographic information about the city or town. The binder also may include any newspaper articles about the neighborhood or community that highlights key features.

> "There is always the danger of information overload. But in real estate, more is usually better. Rule of thumb: If a buyer cannot find important information on the fact sheet, there is too much information provided. Packing too much information on a sheet–to the point that the buyer cannot locate important information–in this case, less may be better. To remove unnecessary information, start by taking a quarter of the information off to give the sheet a more airy and clean look."
>
> Professional Realtor
> Flat Fee Realty Company

How Much Information Is Too Much?

Can you really provide too much information? Some real estate agents will simply answer yes. A home brochure should include just enough information to pique the buyer's curiosity. The last thing you want to do is turn off a buyer with information overload or too many photographs. Nothing substitutes for an on-site

"To help buyers identify with a home, a fact sheet should include a photo of the outside of the house, the number of bedrooms and baths. Some sellers list all information, including lot sizes, taxes, room sizes, key features and schools. Other sellers provide only a description of rooms, upgrades and location. Agents suggest sellers provide only enough information to entice the buyer to walk through the door—no more and no less. Others will argue that by providing less information, you attract more buyers but fewer qualified buyers. Maybe that is the intent of the agent showing your home—to try to get new clients, but that is a bad use of time by the seller who wants only qualified buyers to walk through his or her home."

Professional Realtor
Flat Fee Realty Company

review, not even with the most photogenic homes.

Consider creating more than one version of the flier to use in different situations.

Create a one-page flier to pin onto bulletin boards at the local grocery store, train station and other public places. This flier can also be left out during open houses as a takeaway for casual buyers.

A second, more detailed flier may be created that includes more information about the neighborhood, town or schools. The more comprehensive flier can be given to buyers who visit your home with an agent, buyers who express a greater interest in your home or agents who preview your home on behalf of their buyers.

For prospects that express more interest in your home, you may want to create a home information packet as a take along after each showing. Include the following information in the packet:

- detailed flier describing the home, features, room sizes, etc.
- lead-based paint form
- seller's disclosure form
- radon disclosure form
- schools in the area
- plat of survey
- relevant articles about the community, such as a newspaper clipping touting how hard the city has worked to lower your taxes or articles about awards presented to the local schools for academic excellence, etc.

Information to Include in the Brochure

Include the following information in your brochure:

- address, including zip code
- square footage of the home—combine the first and second floor living space. List basement or subbasement square footage separately.
- year the home was built
- primary exposure
- amount of your most recent tax bill and date of bill
- number of bedrooms and room sizes

- number of bathrooms
- list of other rooms—dining room, living room, den, kitchen, breakfast room, foyer, landing, etc. (with dimensions)
- amenities—basement, fireplace, attic, sun porch, greenhouse, enclosed porch, hardwood floors, whirlpool, swimming pool, central air, walk-in closets, etc.
- list of mechanicals and appliances that will stay with the home, including light fixtures, washer and dryer, etc.—list any exclusions here as well.
- school districts with names of schools
- assessments, special assessments and other condo/co-amenities, including health club or workout rooms, beach rights, clubhouse rights, swimming pool, 24-hour doorman or security system, live-in engineer, parking garage assessments, etc.—itemize the cost of each item included in the assessment such as heat, taxes, water, cable and special assessments
- description of parking space/garage or condo-deeded garage spaces
- distance to sources of transportation—bus, train and highway
- distance to parks or recreational services

If you live in a condo or co-op, provide all relevant documents to potential buyers. Monthly assessments may include real estate taxes, heat, hot water, electricity and cable. Itemizing each element of your monthly bill helps buyers to compare each building's services and how much they cost.

	Condo A	Condo B
Basic monthly assessment (cable, doorman and heat)	$650	$750
Special assessments (5 years)	$150	$ 0
Real estate taxes	$550	$650 paid separately
Parking garage assessment	$150	$250
Hot water/heating	$ 50	$ 75
Total:	$1,550	$1,725

Condo A may look like it has a lower basic monthly assessment charge than Condo B, but examine each breakout carefully. Many variables go into monthly assessments, and as the seller, you should be able to explain why your monthly assessment may be higher or lower than a similar unit in the building. Reasons may be square footage differences, one car space vs. two, etc.

Fair Housing Act

In 1988, the U.S. Congress passed the Fair Housing Act in order to provide all Americans with an equal opportunity to obtain housing. The act was created to strengthen the Civil Rights Act of 1968.

The Fair Housing Act, 42 U.S.C. §3601 et seq., prohibits discrimination by direct providers of housing, such as landlords and real estate companies. It also applies to property sellers, as well as other entities, such as municipalities, banks or other lending institutions and homeowners insurance companies. The act protects against discriminatory practices that make housing unavailable to persons because of:

- race or color;
- religion;
- sex;
- national origin;
- familial status; or
- disability.

In cases involving discrimination in mortgage loans or home improvement loans, the Department of Justice may file suit under both the Fair Housing Act and the Equal Credit Opportunity Act.

Under the Fair Housing Act, the Department of Justice may bring lawsuits where there is reason to believe that a person or entity is engaged in a pattern or practice of discrimination or where a denial of rights to a group of persons raises an issue of general public importance.

Where force or threat of force is used to deny or interfere with fair housing rights, the Department of Justice may institute criminal proceedings.

The Fair Housing Act also provides procedures for handling individual complaints of discrimination. Individuals who believe that they have been victims of an illegal housing practice may file a complaint with the Department of Housing and Urban Development (HUD) or file their own lawsuit in federal or state court. The Department of Justice brings suits on behalf of individuals based on referrals from HUD. To view the entire manual, visit **www.usdoj.gov/crt/housing/housing_coverage.htm**.

Fair Housing Act Advertising Guidelines

Sections of the Fair Housing Act specifically cover the advertisement of any dwelling for sale or rent. The act does not apply to just real estate professionals, bankers or landlords; it applies to everyone.

Incorporating key words or phrases into your advertising or promotion materials may violate Fair Housing Regulations. Failure to follow the Fair Housing Act guidelines may result in a fine. Fines start at $10,000 per violation, and civil damages may be awarded to injured parties. Some items on the list of restricted phrases or words that could get you into trouble may seem quite obvious while others may leave you wondering why.

Avoid the following words in ads, descriptions or promotional materials:

Ethnic words, such as:

- Indian
- Jewish
- Hispanic
- Latino
- Gays

- Irish
- Chinese
- Caucasian
- Catholic
- Mexican-Americans

This is an incomplete list. Avoid any ethnic reference.

Also avoid these other less obvious words and phrases:

- Community
- Mother-in-law apartment
- Handyman's dream
- Near
- Private
- Starter home

- Close to
- Near country club
- Grandma's house
- Prestigious
- Within walking distance of
- Sophisticated

The following words and phrases can be included in your ads:

- Beautiful
- Do not let this one get away
- Tucked away
- Move right in
- Look no further!
- Fixer-upper

- Larger than it looks!
- English beauty
- Steps from the lake
- Stunning views
- Paintbrush special

Free Forms and Checklists

Visit Socrates.com and register to receive a variety of useful FREE forms, letters and checklists. See page iv for details on how to register (you will need the 7-digit registration code provided on the enclosed CD).

5

· · · · · ·

Disclosures

Many states mandate that a written seller's disclosure form be included with each real estate transaction completed. Even if a disclosure is not required, sellers are wise to fill out and date a disclosure form to provide to the buyer. Seller disclosure forms ask questions about the condition of the home's electrical, plumbing and mechanical systems; foundation structure and condition; septic, well and sewer systems; and the general condition of the structure. The questions included on the form are detailed and require the seller to voluntarily disclose any flaws or known structural inconsistencies with the home.

A few states, such as Indiana, use the information to conduct sales ratio studies, to promote tax equalization and to ensure that all parties involved in the sale have completed, received and signed a copy of the disclosure. The state also may charge a small disclosure filing fee of five or 10 dollars to include the document with other information about the parcel of land or home.

Seller's Disclosure

Required in most states, the seller's disclosure mandates that you, the seller, must disclose any known material or latent defects of your property. This means you must disclose whether your property has any hidden or unseen defects that could adversely affect its value. The disclosure form is usually a preprinted form with specific questions and check boxes stating that the seller is aware or unaware–or that the question does not apply–of any defects in electrical, structural, mechanical or other systems. Sellers must answer all the questions honestly. Questions asked are specific to an area. The form may include only one sheet or several, depending on the detail of the questions asked.

Buyers like sellers' disclosures because they tell them up front about the condition of the property. Sellers also like having the disclosures because they protect sellers from having buyers discover a defect during an inspection and then asking for money to fix it.

System components typically included on the disclosure form are listed below:

- **Water and sewer system and appliances**
  Built-in vacuum system, clothes washer and dryer, dishwasher, disposal, freezer, gas grill, hood, microwave oven, oven, range, refrigerator, room air conditioner(s), trash compactor, TV antenna/dish, cistern, septic field/bed,

hot tub, plumbing, aerator system, sump pump, irrigation systems, water heater (electric), water heater (gas), water heater (solar), water purifier, water softener and well water.

Are the improvements connected to a public water system?

Are the improvements connected to a public sewer system?

Are the improvements connected to a private/community water system?

Are the improvements connected to a private/community sewer system?

- **Electrical system**
  Air purifier, burglar alarm, ceiling fan(s), garage door opener/controls, inside telephone wiring and blocks/jacks, intercom, light fixtures, sauna, smoke/fire alarm(s), switches and outlets, vent fan(s) and type of electrical service (60/100/200 amp service).

- **Heating and cooling system**
  Attic fan, central air conditioning, hot water heat, furnace heat (gas), furnace heat (electric), solar house-heating, wood-burning stove, fireplace, fireplace insert, cleaner, humidifier, propane tank and other heating source.

Note
The term defect means a condition that would have a significant adverse effect on the value of the property. The condition would significantly impair the health or safety of future occupants of the property or, if not repaired, removed or replaced, would significantly shorten or adversely affect the expected normal life of the premises.

Seller's Residential Real Estate Sales Disclosure—State Form

Are there any additions that may require improvements to the sewage disposal system? If yes, have the improvements been completed on the sewage disposal system?

Other disclosures:

- Roof: Age, if known: _____ years
- Does the roof leak?
- Is there present damage to the roof?
- Is there more than one roof on the home? If so, how many layers?

Hazardous conditions:

- Have there been or are there any hazardous conditions on the property, such as methane gas, lead paint, radon gas in home or well, radioactive material, landfill, mine shaft, expansive soil, toxic materials, mold, other biological contaminants, asbestos insulation or PCBs?
- Do improvements have aluminum wiring?
- Are there any foundation problems with the improvements?
- Are there any encroachments?

- Are there any violations of zoning, building codes or restrictive covenants?
- Is the present use a nonconforming use? Explain:
- Have you received any notices by any governmental or quasi-governmental agencies affecting this property?
- Are there any structural problems with the buildings? Have any substantial additions or alterations been made without a required building permit?
- Are there moisture and/or water problems in the basement, crawl space area or any other area?
- Have any improvements been treated for wood-destroying insects?
- Is there any damage due to wind, flood, termites or rodents?
- Are the furnace/wood-burning stove/chimney/flue all in working order?
- Is the property in a flood plain?
- Do you currently pay flood insurance?
- Does the property contain an underground storage tank(s)?
- Is the homeowner a licensed real estate salesperson or agent?
- Is there any threatened or existing litigation regarding the property?
- Is the property subject to covenants, conditions and/or restrictions of a homeowners' association?
- Is the property located within 1 mile of an airport?

The form will usually start out with a statement similar to this:

Seller states that the information contained in this disclosure is correct to the best of seller's current actual knowledge as of the above date. The prospective buyer and the owner may wish to obtain professional advice or inspections of the property and provide for appropriate provisions in a contract between them concerning any advice, inspections, defects or warranties obtained on the property. The representations in this form are the representations of the owner and are not the representations of the agent, if any. This information is for disclosure only and is not intended to be a part of any contract between the buyer and the owner. The law generally requires sellers of one- to four-unit residential property to complete this form regarding the known physical condition of the property. An owner must complete and sign the disclosure form and submit the form to a prospective buyer before an offer is accepted for the sale of the real estate. Property address—number and street, city, state, and zip code.

Questions included on the disclosure are presented in a check box fashion with the seller checking a box: Yes/No/Do Not Know/Not Applicable (N/A).

Question	Yes	No	Do Not Know	N/A
Seller has occupied the property within the past 12 months. (No explanation is needed.)				
I am aware of flooding or recurring leakage problems in the crawl space or basement.				
I am aware that the property is located in a flood plain or that I currently have flood hazard insurance on the property.				
I am aware of material defects in the basement or foundation, including cracks and bulges.				
I am aware of leaks or material defects in the roof, ceilings or chimney.				
I am aware of material defects in the walls or floors.				
I am aware of material defects in the electrical system.				
I am aware of material defects in the plumbing system—this includes such things as water heater, sump pump, water treatment system, sprinkler system and swimming pool.				
I am aware of material defects in the well or well equipment.				
I am aware of unsafe conditions in the drinking water.				
I am aware of material defects in the heating, air conditioning or ventilation system.				
I am aware of material defects in the fireplace or wood-burning stove.				
I am aware of material defects in the septic, sanitary sewer or other disposal system.				

I am aware of unsafe concentrations of radon on the premises.				
I am aware of unsafe concentrations of or unsafe conditions relating to asbestos on the premises.				
I am aware of unsafe concentrations of or unsafe conditions relating to lead paint, lead water pipes, lead plumbing pipes or lead in the soil on the premises.				
I am aware of mine subsidence, underground pits, settlement, sliding, upheaval or other earth stability defects on the premises.				
I am aware of current infestations of termites or other wood-boring insects.				
I am aware of a structural defect caused by previous infestations of termites or other wood-boring insects.				
I am aware of underground fuel storage tanks on the property.				
I am aware of boundary or lot line disputes.				
I have received notice of violation of local, state or federal laws or regulations relating to this property, which violation has not been corrected.				

The final paragraph on the form indicates that the seller has provided accurate information:

The information contained in this disclosure has been furnished by the seller, who certifies to the truth thereof, based on the seller's current actual knowledge. A disclosure form is not a warranty by the owner or the owner's agent, if any, and the disclosure form may not be used as a substitute for any inspections or warranties that the prospective buyer or owner may later obtain. At or before settlement, the owner is required to disclose any material change in the physical condition of the property or certify to the purchaser at settlement that the condition of the property is substantially the same as it was when the disclosure form was provided. Seller and purchaser hereby acknowledge receipt of this disclosure by signing it.

Most states require the seller to provide a signed copy of the disclosure sheet to the buyer. The buyers and the sellers must both sign the disclosure sheet to indicate that the sellers have disclosed the present condition of the home to the buyer and that the buyer has received the disclosure statement. This form must be signed by both the seller and the buyer before the purchase contract may be signed. If the disclosure is given to the buyer after the contract is signed, the buyer usually has a short period of time–3 to 5 business days–to cancel the contract if the seller's disclosure turns up a serious defect.

During closing procedures, the seller again will sign the form at the time of closing to indicate that there have not been any changes to the condition of the home between the time the buyer's purchase bid was accepted and the actual closing date.

The seller hereby certifies that the property is substantially the same as it was when the seller's disclosure form was originally provided to the buyer. If not the same, explain any changes.

Tip
Even sellers of as-is homes must provide a seller's disclosure form to the buyer before a contract is signed. When selling a home as-is, the seller must honestly disclose all problems to the buyer. If you are the seller and will not allow a home inspection prior to closing, you must disclose all known problems associated with your home. By disclosing problems up front and letting the buyer know that the sale price reflects the home's true condition, you will avoid renegotiations during the closing and the threat of future lawsuits.

Lead-Based Paint Disclosure

Lead paint is most often found in homes built before 1978, when lead additives were banned from paint. Every purchaser of a property on which a residential dwelling was built prior to 1978 must be notified that the property may have been painted with lead-based paint and may place young children at risk of developing lead poisoning. When ingested or inhaled by young children, lead may produce permanent neurological damage, including learning disabilities, reduced intelligence quotient, behavioral problems and impaired memory. Lead poisoning also poses a particular risk to pregnant women. The seller of the residential property is required to provide the buyer with any information on lead-based paint hazards based on risk assessments or inspections in the seller's possession and notify the buyer of any known lead-based paint hazards. In HUD homes or those financed with a FHA mortgage, lead paint must be removed, covered or painted over or the agency will not back a mortgage for the home.

Tests to discover lead in paint may be conducted by a qualified company and generally cost between $50 and $500 depending on the number of samples tested. You also can purchase inexpensive lead testing kits from a local hardware store to determine if painted surfaces contain lead. A simple way to solve the problem is to repaint the interior of your home, especially in areas that have not been painted for many years and may be cracking or chipping.

The Lead-Based Paint Disclosure form provides information to the seller regarding known lead exposure in the home. The disclosure includes a lead warning statement that may read:

Lead Paint Warning Statement

Every purchaser of any interest in residential real property on which a residential dwelling was built prior to 1978 is notified that such property may present exposure to lead from lead-based paint that may place young children at risk of developing lead poisoning. Lead poisoning in young children may produce permanent neurological damage, including learning disabilities, reduced intelligence quotient, behavioral problems and impaired memory. Lead poisoning also poses a particular risk to pregnant women. The seller of any interest in residential real property is required to provide the buyer with any information on lead-based paint hazards from risk assessments or inspections in the seller's possession and notify the buyer of any known lead-based paint hazards. A risk assessment or inspection for possible lead-based paint hazards is recommended prior to purchase.

Seller's Lead-Based Paint Disclosure Form

The disclosure indicates that the seller is either aware or not aware of lead-based paint hazards in the home and has provided the buyer with any available documentation regarding lead-based paint hazard reports as indicated in the form below:

1. The presence of lead-based paint and/or lead-based paint hazards (initial one):

   ____ (a) Known lead-based paint and/or lead-based paint hazards are present in the housing.

   ____ (b) Seller has no knowledge of lead-based paint and/or lead-based paint hazards in the housing.

2. Records and reports available to the seller (initial one):

   ____ (a) Seller has provided the purchaser with all available records and reports pertaining to lead-based paint and/or lead-based paint hazards in the housing (list documents).

   ____ (b) Seller has no reports or records pertaining to lead-based paint and/or lead-based paint hazards in the house.

The purchaser will then verify receipt of such reports or having been given the opportunity to conduct an independent inspection.

Purchaser's acknowledgement (purchaser must initial):

1. Purchaser has received copies of all information listed above.

2. Purchaser has (initial one only):

   ____ (a) received a 10-day opportunity, or mutually agreed upon period, to conduct a risk assessment or inspection for the presence of lead-based paint and/or lead-based paint hazards.

   ____ (b) waived the opportunity to conduct a risk assessment or inspection for the presence of lead-based paints and/or lead-based paint hazards.

Homeowners' Association Disclosure Summary

Like the seller's disclosure sheet, the Homeowners' Association Disclosure Summary also is required in most states. The summary includes information about dues, homeowner and association responsibilities, and homeowner restrictions or rules the new owner must follow. A typical homeowners' association disclosure summary may look like the following:

Homeowner's Association Disclosure

Purchaser(s) should not execute a real estate sale or purchase contract until receiving and reading this disclosure summary.

1. This is a disclosure summary for _____ (name of community).

2. As Purchaser of property in this community, you will be obligated to be a member of a homeowner's association.

3. There have been, or will be recorded, restrictive covenants governing the use and occupancy of properties in this community.

4. You ❑ will ❑ will not be obligated to pay assessments to the association, which assessments are subject to periodic change. If applicable, the current amount is _____ Dollars ($_____) per _____.

5. Your failure to pay these assessments could result in a lien on your property.

6. There [check only one] ❑ is ❑ is not an obligation to pay rent or land use fees for recreational or other commonly used facilities as an obligation of membership in the homeowner's association. (If such obligation exists, then the amount of the current obligation is _____ _____ Dollars ($_____).

7. The restrictive covenants [check only one] ❑ can ❑ cannot be amended without the approval of the association membership.

8. The statements contained in this disclosure form are only summary in nature, and, as a prospective Purchaser, you should refer to the covenants and the association governing documents.

_____   _____
Date   Purchaser

_____   _____
Date   Purchaser

This disclosure must be supplied by the developer, or by the parcel owner if the sale is by an owner that is not the developer.

Page 1 of 1

www.socrates.com

© 2005 Socrates Media, LLC
LF609-1 • Rev. 01/05

Radon

Found all over the United States, radon is a naturally occurring radioactive gas without color, odor or taste that comes from the radioactive decay of uranium in soil, rock and groundwater.

Radon is the second leading cause of lung cancer and a serious public health problem. The National Academy of Science estimated that radon causes more than 20,000 lung cancer deaths each year. The average level of radon found in a home in the United States is 1.3 picocuries per liter (pCi/L). The average outdoor level is about 0.4 pCi/L. Lung cancer is the only health hazard that has been definitively linked with radon exposure and can occur as many as 5 to 25 years after exposure. There is no evidence that other respiratory diseases, such as asthma, are caused by radon exposure and there is no evidence that children are at any greater risk of radon-induced lung cancer than adults.

Elevated radon levels can be remedied easily and inexpensively by an Environmental Protection Agency (EPA) or state qualified radon mitigation contractor. If high radon levels are found, the contractor will install a radon mitigation system typically consisting of a fan connected to a ventilation system that vents the radon above the roofline. Although the cost may vary depending on the size and design of the home, radon mitigation systems typically cost between $800 and $1,500. Radon testing is becoming more routine in real estate transactions as disclosure of EPA's test recommendation becomes more widespread.

Most corporate relocation services require that the seller assume all responsibility for radon testing and remediation. Home buyers who do not address this issue at the time of purchase may be forced to deal with it when they become home sellers. Increasingly, knowledgeable buyers are asking for a radon inspection and remediation clause in the sales contract.

Radon is invisible and odorless, so a test is the only way to determine if a home has high radon levels. The EPA and the Office of the U.S. Surgeon General recommend that all homes below the third floor be tested for radon and repaired when elevated levels are found. Radon testing is inexpensive and easy. Reliable test kits are available through the mail, in hardware stores and other retail outlets and are generally inexpensive, ranging in price from $8 to $10.

An example of a radon disclosure statement might look like the following:

Seller's Name: _____

                    _____

Property Address: _____

                    _____

                    _____

                    _____

PURCHASERS ARE HEREBY NOTIFIED AND UNDERSTAND THAT RADON GAS AND SOME MOLDS HAVE THE POTENTIAL TO CAUSE SERIOUS HEALTH PROBLEMS.

Purchaser acknowledges and accepts that the property described above (the Property) is being offered for sale AS IS with no representations as to the condition of the Property. The seller has no knowledge of radon or mold in, on, or around the Property other than what may have already been disclosed.

Radon is an invisible and odorless gaseous radioactive element. Mold is a general term for visible growth of fungus, whether it is visible directly or is visible when barriers, such as building components (for example, walls) or furnishings (for example, carpets), are removed.

Purchaser represents and warrants that Purchaser has not relied on the accuracy or completeness of any representations that have been made by the Seller as to the presence of radon or mold and that the Purchaser has not relied on the Seller's failure to provide information regarding the presence or effects of any radon or mold found on the Property.

Real Estate Agents and Agents are not generally qualified to advise purchasers on radon or mold treatment or its health and safety risks. **PURCHASERS ARE ENCOURAGED TO OBTAIN THE SERVICES OF A QUALIFIED AND EXPERIENCED PROFESSIONAL TO CONDUCT INSPECTIONS AND TESTS REGARDING RADON AND MOLD PRIOR TO CLOSING**. Purchasers are hereby notified and agree that they are solely responsible for any required remediation and/or resulting damages, including, but not limited to, any effects on health, due to radon or mold in, on or around the property.

In consideration of the sale of the Property to the undersigned Purchaser, Purchaser does hereby release, indemnify, hold harmless and forever discharge the Seller, as owner of the Property from any and all claims, liabilities, or causes of action of any kind that the Purchaser may now have or at any time in the future may have against the resulting from the presence of radon or mold in, on or around the Property.

Purchaser has been given the opportunity to review this Release Agreement with Purchaser's attorney or other representatives of Purchaser's choosing, and hereby acknowledges reading and understanding this Release. Purchaser also understands that the promises, representations and warranties made by Purchaser in this Release are a material inducement for Seller entering into the contract to sell the Property to Purchaser.

Dated this _____ day of _____, 20_____.

_____   _____
Purchaser's Signature   Purchaser's Signature

_____   _____
Purchaser's Printed Name   Purchaser's Printed Name

Asbestos Disclosure

Asbestos is generally not a problem associated with homes built after 1980. Older homes however, are likely to contain some form of asbestos. Asbestos is common in older ceiling tiles, linoleum floor tiles and pipe or vent wrapping. The good news is that asbestos is not a big threat if undisturbed.

Asbestos is a microscopic fiber that can become airborne if disturbed. It is easily ingested through the nose or mouth and lodges in the lung. Asbestos has been linked to lung cancer. If you discover during an inspection that asbestos is present in your home, you can have an asbestos specialist tell you the safest way to remove it.

Termite Disclosure

Termites and other wood destructive pests may be a hidden danger in many areas. A termite disclosure form may be requested by the buyer and may look like the following:

Termites/Wood Destroying Insects, Dry Rot, Pests Disclosure Statement

1. Are you aware of any termites/wood destroying insects, dry rot or pests affecting the property?   Yes _____ No _____

2. Are you aware of any damage to the property caused by termites/wood destroying insects, dry rot or pests?   Yes _____ No _____

3. Is your property currently under contract by a licensed pest control company?   Yes _____ No _____

4. Are you aware of any termite/pest control reports or treatments for the property in the past five years?   Yes _____ No _____

Explain any Yes answers that you gave in this section:

_____

_____

Seller's Certification

Seller certifies that the information in this Termites/Wood Destroying Insects, Dry Rot, Pests Disclosure Statement is true and complete to the Seller's actual knowledge as of the date signed by the Seller. If a seller of residential real property acquires knowledge, which renders materially inaccurate a Termites/ Wood Destroying Insects, Dry Rot, Pests Disclosure Statement provided previously, the Seller shall deliver a revised Statement to the buyer as soon as possible. In no event, however, shall a seller be required to provide a revised Disclosure Statement after the transfer of title from the Seller to the Buyer or occupancy by the Buyer, whichever is earlier.

Seller's Signature

X _____   Date _____

X _____   Date _____

Buyer's Acknowledgment

Buyer acknowledges receipt of a copy of this statement and buyer understands that this information is a statement of certain conditions and information concerning the property known to the Seller. It is not a warranty of any kind by the Seller or Seller's agent and is not a substitute for a pest inspection or testing of the property or inspection of the public records.

Buyers Signature

X _____   Date _____

X _____   Date _____

6

· · · · · ·

Getting Down to Business

Do Not Disclose Why You Are Selling

Buyers want to know why a seller is selling, and the first question they ask is, "Why are you moving?" It is a natural question and the buyer may seem genuinely interested. Most likely, however, the buyer really wants to know your reasons for selling. How you answer that question provides the buyer with a number of clues as to how serious, flexible or desperate you are to sell your home. Think carefully before giving away important information. Your answer will have an impact on price negotiations.

How would you answer these questions?

"Why are you moving?"

"To move closer to family." This is a generic response that provides a neutral reason for selling. The seller may or may not have a deadline to sell.

"Job transfer" or "Accepted a new job." Indicates the seller must sell quickly and may be willing to give a little on the price.

"Move closer to an ill family member." Indicates a deadline has been set and there is a sense of urgency. The seller has more important issues to deal with and may be open to accepting a lower price to be able to assist the family member sooner.

"Loss of job (divorce, bankruptcy, illness)." Indicates the immediate need to sell, but it also means the buyer wants and needs to get top dollar.

"When do you want to be out?"

"We are in no hurry." Tells the buyer you are not serious about selling.

"By the beginning of the school year. We want the kids to be enrolled in their new schools." Another urgent deadline has been set.

"When we sell." The seller just told the buyer he or she is willing to sit on the property until the seller's bottom price is met.

"As soon as possible." The seller has the upper hand during negotiations and may present a low-ball initial offer to test the waters.

Be prepared to be asked these types of questions by a buyer. Choose your answers carefully. If you give the buyer an indication that there is a deadline or that you must sell quickly, you are giving the buyer the go-ahead to present a lower initial offer or to see how low you will go.

Responding to Phone Inquiries

Be prepared to handle phone calls. Write up a script to follow in advance so that you are sure to tell the potential buyer everything you think is important.

If a buyer calls about your home, instruct your children to let the prospect know that you will be at the phone soon to answer their questions. If you are not home, instruct your children to take messages and put them in a visible spot, such as taped to the refrigerator or the back door. Let them know that they need to write down the caller's name and phone number and not just tell them to call back later.

To determine the effectiveness of your marketing, ask the callers a few questions, such as how they heard about the home. Ask if they are working with an agent. If they are, ask for the agent's name and agency affiliation.

After giving the particulars about the house, i.e., size, number of bedrooms and bathrooms and price—ask if the caller is interested in scheduling an appointment to see the house.

Pricing—The Value of Your Home

Buyers and sellers are dreamers. Buyers want to believe there is an affordable home in their dream neighborhood, and sellers always want to believe their home is worth more than it really is. On average, the difference between the list price of a home and the sales price of a home is only about 6 percent. This means that most homes sell within 6 percent of their listing price. Many sellers think the list price is the price someone should pay for their home and often are insulted if a buyer offers anything less.

> "Do your homework to determine a comparable price for your home. If you price your home right, it will sell. Be advised, however, that if you sell too soon you may be losing money. If your price is too high, the home will continue to sit. Price it right and stick to the price."
>
> Robert Picarellaro
> Prello Realty
> Flat Fee Realty Company

That kind of thinking can create obstacles to a sale, especially if the seller has an overly optimistic view of the value of his or her home. That is why the CMA is so important. It is a reality check for sellers who may want to price their home at $250,000 when the highest priced home on the block has sold for only $200,000.

Overpricing a home is a certainty when a seller has misread the market. When demands for homes are high, as in a sellers' market, it is easier to get list price, even if the home is overpriced. It is much more difficult to get list price during a buyers' market when there are many other properties competing for the same buyer.

Preselling Inspections

Home inspections usually are ordered by the buyer upon signing a purchase agreement. As soon as the contract is signed by the buyer and seller, the buyer will have an agreed upon number of business days–usually 5–to order and complete the home inspection and submit a punch list requesting the seller to make repairs identified in the inspection report.

Home inspection language included in the contract generally reads something as follows:

Inspection: This contract is contingent upon approval by Purchaser of the condition of the real estate as evidenced by an inspection, conducted at Purchaser's expense and by a contractor selected by Purchaser, within 5 working days after Seller's acceptance of this contract. Purchaser shall indemnify Seller from and against any loss or damage to the real estate caused by the acts or negligence of Purchaser or the person performing such inspection. Unless written notice of disapproval is given within the time period specified, this contingency shall be deemed waived, and this contract will remain in full force and effect. If written notice of disapproval is given within the time period specified above, then this contract shall be null and void and the earnest money shall be returned to Purchaser. For purposes of this contingency, the written notice of disapproval must be personally delivered and shall be deemed given and be effective as to the date when such notice is received by Seller.

Home inspectors thoroughly examine every portion of the home from foundation, roofing, wall condition, electrical and plumbing to heating and air conditioning systems. They search for things that are broken, out of date or out of compliance with local housing codes and then report back to the homeowner a list of items that should be fixed or looked at more thoroughly by a specialist. Inspectors also may find evidence of infestation by pests–such as termites or carpenter ants–lead pipes, lead paint, underground storage tanks, etc.—all things that should be disclosed if known by the seller.

Many states require sellers to disclose problems with their home's condition to the buyer before closing. To meet these requirements, to find out any problems in advance, to circumvent surprise problems that a buyer's inspection may turn up or to avoid long punch lists, sellers are increasingly ordering home inspections before putting their homes up for sale.

If you are unsure about the condition of your home or want to be proactive and avoid negotiating on small repairs, order a preinspection for yourself. The inspection allows you to make minor repairs or identify repairs that may be considered dangerous to the occupants. You may decide simply to disclose the problem and not to make the repair at all, instead adjusting the asking price to reflect the condition of the home.

In some instances, the home inspector may see evidence of deterioration of the foundation or notice unusual cracking or settling that may require examination by a licensed structural engineer. A structural engineer may be hired by the seller or buyer to examine the foundation of the home and to ensure that the structure is in good condition. If there is any shifting or settling of the structure, they will recommend a course of action such as jacking up the sagging portion of the home or stabilizing the affected areas to stop additional settling.

Hire a Good Inspector

Hiring a home inspector is similar to hiring any other type of contractor to work on your home. Dozens of home inspection companies are listed in the phone book. Do your homework—some professional inspectors are anything but. Look for an inspector that is a member of the American Society of Home Inspectors (ASHI), a nationwide, nonprofit professional trade association founded in 1976. ASHI admits only those home inspectors who have:

- passed the National Home Inspector Examination and ASHI Standards and Ethics Examination;
- had inspection reports successfully verified for compliance with ASHI Standards of Practice; and
- submitted valid proof of performance of at least 250 fee-paid home inspections that met or exceeded the ASHI Standards of Practice.

Few states require the licensing of home inspectors. Structural engineers are licensed by every state, and many also perform home inspections for the same fee as a professional home inspector. It is a good idea to hire a structural engineer to perform a home inspection if the property has been in an earthquake, fire, flood or any other major natural disaster.

Ask your lawyer, neighbors or real estate agent to recommend a reliable home inspector. Before hiring an inspector ask the following questions:

- What is the current fee structure?
- What is included in the fee, and how long should the inspection take? A good inspection will take between 2 and 3 hours.
- Is the inspector bonded, licensed and insured?
- What professional organizations does the inspector belong to? Is he or she a member of ASHI? If not, is he or she working toward membership?
- Will you receive a written summary of the inspector's findings? How soon after the inspection can you expect to receive the report?
- Can the inspector provide references from at least three people that he or she has done work for?

The Home Inspection Report

The home inspection report summarizes the inspector's findings. The home inspection report is broken out into several different categories. The inspector examines each system of the house to ensure it is working properly or to make recommendations to the buyer. An example of a home inspection report is included on page 106.

Who Pays the Cost of Repairs?

When the inspector has completed the examination, he or she will create a written summary for the client. The summary will note the condition of the systems reviewed by the inspector. The inspector will make note of each item examined and provide recommendations to the seller or buyer or list necessary repairs in order of importance. The buyer can then take this summary and determine which items on the list should be repaired or replaced prior to the closing. This list often is referred to as a punch list.

A punch list can be short, or it can be many pages long and include minor repairs to every room in the house. A short punch list may include items such as repairing electrical outlets that may not be grounded or replacing a gauge wire that is the wrong size, windows panes that may have become cracked or bricks that need tuck-pointing. It is not uncommon for a buyer to create a punch list of several pages requesting the seller to repair every item listed by the inspector. From the list, the seller is able to pick and choose which repairs to make and which items to leave to the buyers to take care of.

A buyer also may use the punch list as a negotiating tool. During one home inspection, the inspector found evidence of soft wood in the fascia over the garage. The buyer wanted the seller to either make the repair or else knock $5,000 off the negotiated selling price. The seller knew the buyer was planning to build a big addition off that side of the house. Instead of giving the $5,000 credit, the seller opted to make the less expensive repairs. In this instance, the buyer was trying to knock more money off the sales price of the home. The seller did not want to further reduce the price of the home and opted to make the less costly repairs instead. Six months later the wall was torn down when construction for the addition began.

In response to punch lists that are too long or request items that are considered more decorative than essential, sellers are inserting language into sales contracts that limits the scope of the home inspection. For example, language may be inserted into the contract to read:

> The home inspection shall cover only major components of the Real Estate, including but not limited to, central heating system(s) central cooling system(s), plumbing and well system, electrical system, roof, walls, windows, ceilings, floors, appliances and foundation. A major component shall be deemed to be in operating condition if it performs the function for which it is intended, regardless of age, and does not constitute a threat to health or safety. Buyer agrees that minor repairs and routine maintenance items are not part of this contingency.

This language limits the buyer from requesting repairs on minor components of the home and does not allow decorating or aesthetic changes. Home inspections often turn up minor problems in the home. The most common things inspectors uncover are problems with the furnace or air conditioner, broken windows or cracked windowpanes, leaking faucets, missing screens, damaged exterior siding, evidence of termites or other pests, asbestos, gas leaks or a hot water heater that has reached the end of its usefulness. Other problems may be more significant and include foundation problems or tuck-pointing issues.

Some buyers feel that any problems found during the inspection are an opportunity to go back to the bargaining table and renegotiate the purchase/sales contract. You must be prepared for this type of situation if an inspector or structural engineer reports any problems with the home. When a buyer comes back with their punch list requesting you to fix each item, you have four options:

1. fix the problems;
2. give the buyer a cash credit toward repairs and closing;
3. reduce the price of the home to offset future repairs; or
4. do nothing.

Fix the Problem

Minor problems reported during the home inspection may be things you have lived with for years. They never bothered you but are unacceptable to the buyer. In many instances, these will be inexpensive repairs you can make easily.

Give a Cash Credit to the Buyer at Closing

If the inspector reports that the hot water heater is approaching the end of its useful life, the buyer may ask you to replace it. You may agree to pay for the entire replacement or agree only to split the cost with the buyer. After all, the hot water heater is not broken. It is working fine, and you do not want to go through the cost or the trouble to replace it. Instead, you may opt to give a cash credit at the time of closing to cover the cost of a new hot water heater. This allows the buyer to purchase his or her own system—such as a 70-gallon heater instead of a 40-gallon heater—with a full warranty, and you do not have to be responsible for the purchase.

Of course, it is a different story altogether if the hot water heater breaks down after the inspection and before the closing. In this instance, you are fully responsible for replacing the unit before settlement.

A cash credit may be given to the buyer at the time of closing in the form of money back or a check. This money can then be used to make the noted repairs. The buyer can hire a repair person of his or her choice, or may decide to take the money and skip the repairs. A cash credit may be given to keep the recorded sale price of the home higher.

Reduce the Price to Offset Future Repairs

If the repairs are substantial or the inspection report turns up something that may become more serious in the future, the seller may reduce the price of the home to keep the sale alive.

> **Example**
>
> The inspection report discovered the roof was wearing unevenly. A tree over the roof was dropping sap on the back half, causing those shingles to age faster than the front half of the roof. Even though the roof was only 10 years old, the inspector stated that it would need to be replaced in another 5 years. The seller hired a roofer who confirmed the diagnosis. The buyer was concerned she would have an expensive repair in 5 years. The buyer and seller had already signed a contract with the negotiated sale price. To keep the sale alive, the seller offered to discount the price of the home another $7,000–about half the cost of the repair–as a good faith gesture against the future repair. The buyer took the offer knowing that in 5 years she would be in better financial shape to make the repair than she was today.

Although the seller had to reduce the price of the home to keep the buyer interested, the agreed upon sale price was higher than expected, so the seller had the wiggle room to make the offer.

Do Nothing

Just because a buyer asks for a credit or repair does not mean you have to agree to it. You may say "No, I am not going to fix those problems. Just because the hot water heater is old does not warrant a total replacement. It is working fine." If your sales contract specifies that only structural or mechanical defects will be covered, a request for missing screens or other nonstructural items may be denied.

Much of the decision regarding whether or not to make repairs depends on how much a buyer is paying for your home. If the buyer is paying almost full price, then you should seriously consider making all reasonable repairs. If the buyer is paying close to your bottom price, you may be reluctant to do anything more for the buyer.

There is a lot to be said, however, for going that extra mile to make the home as pleasant for the buyer as it was for you. Fixing a leaky faucet or changing the air filter on the furnace before closing is a small but appreciated gesture to a buyer. The buyer will be busy unpacking the first few weeks. Knowing the small details have been taken care of makes for a smooth and pleasant closing. There is nothing worse than dickering over trivial points during closing, such as a stain in the carpet or a hot water heater that does not reach 140 degrees.

If you are concerned that any of the mechanical systems or units may pose a future problem for the buyer, consider purchasing a home warranty to cover repairs of heating, air conditioning and appliances. This will give the buyer extra security in the event of a breakdown.

The Home Warranty

According to a Gallup Poll, 79 percent of both buyers and sellers rate home warranties as one of the most important considerations when buying or selling a home, second only to location, design and financing options. Home warranty plans provide coverage for the breakdown of major appliances and systems not usually covered under a homeowners insurance policy. Home warranties do not cover structural problems, such as a crack in the basement or a leaky roof. The seller or buyer pays a premium for the policy, which insures that all covered appliances are working on the day of closing and will be covered under a warranty to fix or replace for a period of 1 year after the closing. In some parts of the country, home warranties are included in more than half of all homes sold. Top producing agents recommend that any seller or buyer purchase a home warranty as an insurance policy against unexpected problems and to impart peace of mind. Buyers like the assurance that if anything goes wrong, they can call someone to fix the problem. Warranties also offer a measure of legal protection, because buyers who sue sellers usually do so because they feel the condition of the home was misrepresented to them.

There are two types of home warranties: a home warranty for new construction and a home warranty for the mechanical systems and appliances in existing homes.

Pre-Owned Home Warranties

Both sellers and buyers benefit from the pre-owned home warranty. Existing home policies cover single family homes, condos, town homes or duplexes of any age. For everyone involved, there are only pluses:

- Homes with a warranty sell faster than homes without a warranty.
- Homes with a warranty sell for a higher value than homes without a warranty.
- Homes with a warranty are more attractive to buyers.
- Buyers rest easier knowing that unexpected repair costs are shared by the warranty provider.

Extended warranty protection plans are available for systems and appliances, including coverage for systems–central air and heat, electrical and plumbing–and appliances–stove, refrigerator and dishwasher, etc.

Having a home warranty protects sellers during the listing period and helps the home sell faster. For home buyers, a home warranty safeguards what is likely their largest single investment and protects them against unexpected repair or replacement expenses. Pre-owned home warranties vary from company to company, but a general pre-owned home warranty may cover unlimited square footage and multiple systems. Warranty coverage varies depending upon the state.

A pre-owned home warranty is a 1-year limited home service agreement that helps protect homeowners against the costs of repair or replacement of covered appliances and major systems that break down due to normal wear and tear. In some policies, there is a small deductible that the homeowner is required to pay for each replaced appliance.

A plan may be renewable. If the renewal option is available, the warranty provider will notify you prior to the expiration of the warranty of the option to renew for 1 year.

Usually, the seller purchases a home warranty, which is paid for out of the closing proceeds. Increasingly, buyers who are not given a warranty with the home will purchase one themselves.

Inspections are not required to obtain warranty coverage. However, covered items must be in good working condition when the warranty period begins. There is a service fee each time a service contractor visits your home. The fee usually runs between $35 and $75.

Basic seller and buyer coverage may include:

- central heating
- water heater
- electrical system
- plumbing
- attic/exhaust fans
- ductwork

Basic buyer-only coverage may include:

- roof leak
- septic system
- dishwasher
- oven
- trash compactor
- garage door opener
- central vacuum
- fire/burglar alarm system
- central air conditioning
- refrigerator
- range
- garbage disposal
- built-in microwave
- doorbell
- lighting fixtures

Buyers may purchase optional coverage to include:

- washer/dryer
- pool
- pool/spa combo
- water well

New Construction Warranties

New construction warranties cover single family homes, condos and town homes up to 1 year old. The home warranty stays with the home and automatically transfers to the new owner upon change of ownership. The cost of the warranty coverage is paid for by the home builder or manufacturer.

This warranty typically covers any structural defects. A structural defect is defined as actual physical damage to the designated load-bearing elements of the home that affects their load-bearing functions to the extent that the home becomes unsafe, unsanitary or otherwise unlivable. A warranty generally covers workmanship and material through year 1, major mechanical systems through year 2 and major structural defects through year 10.

Calculating Your Net Profit

How much can you expect to net from the sale of your home? It is easy to forget that the sale price of your home less any outstanding mortgages will not make up your actual profit. There are other costs to deduct before you arrive at your actual cash profit. Lenders estimate that closing costs, whether absorbed by the buyer or the seller, can represent as much as 6 percent of the total sale price. The worksheet below will help you determine your net profit.

Calculating Your Net Profit Worksheet

Expenses	
Expected selling price	$
Municipal fees and taxes	$
Real estate transfer tax (tax stamps)	$
Attorney fee	$
Title search	$
Survey	$
Special assessments, liens or judgments	$
Prorated real estate taxes, association fees, utility bills	$
Heating/septic/well inspection or testing	$
Additional inspections	$
Points	$
Pay-out on existing mortgage	$
Pay-out on equity line of credits or other loans	$
Miscellaneous closing costs (messengers, recording fees, etc.)	$
Prepayment penalty	$
Expenses related to getting your house on the market	$
Advertising	$
Flat-fee listing	$
Other	$
Real estate agent's commission	$
Repairs from home inspection report	$
Home warranty	$
Moving	$
Septic inspection	$
Well inspection	$
Other	$

Other	$
Other	$
Total	$
Minus Total Expenses	$
Net Profit	$

Municipal Fees and Taxes

Real Estate Transfer Tax—RETT-Tax Stamps

Real estate transfer taxes–RETTs, also known as real property transfer taxes–are state, county, and/or municipal sales taxes most often levied on the sale of residential, commercial or industrial property. The amount of the tax is determined by the value of the property being sold. The transfer tax may be equal to a percentage of the total amount of the sale, or it may it be a predetermined amount. A recording fee also may be assessed to record the transfer of the property. In some areas, the buyer pays the tax; in other areas it is the seller's responsibility. Tax rates and dispositions vary from state to state: Some states have no real estate transfer tax enabling legislation; some direct the revenues to the state general fund, although collection remains a county responsibility; and still others give local governments the authority to collect and keep tax revenues.

At the local level, the real estate transfer tax can create substantial funds for affordable housing development or park and open space acquisition, particularly in fast-growing communities.

Attorney Fees

There is no standard closing fee charged by attorneys. Each law firm sets its own closing fees. Some attorneys charge a percentage of the sale price to prepare the closing documents for you. If you do not already have an experienced real estate attorney, ask around for recommendations for attorneys to represent you at the sale. Be sure you know exactly what services are included in the fee so that you can make accurate fee and services comparisons.

Title Search

Soon after a contract to purchase has been signed and an escrow account has been opened, your attorney will request a title search on the property. Title is the evidence that a homeowner has the right to or possession of the land. A title search examines the chain of titles–previous ownership records–to insure there are no problems with obtaining a clear title to the property. The search also will include a list of items such as loans secured by the property, public utility company easements to run power lines over the property or municipal assessments for future improvements–such as a planned sidewalk in front of the property–that may affect the title or limit the use of your property. It is possible for the title ownership chain to go back hundreds of years. Conducting a title search will uncover any ownership disputes that may have occurred in the past.

Abstract of Title

The title, also known as an abstract of title, is a complete summary of the history of a title. It includes all changes of ownership of the property, including liens, mortgages, assessments, encroachments, encumbrances and any other issues that may prevent a clear title.

Five Common Title Problems

A property must have a clear title for a sale to proceed. Occasionally, problems arise with the title that must be cleared up before the property can be transferred to a new owner. The following are basic problems that will obstruct the transfer of a title.

1. Mechanic's Lien

A mechanic's lien is filed against a homeowner by a contractor who was hired to do work for the owner but did not receive full payment for the work completed. The contractor or subcontractor may file a lien against the property. Once the lien is filed, the contractor has a certain period of time to take action against you to collect payment. If the lien is still active against the property, the title company can hold back money at the closing. The seller may present a signed waiver of lien from the contractor or the title company can use the money held back to pay off the contractor.

2. Deceased Sole Owner

If the sole owner of a property dies after a contract is signed but before the closing, the title company will insure the buyer against possible claims against the property for an additional fee.

3. Delinquent Taxes

If the seller has not paid real estate taxes, the title company may hold back cash from the sale of the home to satisfy those taxes.

4. Encroachments and Easements

A neighbor's fence erroneously built on your property, a neighbor's garage built right in the middle of the lot line and driveways poured three inches into your lot are all small mistakes but may become problematic in the future. Before insisting that the neighbor rip out the fence, tear down the garage or tear up the driveway, talk with the title company. They may be able to work with the seller to issue a policy that will insure the buyer against issues resulting from encroachments on the property.

5. Unreleased Mortgages

When you pay off your mortgage or refinance your loan, the mortgage company releases you from your obligations to make monthly payments. Written notification of the release is usually sent to the seller by mail, but in some instances the release may be recorded improperly or not recorded at all, and an old mortgage will turn up in the title search. If an unreleased mortgage does turn up, contact the lender and request a copy of the release of mortgage. If the lender cannot find a copy of the release, your title company should contact the lender and work out a solution.

Other charges that must be paid at settlement or closing include outstanding special assessments, such as sidewalk or sewer fees imposed by the municipality or liens or judgments against the property. If there are any mechanic's liens or outstanding assessments against the property, those must be paid in full before the property can be transferred to the new owners.

Title Insurance

Title insurance covers the legal fees and expenses incurred to defend a property's title against claims that dispute ownership of the property. Title insurance protects you during the time you own the home and well after you may have sold the property.

A title insurance policy protects you, the seller, from previous ownership claims. Most title insurance policies are based on the cost of the insured home. It is unlike a hazard insurance policy that may only insure the structure. A title insurance policy insures the land and buildings against any ownership claims that may be filed on the property long after you have sold it.

Plat of Survey

Most lending institutions require a survey of the property before agreeing to give a mortgage. Condominium units are an exception. It is common for the seller to order a plat of survey of the property as a requirement of closing. A plat is a drawing of the property that shows the position of the house on the lot and the lot lines. The purpose of the survey is to determine whether the house is within the property borders, whether there are any encroachments on the property by the neighbors and whether there are any easements on the property that may affect legal title. In some instances, it is the buyer who orders the survey; in others, it is the seller. If a survey has been completed within 90 days of the closing, the lending institution will accept the current survey. Surveys older than 90 days will require updating.

Anytime substantial structural or landscaping changes have been made to the property, a new survey must be ordered prior to settlement. If you have not made any changes to the structure or surrounding property, ask your attorney to contact the buyer's attorney or the lender's attorney to see if the old survey with a notarized affirmation of no change would be acceptable.

In many states and in rural areas, a plat of survey is not ordered with each sale due to the expense involved. The cost to conduct a survey may range from $250 to $3,000, depending on the size of the plot and the area. In urban areas, surveys are required with each transaction, refinancing or closing. Because urban lots are generally smaller, the survey is relatively inexpensive, and the work can be completed in a matter of days. In rural areas, where lot sizes may be irregular or larger, the cost of conducting a survey may range between $1,500 and $3,000. Surveys are ordered only when there are boundary line disputes, easement issues or property lines are unclear. Sellers provide a copy of the survey and make sure the property markers are visible for buyer inspection prior to settlement.

Prorated Real Estate Taxes, Association Fees and Utility Bills

In some counties, taxes are prepaid by the buyer, while in others, taxes are collected in arrears. Real estate contracts generally request fair appropriation of taxes. Annual association fees typically are prorated, with both the buyer and seller paying their portion at the closing. Utility bills may be prorated and paid by the seller at closing or paid in advance, with the seller presenting proof of payment at the closing.

Points

Points are fees that some lending institutions charge for originating mortgages. Points make a mortgage more profitable for the lender and enable the mortgage holder to obtain a lower interest rate. One point is usually 1 percent of the mortgage amount and is paid at the closing. Buyers usually pay mortgage points. In some markets, buyers will negotiate with the seller to absorb points they are being charged by their lender.

Payout on Lines of Credit, Existing Mortgages and Other Home Loans

If you have multiple mortgages, a home equity loan or line of credit, these loans must be repaid in full before the property can be transferred to the new owner. Contact your lender to request a payout amount and notify them of the closing date. The lender will be able to calculate what you will owe on the mortgage, complete with interest and other fees, based on the proposed closing date. This is the amount you will owe the lender at the time of closing. Be aware, however, if the closing date is moved, the amount owed the lender is will also change.

Miscellaneous Closing Costs—Messengers and Recording Fees

Lenders are obligated by law to disclose all fees associated with a real estate transaction. These may include messenger fees, recording fees, overnight delivery fees, application fees and more. Ask your lawyer to provide an estimate of all fees associated with the closing that you, the seller, will be obligated to pay and use it as an estimate of the costs you will be responsible for.

Prepayment Penalty

Some lenders charge prepayment penalties if you have owned the home less than 5 years before selling it for. Prepayment penalties, also known as mortgage cancellation fees or repayment penalties, may be as high as 1, 2 or 3 percent of the outstanding balance. Check with your lender whether your mortgage agreement includes a prepayment clause.

Expenses Related to Getting Your House Ready to Market

Itemize all expenses associated with getting your home ready to market. Expenses may include costs associated with advertising the home, creating and copying informational fliers, signing up with a flat-fee listing service and making improvements to the home.

Agent's Commission

If the property is listed with a flat-fee realty company, a real estate agent's commission will be deducted from the sale amount at the time of closing only if a licensed real estate agent brought the buyer to see your home. If the home sold without the assistance of a real estate agent, no commission is due at the time of closing.

Repairs Made Based on Home Inspection Report

Itemize all the costs incurred from repairs made as a direct result of the home inspection report. Costs may range from smaller costs, such as replacing window or door screens, to larger costs, such as pouring a new cement garage floor or replacing a furnace or air conditioning unit.

Home Warranty

Include any home warranty policies you may have purchased for the home.

Home Inspection Report

An example of a typical home inspection report follows. Some inspectors will summarize the entire report in a two-page summary sheet attached to the front of the report. This report merely shows you what a report may look like.

Home Inspection Report

123 Main Street, Anytown

Inspection Date: June 30, 2005

Prepared For: The Buyer

Prepared By: Home Inspection Company
1.555.555.5555
1.555.555.5555 FAX

Report Number: 091

Inspector: Bob Jones
State License # 050000350

Report Overview

The House in Perspective

This is a well-built home. Some of the systems of the home are aging and will require updating over time. As with all homes, ongoing maintenance is also required. Despite the older systems, the improvements that are recommended in this report are not considered unusual for a home of this age and location. Please remember that there is no such thing as a perfect home.

Conventions Used in This Report

For your convenience, the following conventions have been used in this report:

Major Concern: This denotes a system or component that is considered significantly deficient or is unsafe. Significant deficiencies need to be corrected and except for some safety items, are likely to involve significant expense.

Safety Issue: This denotes a condition that is unsafe and in need of prompt attention.

Repair: This denotes a system or component that is missing or needs corrective action to ensure proper and reliable function.

Improve: This denotes improvements that are recommended but not required.

Monitor: This denotes a system or component needing further investigation and/ or monitoring in order to determine if repairs are necessary.

Please note that those observations listed under Discretionary Improvements are not essential repairs but represent logical long-term improvements.

 • For the purpose of this report, it is assumed that the house faces east.

Improvement Recommendation Highlights/Summary

The following is a synopsis of the potentially significant improvements that should be completed or budgeted for over the short term. Other significant improvements that are outside the scope of this inspection also may be necessary. Please refer to the body of this report for further details on these and other recommendations.

Foundation

 • **Major Concern, Monitor:** Substantial foundation settlement was observed at the rear southwest corner of the original house. The slope from the front dining room to the rear kitchen corner is greater than two and a half inches. Structural movement of the building has occurred. Since repairs are needed to protect the building from more serious damage, a structural engineer who is familiar with foundation repair or a company specializing in foundation repairs should be consulted to evaluate the condition and to suggest corrective measures. The rate of movement cannot be predicted during a one-time inspection.

Floors

- **Major Concern, Monitor:** The support of the floor joists at the rear exterior wall of the addition appears to lack adequate bearing. While this does not pose a serious short-term problem, the rear floor is sloped, and the rear upper walls show movement. For example, the southwest master bedroom window is one-half inch out of square and will not seal properly. Additional support may be needed. Review by a structural engineer is recommended.

Crawl Space

- **Repair:** Loose ductwork in the crawl space beneath the kitchen should be secured to avoid damage or improper and potentially unsafe system operation.

Windows

- **Repair:** Localized evidence of minor rot was visible at front dining room window framing. Repairs should be undertaken when painting.

Main Panel

- **Repair:** Oversized breakers within the main distribution panel should be replaced. All breakers serving 14-gauge household branch circuits should be sized at 15 amps. One position is oversized.

Outlets

- **Repair:** Ungrounded three-prong outlets in the southwest dining room should be repaired. In some cases, a ground wire may be present in the electrical box and simply needs to be connected. If no ground is present, repair can be as simple as filling the ground slot with epoxy. Since having a ground increases safety, it would be better if a grounded circuit could be strung to this outlet or a separate ground wire connected. Some electrical codes allow the installation of a ground fault circuit interrupter (GFCI) type outlet where grounding is not provided. In this case, the GFCI may work but cannot be tested by normal means.

- **Repair:** An outlet at the front wall of the dining room has reversed polarity, i.e., it is wired backward. This outlet and the circuit should be investigated and repaired as necessary.

Lights

- **Repair:** Light fixtures at the rear ceiling of the laundry area should not be supported by wiring.

Furnace

- **Repair:** The blower and motor serving the heating system in the addition ignite slowly. They should be checked by a heating technician to ensure reliable heat.

Attic/Roof

- **Improve:** Insulation improvements may be cost-effective, depending on the anticipated term of ownership.
- **Repair:** Insulation should be installed where missing in the center of the attic.
- **Improve:** The level of ventilation is marginal. It generally is recommended that one square foot of free vent area be provided for every 150 square feet of ceiling area. Proper ventilation will help to keep the house cooler during warm weather and will extend the life of roofing materials. In cold climates, it will help reduce the potential for ice dams on the roof and condensation within the attic.

Supply Plumbing

- **Repair:** The supply pipe lacks adequate support across the front crawl space.

Windows

- **Improve:** The side kitchen window(s) are cracked at two panes. Improvement is recommended.
- **Improve:** The front dining room window(s) have lost their seal at several panes. This has resulted in condensation developing between the panes of glass. This fogging of the glass is primarily a cosmetic concern and only need be improved for cosmetic reasons.

Fireplaces

- **Repair; Safety Issue:** The fireplace chimney should be inspected and cleaned prior to operation.

Structure

Description of Structure

Foundation:	• Poured concrete
	• Basement and crawl space configuration
	• Front crawl space(s) viewed from entry opening
Columns:	• Steel
Floor Structure:	• Wood joist
Wall Structure:	• Masonry
	• Wood frame
Ceiling Structure:	• Joist
Roof Structure:	• Rafters
	• Plywood sheathing
	• Solid plank sheathing

Structure Observations

Positive Attributes

The visible joist spans appear to be within typical construction practices.

Recommendations/Observations

Floors

- **Major Concern; Monitor:** The support of the floor joists at the rear exterior wall of the addition appears to lack adequate bearing. While this does not pose a serious short-term problem, the rear floor is sloped and the rear upper walls show movement. Additional support may be needed. Review by a structural engineer is recommended. .

Crawl Space

- **Repair:** Loose ductwork in the crawl space beneath the kitchen should be secured to avoid damage or improper and potentially unsafe system operation.

Discretionary Improvements

Leveling of floors within the home might be desirable during any renovations, but in general jacking of floors is not advisable unless extensive renovations are planned. Damage to the interior walls, ceilings and floors usually results when jacking is performed.

Roofing

Description of Roofing

Roof Covering:	• Asphalt shingle
	• Metal
Roof Flashings:	• Asphalt
Chimneys:	• Masonry
Roof Drainage System:	• Aluminum
	• Copper
	• Downspouts discharge above grade
Skylights:	• Plastic bubble type
Method of Inspection:	• Walked on roof

Roofing Observations

General Comments

In all, the roof coverings show evidence of normal wear and tear for a home of this age.

Recommendations/Observations

Sloped Roofing

- **Monitor:** The design of the roofing system is such that a vulnerable area exists at the rear center roof. There is a higher potential for leaks. Annual inspections and ongoing maintenance will be critical.

Flashings

- **Monitor:** The tar flashing on the brick chimney is vulnerable and should be monitored carefully for leaks.

Exterior

Description of Exterior

Wall Covering:	• Brick
	• Wood siding
Eaves, Soffits and Fascias:	• Wood
Exterior Doors:	• Solid wood
Window/Door Frames and Trim:	• Wood
	• Vinyl-covered
Entry Driveways:	• Asphalt
Entry Walkways and Patios:	• Stone
Porches, Decks, Steps, Railings:	• Concrete
Overhead Garage Door(s):	• Wood
	• Automatic opener installed
Surface Drainage:	• Level grade
Fencing:	• Chain link

Exterior Observations

Positive Attributes

Window frames are clad, for the most part, with a low-maintenance material. There is no significant wood/soil contact around the perimeter of the house, thereby reducing the risk of insect infestation or rot. The auto reverse mechanism on the overhead garage door responded properly to testing. This safety feature should be tested regularly, as a door that does not reverse can injure someone or fall from the ceiling. Refer to the owner's manual or contact the manufacturer for more information. The lot drainage was good and conducted surface water away from the building.

General Comments

The exterior of the home shows normal wear and tear for a home of this age.

Recommendations/Observations

Windows

- Repair: Localized evidence of minor rot was visible at front dining room window framing. Repairs should be undertaken when painting.

Electrical

Description of Electrical

Size of Electrical Service:	• 120/240-volt main service—Service size: 200 amps
Service Drop:	• Overhead
Service Entrance Conductors:	• Aluminum
Service Equipment and Main Disconnects:	• Main service rating 200 amps • Breakers • Located: in the garage
Service Grounding:	• Copper • Water pipe connection
Service Panel and Overcurrent Protection:	• Panel rating: 200 Amps • Breakers • Located: in the garage
Sub-Panel(s):	• Panel rating: 60 Amps • Breakers • Located: in the furnace room
Distribution Wiring:	• Copper
Wiring Method:	• Armored cable BX • Conduit
Switches and Receptacles:	• Grounded
Ground Fault Circuit Interrupters:	• Bathroom(s) • Exterior
Smoke Detectors:	• Present

Electrical Observations

Positive Attributes

The size of the electrical service is sufficient for typical single family needs. Generally speaking, the electrical system is in good order. The distribution of electricity within the home is good. Dedicated 220-volt circuits have been provided for all 220-volt appliances within the home. All visible wiring within the home is copper. This is a good quality electrical conductor.

General Comments

Inspection of the electrical system revealed the need for several minor repairs. Although these are not especially costly, they should be high priority for safety reasons. Unsafe electrical conditions represent a shock hazard. A licensed electrician should be consulted to undertake the repairs recommended below.

Recommendations/Observations

Main Panel

- **Repair:** Oversized breakers within the main distribution panel should be replaced. All breakers serving 14-gauge household branch circuits should be sized at 15 amps. One position is oversized.

Outlets

- **Repair:** Ungrounded three-prong outlets in the southwest dining room should be repaired. In some cases, a ground wire may be present in the electrical box and simply needs to be connected. If no ground is present, repair can be as simple as filling the ground slot with epoxy. Since having a ground increases safety, it would be better if a grounded circuit could be strung to this outlet, or a separate ground wire could be connected. Some electrical codes allow the installation of a GFCI type outlet where grounding is not provided. In this case, the GFCI may work but cannot be tested by normal means.

- **Repair:** An outlet at the front wall of the dining room has reversed polarity, i.e., it is wired backward). This outlet and the circuit should be investigated and repaired as necessary.

Lights

- **Repair:** Light fixtures at the rear ceiling of the laundry area should not be supported by wiring.

Heating

Description of Heating

Energy Source:	• Gas
Heating System Type:	• Forced air furnace (2)
	• Manufacturer: Carrier
	• Serial Number: 3396A10848
	• 132,000 BTU
	• Manufacturer: Arcoaire
	• Serial number: 0000246540
	• 100,000 BTU
Vents, Flues, Chimneys:	• Metal-single wall • Masonry-lined
Heat Distribution Methods:	• Ductwork
Other Components:	• Humidifier

Heating Observations

Positive Attributes

Adequate heating capacity is provided by the system. Heat distribution within the home is adequate. The distribution of heat is divided into zones that allow for greater ease of balancing heat flow.

General Comments

Minor repairs to the heating system are necessary.

Recommendations/Observations

Furnace

- **Repair:** The blower and motor serving the heating system in the addition are in suspect condition. The unit would not start properly; this indicates a problem. They should be checked by a heating technician to ensure reliable heat.

Limitations of Heating Inspection

As we have discussed and as described in your inspection contract, this is a visual inspection and is limited in scope by, but not restricted to, the following conditions:

- The adequacy of heat supply or distribution balance is not inspected.
- The interior of flues or chimneys, which are not readily accessible, are not inspected.
- The furnace heat exchanger, humidifier or dehumidifier and electronic air filters are not inspected.

• Solar space heating equipment/systems are not inspected.

Please also refer to the preinspection contract for a detailed explanation of the scope of this inspection.

Cooling/Heat Pumps

Description of Cooling/Heat Pumps

Energy Source:	• Electricity •240-volt power supply
Central System Type:	• Air cooled central air conditioning (2)
	• Manufacturer: Carrier
	• Serial number: 2696E14063 •36,000 BTU
	• Manufacturer: Lennox
	• Serial Number: 5899F38193 •30,000 BTU

Cooling/Heat Pumps Observations

Positive Attributes

The capacity and configuration of the system should be sufficient for the home. Upon testing in the air conditioning mode, a normal temperature drop across the evaporator coil was observed. This suggests that the system is operating properly. The system responded properly to operating controls.

General Comments

The system shows no visible evidence of major defects.

Recommendations/Observations

None.

Insulation/Ventilation

Description of Insulation/Ventilation

Attic Insulation:	• R15 fiberglass in main attic
	• R30 fiberglass in rear attic
Exterior Wall Insulation:	• Not visible
Vapor Retarders:	• Kraft paper
Roof Ventilation:	• Roof vents
	• Gable vents
Crawl Space Ventilation:	• Exterior wall vents
Exhaust Fan/Vent Locations:	• Dryer

Insulation/Ventilation Observations

Positive Attributes

Insulation levels are typical for a home of this age and construction.

General Comments

Upgrading insulation levels in a home is an improvement rather than a necessary repair.

Recommendations/Energy Saving Suggestions

Attic/Roof

- **Improve:** Insulation improvements may be cost-effective, depending on the anticipated term of ownership.
- **Repair:** Insulation should be installed where missing in the center of the attic.
- **Improve:** The level of ventilation is marginal. It generally is recommended that one square foot of free vent area be provided for every 150 square feet of ceiling area. Proper ventilation will help to keep the house cooler during warm weather and extend the life of roofing materials. In cold climates, it will help reduce the potential for ice dams on the roof and condensation within the attic.

Crawl Space

- **Repair:** A moisture barrier should be installed on the front crawl space floor.

Plumbing

Description of Plumbing

Water Supply Source:	• Public water supply
Service Pipe to House:	• Lead
Main Water Valve Location:	• Front wall of basement
Interior Supply Piping:	• Copper • Steel
Waste System:	• Public sewer system
Drain, Waste and Vent Piping:	• Cast iron • Steel • Plastic
Water Heater:	• Gas
	• Manufacturer: A.O. Smith
	• Serial number: ML950061415
	• Approximate capacity (in gallons): 50
Fuel Shut-off Valves:	• Natural gas main valve at the exterior wall

Plumbing Observations

Positive Attributes

The plumbing system is in generally good condition. The water pressure supplied to the fixtures is reasonably good. A typical drop in flow was experienced when two fixtures were operated simultaneously.

General Comments

The plumbing system is showing signs of age. Updating the system will be required over time.

Recommendations/Observations

Water Heater

- **Monitor:** Water heaters have a typical life expectancy of 7 to 12 years. The existing unit is approaching this age range. One cannot predict with certainty when replacement will become necessary.

Supply Plumbing

- **Repair:** The supply pipe lacks adequate support across the front crawl space.
- **Monitor:** The old steel piping is subject to corrosion on the interior of the pipe. As corrosion builds up, the inside diameter of the pipe becomes constricted, resulting in a loss of water pressure. This piping typically is replaced when the loss of pressure can no longer be tolerated.

Interior

Description of Interior

Wall and Ceiling Materials:	• Drywall • Plaster • Wood
Floor Surfaces:	• Carpet • Tile • Wood
Window Type(s) and Glazing:	• Fixed Pane
	• Double/single hung
	• Double glazed
	• Single pane with storm window
Doors:	• Wood-solid core • Storm door(s)

Interior Observations

General Condition of Interior Finishes

On the whole, the interior finishes of the home are in average condition. Typical flaws were observed in some areas.

General Condition of Windows and Doors

The doors and windows are of average quality.

General Condition of Floors

The flooring system of the home exhibits signs of unusual movement and/or unevenness. Refer also to the Structural Components section of this report.

Recommendations/Observations

Wall/Ceiling Finishes

- **Monitor:** Minor cracks were noted.

Floors

- **Monitor:** Floor slopes are apparent to the southwest corner and at the rear family room.

Windows

- **Improve:** The rear southwest master bedroom window is out of square and will not seal properly. Improvement can be undertaken as desired.
- **Improve:** The side kitchen window(s) are cracked at two panes. Improvement is recommended.
- **Improve:** The front dining room window(s) have lost their seal at several panes. This has resulted in condensation developing between the panes of glass. This fogging of the glass is primarily a cosmetic concern and only need be improved for cosmetic reasons.

Basement Leakage

- **Monitor:** No evidence of moisture penetration was visible in the basement at the time of the inspection. It should be understood that it is impossible to predict whether moisture penetration will pose a problem in the future. The vast majority of basement leakage problems are the result of insufficient control of storm water at the surface. The ground around the house should be sloped to encourage water to flow away from the foundation. Gutters and downspouts should act to collect roof water and drain the water at least five feet from the foundation or into a functional storm sewer. Downspouts that are clogged or broken below grade level or that discharge too close to the foundation are the most common source of basement leakage. Please refer to the Roofing and Exterior sections of the report for more information.

In the event that basement leakage problems are experienced, lot and roof drainage improvements should be undertaken as a first step. Please beware of contractors who recommend expensive solutions. Excavation, damp-proofing and/or the installation of drainage tiles should be a last resort. In some cases, however, it is necessary. Your plans for using the basement also may influence the approach taken to curing any dampness that is experienced.

Appliances

Description of Appliances

Appliances Tested:	• Gas range • Dishwasher
	• Waste disposer • Refrigerator
Laundry Facility:	• Gas piping for dryer
	• Dryer vented to building exterior
	• 120-volt circuit for washer
	• Hot and cold water supply for washer
	• Washer discharges to laundry tub/sink
Other Components Tested:	• Kitchen exhaust fan

Appliances Observations

Positive Attributes

Most of the major appliances in the home are newer. All appliances that were tested responded satisfactorily.

Recommendations/Observations

None.

Limitations of Appliances Inspection

As we have discussed and as described in your inspection contract, this is a visual inspection and is limited in scope by, but not restricted to, the following conditions:

- Thermostats, timers and other specialized features and controls are not tested.
- The temperature calibration, functionality of timers, effectiveness, efficiency and overall performance of appliances are outside the scope of this inspection.

Please also refer to the preinspection contract for a detailed explanation of the scope of this inspection.

Fireplaces/Wood Stoves

Description of Fireplaces/Wood Stoves

Fireplaces:	• Masonry firebox
Vents, Flues, Chimneys:	• Outside combustion air not provided
	• Masonry chimney-lined

Fireplaces/Wood Stoves Observations

General Comments

On the whole, the fireplace and its components were found to be in average condition. Typical flaws were observed in some areas.

Recommendations/Observations

Fireplaces

- **Repair, Safety Issue:** The fireplace chimney should be inspected and cleaned prior to operation.

7

· · · · · ·

There Are Offers and
Then There Are Offers

There is a buyer for every home. A sale may happen quickly or may take a little extra time, but the fact is that every home sells eventually. When you receive a bona fide offer from a prospective buyer, always request it in writing. Never take a verbal offer from a buyer.

There are five basic elements to an offer:

1. address or description of the property

2. date the offer was received

3. price the buyer is prepared to pay

4. date on which the closing will take place

5. signatures of the seller and buyer

Your real estate attorney should be able to provide you with a contract to use when a prospective buyer submits an offer to purchase your home. If you do not have a formal purchase agreement form, you can create your own with only the minimal amount of information required to make the offer legally binding. The information that you need to collect includes: the identification of the property; address, city, state and zip code; the date the offer was received; the amount offered; and the name(s) and signature(s) of the individual(s) making the offer. If more than one individual is purchasing the property, be sure to include all buyers' and sellers' names on the agreement.

A more formal procedure for purchasing real estate entails the buyer presenting an offer on a contract to purchase form. A contract to purchase form is legally binding and details specific property descriptions, a listing of fixtures or exclusions and all the required legal language to transfer the property—rights to sue, contingency provisions, agents' fees, etc.

Date of Closing

This is the date the buyer would like to take possession. Possession is defined as the point at which the buyer accepts the keys to the property. The possession date may be negotiated depending on how anxious the buyer is to move in or how quickly the seller needs to move. The possession date can also mean that the buyer takes possession of the property but also makes the provision to rent the property back to the seller for a predetermined amount each day if the seller and buyer agree. The rent or lease-back date may be as short as 1 or 2 days or much longer.

Earnest Money

The check that accompanies an offer to buy a house generally is referred to as the earnest money deposit. The purpose of the earnest money deposit is to show the seller that the buyer earnestly intends to buy your home. The more money the buyer puts down the more serious he or she is about following through with the sale. The amount of the deposit varies depending on a number of factors. During sellers' markets, deposits are generally larger than during slow markets. In a balanced market, the amount of the deposit is typically less than 2 percent of the purchase price. When the transaction closes, the earnest money is applied to the buyer's down payment and closing costs. As a seller, you want the buyer to put down the largest amount possible in the event that the buyer backs out of the deal and breaks the terms of the agreement. If this happens, and depending upon the specific circumstances, you may be able to keep all or part of the earnest money deposit as compensation for the selling time you lost while off the market.

Inclusions and Exclusions

Each agreement contains a listing of fixtures and personal property to be included with the sale. Fixtures are generally appliances or light fixtures attached to the ceiling, such as wall sconces, hanging pot holders, ceiling fans, chandeliers and hanging lamps. Once a fixture is attached to the wall, it becomes part of the home rather than personal property. The term fixtures covers many different items, such as light fixtures, plumbing, sinks, toilets, doors, door hardware, built-in bookshelves, ceiling fans, overhead lights, central air conditioning units, fireplace screens or andirons, etc. If you do not want to include personal fixtures such as antiques or family heirlooms, replace those items before putting your home up for sale. Make sure you clearly note which items you will be leaving with the home and which items you will be taking with you before a purchase contract is signed.

Date of Possession

This is the day the seller turns the keys to the property over to the buyer. The seller vacates the property, and the buyer becomes the new owner. Possession usually takes place at the closing–also called the settlement–where the deed is exchanged for cash. If possession is scheduled to take place after the closing, language should be inserted into the contract stipulating a per-day fee the seller will pay for living in the home after closing. Almost all contracts now contain an inflated per-day charge that penalizes the seller if he or she does not vacate the premises by midnight on the day of the closing. A high per-day charge discourages the seller from lingering or remaining on the premises after the scheduled closing and encourages a smooth transition.

Prorations of Housing Costs

In most states, real estate taxes are paid annually or in installments. Utility bills are paid monthly or every other month. If a closing is scheduled at any time except the first or last day of the month, the taxes or utility bills associated with the house are prorated over the time between when the seller has left the house and the buyer takes possession. That way both the buyer and the seller are paying their fair share for the time they actually live in the home.

Fees and Costs

The contract outlines the fees the seller will pay and the fees the buyer is responsible for, including inspections, surveys, title insurance, recording fees, transfer taxes and fees and the brokerage commission.

Contingencies

The four most common contingencies buyers include in a deal are:

1. receipt and approval of the home inspection
2. buyer obtaining financing
3. buyer selling current home
4. attorney approval of contract

The home inspection is the most common contingency, but other inspections may be required by the lender—termite, radon, etc. All inspections and attorney approvals must be completed within an agreed upon amount of time, usually 5 business days, as written in the contract.

Purchase Price

It is customary for the buyer to put his or her initial purchase price on the contract and then begin negotiations. Once you have agreed on a price, it is inserted into the contract and initialed by all parties.

Expiration Date of the Contract or Offer

Every real estate offer should include an expiration date. This is the deadline by which the seller must respond to the initial offer, usually 48 to 72 hours. If a counteroffer is given, the buyer should have an equal amount of time to accept or counter again. Contracts that do not include an expiration date give the seller little incentive to review, accept or decline the offer with any amount of urgency. Instead, the seller may shop the offer around to other buyers in an effort to secure a better one.

"All offers presented by agents on behalf of their buying clients must be submitted to the realty agency first. The realty agency will present the offer to the sellers and then will often let the seller and buyer complete their own negotiations. Flat-fee listing services may become involved in the negotiations only by request from the seller."

Professional Agent
Flat Fee Realty Company

Option to Purchase Real Estate

THIS AGREEMENT is made and entered into this _____ day of
_____, 20 _____, by and between _____
as "Optionor," and _____ and/assigns, hereinafter referred to as
"Optionee."

WITNESSETH, that for and in consideration of _____ Dollars ($_____),
and the mutual promises and covenants set forth below, the parties agree as follows:

1. Option to Purchase Real Property. Optionor grants Optionee the exclusive right to purchase the real property
   described as: _____
   _____
   _____
   _____

2. Term of Option. This option shall commence on _____, 20 _____ and
   expire on _____, 20 _____.

3. Terms of Sale. The terms of sale shall be: _____
   _____
   _____
   _____

   The following items shall be prorated at closing: _____
   _____

   All personal property, appliances, attachments and fixtures shall be included in the sale except: _____
   _____
   _____

   The Optionor shall convey title by a good and marketable warranty deed and shall furnish a policy of insurance
   from a reputable title insurance company.

4. Extension of Option Period. Upon payment of _____ Dollars
   ($_____), Optionee shall have the right to extend this option by _____ year(s) under the same
   terms and conditions.

5. Notice of Exercise. This option may be exercised at any time during the option period as described above, and
   Optionee may exercise the option with or without notice to Optionor.

6. Escrow of Closing Documents. All documents necessary for title transfer, including, but not limited to a warranty
   deed and bill of sale, shall be executed and held in escrow with an escrow agent of Optionee's choosing. Optionor
   shall execute a deed of trust or mortgage in favor of Optionee to secure performance of this agreement.

Condo Sales

Condo sales adhere to a different set of rules than single family or town house sales. Some condo homeowners associations have bylaws giving the board first right of refusal when a condo unit is being sold. This means the board may purchase the unit if it decides it is in the best interest of the condo building. The board does not have the right to refuse to approve the interested buyer. In a sales contract, you will have to agree to procure the release or waiver of any option or right of first refusal and to comply with other condo rules and regulations.

Co-Op Sales

Co-ops operate differently than condos in that you are not selling property; rather, you are selling your shares of the corporation that owns the building. Co-op boards also have the right of first refusal when a unit goes up for sale. In addition, they have the right to vote whether a prospective buyer will be allowed to move into the building. Co-op buyers must submit financial and personal records for review by the board. The board will meet personally with the interested buyer, take a vote and either approve or block the sale. When a buyer presents a contract to purchase the co-op unit, the seller should provide a list of documents that the buyer must provide and applications to fill out for the board to review.

Tip
Real estate laws vary from state to state. Be sure to understand your responsibilities and rights before signing any forms. It is your responsibility to know who will pay specific fees.

If you accept the offer, fill in and sign a Seller's Acceptance to Purchase Offer. This signed agreement will get the sale process started. Create two copies of the agreement and give one to the buyer and one to your real estate attorney. This way both parties will have a signed original. The form will look like the following:

Seller's Acceptance of Purchase Offer

Seller accepts Buyer's offer presented to Seller on _____, 20_____,
at _____ a.m./p.m.

The warranties, representations and covenants made within the offer survive closing and the conveyance of the property.

Seller agrees to convey the property on the terms and conditions as set forth within the offer.

Seller hereby acknowledges receipt of a copy of said offer.

Seller 's Signature: _____

Print Name Here: _____

Social Security No. or FEIN: _____

Date: _____

Seller 's Signature: _____

Print Name Here: _____

Social Security No. or FEIN: _____

Date: _____

_____ This offer is rejected

_____ This offer is countered

The contract spells out the agreement between you and the buyer. The terms of that agreement should cover all areas of potential dispute and key contingency dates. The contract should include specific information about the closing date; the amount of earnest money—how much is due and due dates; fixtures and appliances included with the property; date of possession; prorations of taxes and utility bills; who pays transfer taxes, recording fees and costs; notable contingencies; the purchase price; and the date the offer expires.

Low-Ball Offers—Do Not Get Angry

A low-ball offer is one that is far below the property's real value and is frequently perceived as insulting by the seller. If homes in your area are selling at 90 percent of list price and a buyer offers you a low-ball offer at 70 percent of your list price, do not get angry; the buyer is simply testing the market. As a seller, it is important for you to know how close to the asking price homes are selling for in your area so you can counter the offer properly.

Low-ball offers come from buyers who are trying to get a bargain, people who think you may be desperate enough to accept anything to secure a sale or buyers who have not done their homework and think your home is overpriced. They generally come from buyers who are not serious about purchasing your home but just want to see if they can catch you at a weak moment when you might accept their offer.

If you receive a low-ball offer, let the buyer know the offer is not acceptable by countering at full price or by returning the contract unsigned with a note explaining that the offer was unacceptable.

Take-It-or-Leave-It Offers

A take-it-or-leave-it offer completely eliminates any negotiation. The buyers are saying, "This is all we can afford or are willing to pay, so do not try to negotiate—it is not going to happen." Take-it-or-leave-it offers are usually low. Sometimes buyers will make one to try to get the property for less than its market value. Take-it-or-leave-it offers are made by buyers who feel the seller is desperate to sell; they see that the home has been on the market for a long time and assume the seller may be tired of prospective buyers walking through the home, may not have received any offers yet or may need cash from a sale immediately. If the price and contingencies are unacceptable you should contact the buyers and/or the agent and thank them for the offer but explain that you feel your home is worth more money that they have offered.

"Buyers think that because a property is listed by owner they can negotiate down the price of the home. Their reasoning is that the buyer would have paid commission if listed with a full-service agent; therefore, the starting negotiating point for them is the sales price less the perceived commission. Nothing could be further from the truth. If a home is competitively priced–whether listed with a realtor or not–the selling price is the market value. It is an incorrect assumption that a home listed with a flat-fee agency or by owner is worth less than a home listed with a full-service realtor."

Professional Agent
Flat Fee Realty Company

Sometimes buyers simply are testing the waters to see how low you may go. Do not be surprised if the buyer who submitted the take-it-or-leave-it offer comes back 1 or 2 weeks later with a higher offer. In either instance, you should always respond to an offer, no matter how low it is.

> **Tip**
>
> While the terms of a take-it-or-leave-it offer are generally non-negotiable, the terms of the contract may be. The buyer may be willing to close earlier or later or remove certain contingencies.

Is the First Offer the Best Offer?

There is an unwritten rule in real estate that the first offer will be your best offer. While it is not always true–especially when the first offer is a low-ball or take-it-or-leave-it offer–in many instances, the first offer a seller receives may be the best. Many sellers, however, have trouble accepting the first offer, especially if it comes a few days or weeks after the property has been listed. The thinking is that if the offer comes too quickly, the house is priced too low, and a better offer may come from the next buyer. As mentioned earlier, the longer a home sits on the market the lower its perceived value is.

How can you know if the first offer is the best offer? If an offer comes in that is within between 6 and 15 percent of your asking price, negotiate with the buyer to find a comfortable midpoint. Remember, most homes sell within 6 percent of the asking price. Many factors also may play into the validity of the contract. Are there many contingencies attached to the contract? Are the buyers qualified to buy the home? Are the buyers willing to put down a sizable earnest money deposit?

Be Flexible

It is rare that a home will sell for full asking price. If the market is hot or the number of available properties is low–a sellers' market–the chances that the property will sell for close to the full asking price are greater. If the market is slower and the number of available properties is high–a buyers' market–the chances that the property will sell for full asking price are much less. Being flexible about the amount you will accept will help sell your home faster. As a guideline, professional real estate agents advise sellers to price their homes competitively based on the comparable analysis by setting the asking price one negotiation above the lowest offer the seller is willing to accept.

To determine an acceptable range between asking and selling price for your home, compare the asking price versus the actual selling price of homes in your neighborhood. If it appears that homes are selling at 95 percent of the asking price, consider adding 5 percent to your initial asking price. This strategy will afford you the option of lowering your asking price if your property does not sell quickly, while still keeping your one negotiation goal in mind.

> **Example**
>
> Homes for sale within a six-block radius are priced between $300,000 and $550,000. On average, homes are selling for between 5 and 7 percent of their original asking price—between $285,000 and $511,500. If your home is on the market at $500,000 and you want to get close to full asking price, consider increasing the price by $10,000. A sale at 95 percent of your revised selling price will still net you approximately $484,500.

Counteroffers

For every offer there is a counteroffer ready to be presented. A counteroffer occurs when a buyer makes an initial offer on the home, and the seller responds with a new price, new terms or a list of what the seller will agree to repair.

Every real estate purchase agreement has some type of contingency included in the terms of the sale, which opens the door for negotiation and counteroffers. Counteroffers are used to fine-tune the terms and conditions of the offer received by the buyer.

> **Example**
>
> A buyer presents an offer to purchase your home for $150,000 with a 4-week move-in date. Since your asking price is $175,000 and the offer is lower than what other homes in the neighborhood have sold for, you present a counteroffer of $165,000. The buyer is willing to go a little higher, and counters with an offer of $160,000 and asks the seller to leave all appliances and draperies. The buyer offers the seller a 6-week move in date, which allows the seller more time to find something to buy or rent. The seller agrees to the terms and the sale is completed.

When you make a counteroffer, it is usually unnecessary to draw up a new contract. Once you have agreed upon the terms and the price, a new contract may be made up or the existing one simply amended.

Knowing what type of buyer you are working with when making a counteroffer can help the process go smoother.

- The reasonable buyer is a buyer who wants to purchase your home for a fair price. He or she is not trying to get a deal but is willing to pay what your home is worth and no more. The buyer will start the offer at 5 to 10 percent below your asking price and negotiate from there.

- The nonstop negotiator is the type of buyer who will never stop negotiating, even after the contract to purchase has been signed. This buyer will attempt to negotiate everything right down to the last minutes of settlement or closing. The nonstop negotiator will try to get a cash settlement for everything that is wrong with the home. His or her goal is simply to get your home for the lowest possible price.

Contingencies

Every offer contains verbiage outlining some form of escape clause that enables the buyer to back out of the deal. This escape clause is also known as a contingency clause. It gives the buyer the right to pull out of a deal in the event that a home inspection turns up a big problem, the buyers fail to obtain financing or their home does not sell and they are forced to carry two mortgages. Contingencies can create complications for the seller. The more contingencies a contract includes the more opportunities a buyer has to get out of the deal.

The Most Common Contingencies

Following are some of the most common contingencies built into purchase offers:

- **Contingent on the buyer obtaining financing**—The buyer can withdraw from the contract if the mortgage specified in it is not approved by the mortgage lender. This may happen if mortgage interest rates increase while all the closing documents are being assembled or if the buyer suddenly loses his or her job.

- **Contingent on the outcome of the property inspection**—The buyers can withdraw their offer if they do not approve the inspection report or cannot reach an agreement with the seller about corrections to problems uncovered by the inspection. The buyer and seller agree to a period of 5 business days during which to perform a home inspection and receive a report. Anytime during the 5-day period, the buyer or the seller may withdraw their offer or acceptance of the offer if the inspection report includes structural problems with the home. Common inspections include radon, asbestos, lead, toxic substances, water and structural engineering. Pest inspections check for the presence of and damage caused by termites, mice, rats, roaches, carpenter ants, bats and bees.

- **Attorney approval**—An attorney approval rider gives the buyer and seller 5 business days from the date of the contract signing to have their attorneys review the contract and approve the terms for their clients. The attorney may be called upon to fine-tune points of the contract. In some states, attorneys are not hired by buyers or sellers but the real estate agent.

- **Seller 72-hour contingency**—The seller is placing a stipulation on the sale that he or she must be able to find suitable accommodations to purchase or the sale will not occur. This type of offer benefits the seller only and leaves a buyer with little more than hope that the seller will find a suitable home to purchase within 72 hours.

- **Contingent on the buyer securing a contract on his or her property**—The sale cannot be completed until the buyer receives an offer on his or her current residence, and it passes the homeowners inspection and attorney approval stages.

- **Contingent on the buyer's property closing**—Buyers will often insert this contingency to protect themselves from the possibility of owning two properties at the same time. Buyers are worried that the purchaser of their property will back out at the last minute and leave them with the expense of two homes. With this contingency clause in place, buyers can postpone or pull out of the sale and still have their full escrow money returned.

If you accept a contract containing this contingency, be sure to include a seller's release clause. This will allow you to accept a better offer if one comes your way. The clause is called the 72-hour clause because the sellers are specifying that they can cancel a deal 72 hours after notifying the buyers that they have received another offer if the buyers do not respond or cannot match the newer offer.

The 72-hour clause is designed to provide buyers with a reasonable amount of notification. If the seller receives a new offer on a Friday, the buyer will have a reasonable amount of time to consult his or her agent or attorney in the event that they work only on weekdays or are unavailable during the weekend.

- **Approval by a condo or co-op board**—As written into the association's bylaws, the condo or co-op board may have the right to approve each buyer before the sale can be completed.

The Kick-Out Clause

An offer that is riddled with contingencies provides the buyer with many outs. Contracts with contingencies protect the buyer. The seller can protect his or her own interests when dealing with a contract loaded with contingencies by including a kick-out clause. The kick-out clause allows the seller to continue showing the home until the buyer drops or meets all contingencies. If another offer comes in, the seller can go back to the first buyer, inform him or her of the offer and ask the buyer to meet the standards of the new contract. If the buyer refuses to match the standards of the new contract, the seller has the right to cancel, or kick out, the first buyer's contract and sell the home to the buyer who submitted the better offer.

Qualifying a Buyer

You will want to weed out potential buyers who really cannot afford to purchase your home quickly. A number of factors will help determine whether or not you are wasting your time negotiating a sale.

The Deposit or Earnest Money

Typically, an offer is accompanied with a deposit or earnest money equaling between 1 and 5 percent of the purchase price. How much a seller should expect in earnest money–also known as a good faith deposit–from a buyer is a matter of negotiations and agreement between the seller and the buyer. However, the larger the deposit the more committed the seller will be to making the deal work.

A buyer who puts down a deposit of 5 percent will be less likely to give up such a large amount of money. Sellers always want a larger deposit because they know the buyer will be less likely to walk away from a deal if more earnest money is in jeopardy of being forfeited. Ideally, the buyer will put down a 5 percent deposit with the offer. Buyers, on the other hand, often want to make a lower deposit if they are cash poor or are unwilling to tie up their available cash.

There is no hard and fast rule on how large a deposit should be. There are endless stories from sellers and real estate agents who have sold homes only to have the buyers back out of a deal without reason and forfeit their deposit money. Be aware that it is an increasingly common practice for a buyer to put a small deposit on one or two homes simultaneously in order to place a hold on a property before deciding which one to purchase. Real estate agents are reporting that they are selling the same piece of property two to three times before a sale is completed. Losing a small deposit may not be a hardship for the buyer, but it can be problematic to the seller who is ready to move on. Word may spread quickly that the property is under contract, resulting in down selling time for the seller. Buyers will be less likely to look again at a property that is already under contract. The seller will probably lose an entire month of selling time. Even worse, potential buyers may think that something turned up during the house inspection.

If the sale agreement is properly executed and the buyer does not perform as promised, you may be able to keep the money. Most contracts include certain clauses that offer the buyer an out in the event that he or she cannot complete the transaction, with a few exceptions. The buyer's failure to qualify for a mortgage may result in the return of the deposit. The buyer also may receive the deposit back if the home inspection turns up major repair problems that cannot be resolved with the seller. Again, the wording is such that there must be a diligent effort on the part of the buyer to secure a mortgage. A buyer who decides not to buy the home cannot simply refuse to apply for a mortgage and use that clause as an out.

Earnest Money Schedule

Every offer to purchase real estate should be accompanied by an earnest money check. How much earnest money should be given by the buyer is decided during the negotiation stages. A check for a minimum of $1,000 should be included with the original offer presented to the seller. The balance of the agreed upon earnest money should be sent to the seller before the attorney or inspection approval contingency due date.

If a buyer defaults in paying the seller the balance of the earnest money before the due date, the seller may cancel the agreement in writing to the buyers and keep the earnest money. The seller may then put the home back on the market. A general rule of thumb for how much earnest money to offer is as follows:

Sale Price	Amount of Earnest Money to Seller
To $50,000	$1,000 minimum
$50,000 to $150,000	$2,500 minimum
$150,000 to $500,000	$5,000 minimum
Over $500,000	$10,000 minimum

Nontraditional Forms of Deposit or Earnest Money

A contract can be written in any way that is agreeable to both buyer and seller. In some states, however, there must be some type of consideration accompanying a written contract or it is not a valid offer to purchase. A creative approach to financing will solve virtually any problems a cash-poor buyer may have. Suppose you do not have $15,000 cash readably available for a deposit, but you have something else of value that can be put up as collateral—a car, stock, CDs. There is no law or rule stating that you cannot use something other than cash. Of course, once you put up the cash, the other collateral will be returned to you.

Any money submitted with the contract will be held in escrow or in a trust account by a third party or the party handling the closing.

Setting Your Bottom Price

One of the most important things you should do as a seller is to decide in advance the least amount of money you are willing to accept for your house. This is called your bottom or floor price. Setting your bottom price is an important factor when negotiating the price of your home with a buyer. If the initial offer is at or just above your bottom price, you can feel comfortable that you are close to agreeing on a price and the sale will most likely go through. On the other hand, if the initial offer comes in well below your floor price and you are thousands of dollars apart, the possibility that the buyer will come up to your bottom price is remote and agreement is not likely.

Managing Multiple Offers

Every seller's dream is to receive multiple offers and prompt a bidding war. During a sellers' market, multiple offers may be presented to the seller on the same day. A bidding war can get a seller more money than he or she would have received from a single offer.

If the seller knows that two or three people are very interested in making an offer on the property, he or she may attempt to promote multiple offers or create a bidding war by stating that all offers must be presented by 5 p.m. on Friday to be considered. This creates a sense of urgency with the buyer who is sitting on the fence or is waiting to see if anyone else is interested. This strategy gives the buyer only a few days to make up his or her mind to present an offer or risk losing the property to another buyer.

To effectively manage multiple offers on your property, you need to play fair with each buyer. You may need those other buyers if the first buyer pulls out of the contract for any reason. If the buyer withdraws from the contract because he or she cannot get financing or the home inspection turns up an unexpected problem the buyer does not want to address, you will want to have backup offers. If the other bidders feel they were treated unfairly, they may not choose to make a second offer and you could be left empty-handed.

There are two ways you can handle multiple offers: consider each offer separately as it comes in or wait until you receive all of the offers, review them together and choose the buyer who presents the best offer with the best terms and the least amount of contingencies.

The Sealed Bid

When offers come in and are not judged until the time period is up, it is referred to as a sealed bid. Bidders have one chance to submit their best offers. Once you have received the offers, you can decide which ones you want to respond to. Your initial reaction may be to counter each one and hope the buyers come back with a second offer. The flaw in that strategy is that both buyers may accept your written counteroffer, and you will be legally bound to honor both contracts, which you cannot do. The better option is to not respond to either bid but to go back to the buyers and inform them that multiple offers have been submitted. Let them know how much each buyer bid so that the buyers know where they are among the offers and then ask them to submit revised offers. You also may let the bidders know that you will be making a decision on the best offer.

Tip
Never sign more than one contract at a time. A contract is a legally binding document that obligates you to follow through with the deal. Signing two contracts at once will put you in legal jeopardy.

Background and Credit Checks

If you are offering seller financing, it is important for you to be able to distinguish between a good financial risk and a bad one. If a prospective buyer asks if you will finance the purchase of your home, it is your right and duty to ask the person to fill out an application form. After all, you will be lending the buyer a considerable amount of money and, like any bank, you are entitled to check out the buyer's credit history, job stability and ability to repay the loan. Key pieces of information that should be included on the application are:

- borrower's name, address and phone number
- Social Security number
- list of three previous addresses and length of residency
- employer's name, address and telephone number
- length of time at current job
- list of three previous jobs and dates of employment
- copy of last federal and state tax returns
- current pay stub showing income
- whether the borrower is willing to sign an agreement allowing you to request a copy of his or her credit report and pull up their FICO score
- whether the borrower has ever filed for bankruptcy

If the buyer is currently paying rent, call the landlord to inquire whether the buyer pays on time each month. The best candidate for seller financing is the buyer who has already been preapproved for a loan by a local lender but just needs a little extra from you to purchase your property.

It is easy to request a credit check on a potential buyer. If the buyer gives his or her consent, you may request a credit check from one of the three major credit reporting agencies:

Equifax

Equifax Credit Information Services, Inc.
P.O. Box 740241
Atlanta, GA 30374
1.800.685.1111
www.equifax.com

Experian

National Consumer Assistance
P.O. Box 2002
Allen, TX 75013
1.888.397.3742
www.experian.com

TransUnion, LLC

Consumer Disclosure Center
P.O. Box 1000
Chester, PA 19022
1.800.888.4213
www.transunion.com

Prequalifying the Potential Buyer

Clients who are represented by a real estate agent are more likely to be prequalified by the agent. When a buyer contacts you directly, you are at a slight disadvantage because you do not know if the buyer is preapproved to purchase a home in your price bracket. When considering offers, a preapproved buyer is different than a prequalified buyer.

Prequalified Buyer

Anyone can be prequalified by a local lender. Usually this is a free service offered by a bank that is trying to win your business. Prequalified means the lender has taken a cursory look at your assets and liabilities, your debts and your cash and run these numbers through a mathematical calculation to determine if you debt-to-asset ratio meets their lending guidelines. While being prequalified provides an indication to the buyer of how much they may be eligible to borrow, it does not guarantee they will be able to borrow enough to buy your home. The information included on the prequalification worksheet is very similar to any credit card application.

Example

Stephen and Theresa were relocating to the state of Washington upon the sale of their home. As soon as a purchase contract was signed, they visited Washington to scout areas that offered the best potential for their relocation. Before they left for their trip, they wanted to secure a prequalification letter to present to real estate agents. They visited the same lending institution that currently held their home mortgage and requested one. Without even so much as pulling up their current payment history, the loan officer asked how much they thought they could afford and quickly drew up a letter on bank stationary stating that they were qualified to purchase a home in that price range.

Tip

Anyone can obtain a bank approval letter stating that they are qualified to purchase your home. Do not take anything for granted. If you are offering seller financing, and the buyer is not represented by a real estate agent who has prequalified him or her, ask the buyer for bank or landlord references to verify his or her borrowing power, even if the buyer presents such a letter. Most buyers will not be offended, especially if they are serious about the purchase.

Preapproved Buyer

Obtaining preapproval status is a much different process and reviews the buyer's finances more carefully than the prequalification process. The buyer may have to pay a sizeable application fee–often $250 or more–to become preapproved by a lender. If a buyer is preapproved, it means the lender has researched his or her credit history, verified income and is prepared to lend the buyer the loan for a mortgage. The only items needed to complete the loan are a contract for the purchase and the appraisal.

The Art of Negotiations

Negotiation is all about give-and-take. In successful negotiations, emotions are set aside, and everyone walks away a winner. Negotiations begin with the buyer presenting an offer to purchase real estate from the seller. The seller will review the terms of the contract and counter or submit a response to the offer. In a counteroffer, the seller and the buyer have the option to adjust or change the terms of the contract. The buyer will review the counteroffer and will either accept the terms of the contract and the price or counter again. This back-and-forth will continue until both parties agree on the price, terms and key points of the sale.

10 Tips to Conducting Successful Negotiations

To conduct successful negotiations, keep in mind that it is a financial transaction and is not personal. The following are 10 tips to help you negotiate successfully:

1. Know your floor price but remain flexible if the offer and your floor price are no more than or $2,000 apart.

---

2. Find out what is motivating your buyer. Ask the buyer when he or she wants to move in and his or her motivation for picking that date. The reason may be timing the sale to the beginning or end of the school year or working around holidays.

3. Present a seller's disclosure form with your listing sheet. Disclosing any flaws or known defects before negotiations begin eliminates surprises and the possibility of reopening negotiations after the inspection or during attorney approval periods.

4. Know when to keep your mouth shut. In other words, limit your discussion and do not talk too much. The best negotiators let silence work in their favor. Offering too much information will weaken your position. Let the buyers do all the talking. You may be pleasantly surprised at how well this strategy works.

5. Timing is everything. The timing of your counteroffer will speak volumes. If you counteroffer too quickly, the buyer will think you are desperate. If you counteroffer too slowly or just before the offer expires, the buyers may get frustrated at the slowness of the response and quickly lose interest. Upon receipt of an offer, respond within 24 hours, even if you have 48 hours to respond. If you need more than 24 hours to decide, you are not ready to sell.

6. Keep it strictly business. The buyer does not need to know everything about your personal life. Never divulge your bottom price to an agent or to the buyer. Keep all conversation strictly professional and focused on the terms of the sale.

7. Make it clear that you are actively showing the home and that other buyers are interested. Never let a buyer know that activity on your home has ceased.

8. Show your home until all contract contingencies are removed. If the contract includes a financing, approval or sales contingency, always include a rider that allows you to continue showing the home until all contingencies have been satisfied or removed.

9. Avoid the 24-hour walk-through contingency. This contingency allows the buyer to reopen negotiations within 24 hours of the final walk-through. Often, the buyer will try to negotiate a cash credit for something he or she missed during the inspection or a stain that occurred after the inspection but before closing. If something has broken or become stained during this time, you are obligated to bring the home back to original condition. That may mean replacing the furnace that is beyond repair or cleaning the stained carpet.

10. Adopt a go-with-the-flow attitude. Closings can become emotional. For some sellers, it finally sinks in that their home has sold and it is time to move on only when the buyer's possessions are on a moving truck just waiting to enter the premises. Remember why you wanted to sell in the first place. Keep an

open mind and mild manner. Do not let the buyer know it is imperative that the transaction go through; he or she may use this information to take advantage of you during closing by trying to renegotiate the sale.

> **Tip**
>
> If you are a poor negotiator or if emotions are getting in the way, enlist the help of your lawyer to negotiate the deal for you. Outline your bottom price and terms you will accept and let your lawyer finesse the deal on your behalf.

Avoiding Contingencies

One reason sellers like contingency-free offers is that they minimize the possibility of a sale falling through. Typical contingencies benefit the buyer but rarely result in a failed sale. However, sellers should avoid contingencies that leave little or no room to maneuver. If a buyer wants to make the sale contingent on the sale of his or her current home, make sure the contract includes a release clause that will release you from the first contract if an offer without contingencies is presented by another party.

Finessing the Deal

Most lawyers will manage negotiations in consultation with you, especially if you are offering seller financing. Before you jump into negotiating your own deal, however, make sure that you are prepared to discuss your property's weaknesses or whether you can consider a lower price without bristling. Remaining calm and focused is the best tactic in negotiations.

If you are fortunate enough to be selling your home in a sellers' market, you may not feel that you need advice on negotiating the deal. But careful negotiation can be critical, especially if you are considering multiple offers. Conversely, in a buyers' market, you may be glad just to get an offer, let alone have the option to negotiate. But even in this situation, it is important to avoid making unnecessary concessions.

It pays to understand the dynamics of negotiation and recognize that the best real estate transactions are those in which both the seller and buyer believe they got the best deal.

> **Tip**
>
> Hedge your deal. Accepting a backup offer is one way to hedge your bets in an uncertain market. By having a second offer waiting, you create incentive for your first buyer to carry through with the purchase. A backup offer can offset preclosing issues, such as unexpected repair problems and can discourage your first buyer from renegotiating the contract. On the other hand, a backup offer might include troublesome contingencies or other unattractive terms. Be careful. Once you accept a backup offer, you are obliged to go through with the sale if your primary buyer falters.

Why Deals Fall Through

Negotiations gone awry are a major cause of failed real estate transactions. Try to avoid the following negotiating traps.

Moving Too Fast

It can be tempting to push negotiations through quickly, especially if you need to sell for financial or relocation reasons or if the market is fast—if there are many buyers but few listings. Take the time to read offers carefully. If a buyer makes a low offer because the house needs repairs, make sure the buyer's estimate of the cost of those repairs is accurate and not inflated. It may be better to make the repairs yourself before selling rather than accept a big price cut.

Emotions Get in the Way

Remember that the house you are selling is a commodity. Do not take offense at comments about the landscaping or decor, especially when the buyer makes a lower offer based on those factors. If the market is not in your favor, you may have to offer a decorating allowance or accept a lower price. If you are in a sellers' market, counter with a full-price offer. In any case, do not stop dealing with a buyer just because you do not share the same tastes.

Reluctance to Counter

Countering an offer is a time-honored tradition in real estate. Countering means that you come back to the buyer with a different price or different terms. Remember that negotiating to sell a house is a give-and-take process. If you fail to counter offers, you may end up accepting a lower price for your home. Make all counteroffers in writing to avoid misunderstandings.

Bad Faith Bargaining

Bad faith bargaining occurs when one or both parties is not bargaining seriously or with the intention of actually completing the transaction. Bad faith bargaining can not only result in a failed sale but also can result in possible legal action. If you are not serious about selling your property–that is, you will not accept anything but an overpriced offer–you probably should not be on the market. If you are a serious seller, watch out for the bad faith buyer who will waste your time by making unacceptably low offers or engaging in endless negotiations. Even worse are buyers who misrepresent their ability to purchase your home and take you off the market for several weeks before their failure to secure financing nullifies the contract. If you have any qualms about a buyer's financial means, ask for a preapproval letter from a lender.

Failure to Meet Deadlines

Time can be an ally and an enemy in negotiations. It is vital that both sides meet deadlines, but this does not mean that you cannot be flexible. A long line at the lender may hold up a buyer's financing. Make sure that your closing date allows for contingencies that may take a longer time than usual to satisfy. Also, make sure that the buyer or the agent asks to extend contract deadlines promptly so that you can make any adjustments.

Miscommunication

The buyer may not understand the inspector's report or may be scared away by unfamiliar terminology.

Example

A young couple entered into a contract to purchase an older home. The home inspection turned up a couple of small cracks in the foundation. The buyer opted to have a structural engineer look at the foundation to confirm the foundation was solid. During the inspection, the structural engineer outlined three possible repair options to the homeowner, ranging from a simple fix costing $600 to a full-blown fix costing between $15,000 and $22,000. At no time did the inspector say the repairs needed to be done immediately or that the full-blown repair option was necessary. Upon receiving a verbal summary of the inspector's report, the buyer backed out of the deal with the excuse that the inspector said there were major repairs that needed to be done immediately at a cost of $40,000. There was no written inspection report or cost estimate. The seller decided to have a second structural engineer verify the buyer's vendor. The engineer stated that the house had settled at one time but there was no evidence of continued settling. If any additional settling happened in the future, the fix would be four footers to stabilize the portion of the home that had settled at a cost of $2,000 per footer, but that fix was not necessary unless additional settling occurred and certainly was not required in the near future. The foundation did need some minor repairs but at a significantly lower cost. The minor repairs were made, but the damage had been done. The buyer backed out of the deal, and the home had to go back on the market.

Seller Financing—A Good Option for Both Parties

Seller financing options may be beneficial to both parties. A seller may be willing to offer financing to buyers to make a slow moving property more attractive or to obtain a better return on investment than could be obtained from a conventional investment. Seller financing may be attractive to sellers who do not need the cash from the sale of the home to buy another one. The interest rate and length of the loan can be whatever you and the buyer negotiate. There are different types of seller financing that work well to attract buyers to a slow moving property and provide help to the first time buyer.

Purchase Money Mortgage (PMM)

In a PMM arrangement, you, the seller, take the place of a conventional lender and provide the buyer with all the financing needed. In effect, you become the bank. This type of agreement is also known as an installment purchase. The buyer pays for the home a little bit at a time. The buyer receives an interest in the home, but you hold title until the buyer pays the loan back in full. To minimize your risk, you may require the buyer to put down a sizable down payment.

If the buyer can afford a 20 percent down payment, then you, the seller, loan the buyer the other 80 percent of the sale price. It is best in this situation to have your home completely paid off before offering a buyer the PMM option. If you are still paying off your own mortgage, be careful about using a PMM or installment purchase agreement. If your lender finds out that you have sold the home, the lender could foreclose on your home and jeopardize your and the buyer's credit. The reason is that your current mortgage agreement with a bank most likely has a due-on-sale clause that allows the lender to call your loan upon the sale of the property.

The advantage to this type of agreement is that you are the primary lender. If the buyer defaults on the loan, you may foreclose on the house and sell it to pay yourself back first. You will not need to file a lien on the property and wait until all secured creditors are paid, leaving only a few pennies on the dollar to be paid to unsecured creditors such as yourself. With PMM financing, only a federal income tax lien would take priority over your loan and would be paid off first.

Second Mortgage

A second mortgage means that the borrower has gone to a conventional lender for the first loan and then comes to you to make up the difference between the sale price of your home and the loan from the bank. A second mortgage may become an option if the property appraises lower than the sale price and there is a gap between the amount of money the buyer can put down and the amount of mortgage the lender will approve. To save the sale, the seller may step in to offer a second mortgage to the buyer.

Buy Down

This option is technically not considered seller financing, but it is a way to help out a prospective buyer who may be able to put down 20 percent but may not qualify for a loan at the current interest rate. If the interest rate on a loan is 7 percent, you could buy down the rate for 1, 2 or 3 years until the buyer's income would allow him or her to make the full payment. What that means is that you would make up the difference between what the buyer pays and what the regular rate of the loan is. For example, in the first year of a 7 percent loan, if the buyer pays only 4 percent a year, you pay the remaining 3 percent to make up the difference. In year 2, the seller may make up only 2 percent of the difference with the contribution dropping to only 1 percent in year 3. Before jumping into a buy down or financing agreement, always consult a real estate attorney or tax attorney to draw up and file the necessary loan papers.

Assumable Mortgage

An assumable mortgage is a mortgage that can be transferred from one borrower to another with no change in terms. If an assumable mortgage is transferred, the buyer assumes all responsibility for repayment. The original lender must agree to the transfer of an assumable mortgage. The seller should receive a written release from the original lender stating that he or she has no responsibility for further payments. The buyer may be required to meet certain standards to qualify and may be charged an assumption fee. Assumable mortgages can make a property more desirable if interest rates have risen, because the new buyer's payments are at the original rate. By definition, assumable mortgages cannot have a due-on-sale clause.

Assumable mortgages are not technically seller financing, but they are similar in that the seller is providing existing financing. Most mortgages are assumable. That means the mortgage can be assumed by someone else who takes over the payments and finishes paying the loan. The major benefit of assumable mortgages is the lower interest rate relative to current market rates. If the seller has a 5.5 percent mortgage, for example, and the best the buyer can get in the current market is 7 percent, both parties may benefit if the buyer assumes the 5.5 percent loan. An assumption also avoids the settlement costs on a new mortgage.

Until recently, few lenders were asked about assumable mortgages because market rates were so low. As rates continue to rise, interest in assumptions will receive increasing attention. The buyers who do best on assumptions are those who have the cash to pay the difference between the sale price and the balance of the old loan. The seller's benefit is usually in the form of the buyer agreeing to pay a slightly higher price for the house.

The benefit to buyer and seller from assuming a mortgage comes at the expense of the lender. Instead of having the 5.5 percent loan repaid, which would allow the lender to convert it into a new 7 percent loan, the 5.5 percent loan stays on the books.

Because of this, however, many lenders have inserted due-on-sale clauses in their mortgage contracts. These clauses stipulate that if the property is sold, the loan must be repaid. Even with a due-on-sale clause, the lender may allow an assumption–keeping the loan on the books avoids the cost of making a new loan–but the interest rate will increase to the current market rate. FHA and VA mortgages are an exception and do not contain these clauses.

Raising the interest rate to market rate removes most of the assumable mortgage's benefits for the buyer and seller. In some cases, an attempt is made to retain the benefit by agreeing to a sale using a wraparound mortgage without the knowledge of the lender. The seller takes a mortgage from the buyer, which may be for a larger amount than the balance of the old loan and continues to pay the old mortgage out of the proceeds of the new one. The new mortgage wraps around the old one.

This can be risky business, particularly to the seller, who has given up ownership of the house but retained liability for the mortgage. The seller is liable if the buyer fails to pay or if the lender discovers the sale and demands immediate repayment of the original loan.

Balloon Mortgages

Generally, a balloon mortgage is an interest-only loan, with the balance or principal due at the end of the agreed-upon number of years. Interest payments may be paid monthly, quarterly or annually. Balloon mortgages usually run 3 to 7 years, with the balance due at the end of the loan date. Most buyers who take advantage of this type of financing are self-employed or otherwise unable to secure longer-term standard financing.

This type of loan is popular with buyers when interest rates are higher, and the buyer is gambling that rates will be much lower in a few years. At that time, the home will have appreciated in value, and the buyer may be in a better financial position to refinance for the full amount of the loan and then pay the seller the total amount due.

Before you offer seller financing, talk with an attorney or tax advisor to make sure the risk to you is minimal. If you decide on this strategy, be sure to follow the procedures that any regular lender would. Do a credit and income check and always seek professional guidance to draw up legal papers. If something does go wrong in the future, you may foreclose on the property, but it can be a time-consuming and aggravating process. However, if you choose your buyer carefully and conduct the proper credit checks, you can minimize that risk and reap larger financial rewards.

Discounts on Other Socrates Products

In addition to a variety of free forms and checklists, you will find special offers on a variety of Socrates products. Visit **www.socrates. com/books/ForSaleByOwner.aspx** for more information.

8

· · · · · ·

What If There Are No Acceptable Offers?

How Long Is Too Long between Offers?

Real estate agents estimate that the average number of showings before an offer is presented is 40. That number of showings may be reached within the first few days of being listed if the market is hot, or it may take months if the market is slow. If you have not received an offer after the first 40 showings, then either the price or condition of your home is scaring away prospective buyers and you need to take steps to correct whatever is wrong.

A newly available house will have the majority of the showings conducted during the first 3 weeks. All the buyers who are active in your area will want to see it within that time period. If a buyer likes it, then it will probably result in a quick sale.

If the market is strong and your home remains on the market 1 or 2 months without an offer, then you may have to re-evaluate the price and the condition of your home. If there are no pressing reasons to move, then you can wait until the right buyer comes along. If you have not received any offers and your reasons for moving are job related or you need to sell quickly, you should reevaluate your market position as quickly as possible.

Tip
Remember that the longer your home is on the market the less likely you are to get an offer for the full price. Do not hesitate to take steps quickly after the first or second month goes by. If you make major repairs or offer incentives, schedule another open house to renew enthusiasm for the property.

If your home has not sold, you have two options: You can either fix it up or lower your price. Before selecting either option, seek and listen to buyer feedback. Make follow-up phone calls to prospective buyers who have viewed your home. Ask for their feedback. What did they like or not like about your home? What has stopped them from making an offer? Correct any recurring issues. If the consensus is that your home is not selling because of price, reduce the price as soon as possible.

Fix It Up

Make cosmetic changes. Rip up the old shag rug and replace it with a new carpet of neutral color. Refinish or replace worn hardwood floors. Repaint rooms that may have loud colors or look dated. A fresh coat of paint and new carpeting will go a long way toward making the home look bright, fresh and clean.

Decorating Allowance

If you do not want to paint or replace the carpet yourself, offer an appropriate allowance to a buyer who likes everything but your taste in decor.

Revisit Pricing

If all the homes around you are selling, try to find out how much they are selling for. If the average home sale is taking 6 months but the homes are selling within 5 percent of the asking price, you may wish to drop your price only a little bit and be more patient. If homes are taking an average of 6 months to sell but also are taking a 20 percent hit on price, you may wish to hold off selling until the market improves or accept a smaller net profit from the sale than originally planned.

If you decide to lower your price, you may lower it by small amounts until you reach a price that makes buyers take notice, or you may make one big reduction. For example, if your original list price is $575,000 and similar homes have been selling for $550,000, you can cut your price to $555,000 or $560,000. A big price drop signals that you are serious about selling. Smaller, more frequent drops indicate that the seller is serious but is more cautious about dropping the price too much or too quickly. Before you decide to reduce the price, consider the move carefully. It is very easy to sell an underpriced house; it is much more difficult to raise the listing price once it has been lowered.

If your home has been on the market for several months without a buyer and depending on your reasons for moving, you have the option of taking the property off the market and putting it back up for sale when market conditions improve. A home that is on the market too long may result in agents and buyers thinking that something must be wrong with it.

Offer Incentives

If your price is in line with the market and the home is already decorated with neutral colors and newer carpeting, there are other incentives you can offer to attract more buyers.

Presale Inspection and Warranty

A comprehensive home inspection combined with a home warranty reassures buyers that the property is in good condition and that certain repairs will be covered by insurance. Make copies of these documents for buyers to take away.

Lease Option

A lease option allows the buyer to rent the property for a period of time with an option to buy. A percentage of the rent is set aside as the buyer's down payment while you use the remainder to cover your mortgage. To increase the likelihood of a sale, put at least 30 percent of the rent toward a down payment.

Seller Financing

Seller financing is the most advantageous incentive if you have substantial equity in the property. Options include buying down the mortgage rate, putting funds in escrow to cover several months of mortgage payments or carrying back a second mortgage to help a buyer cover a down payment. Before you offer financial assistance to a buyer, consult your agent and a real estate attorney and make sure the buyer is creditworthy.

Closing Costs

You can offer to cover nonrecurring closing costs, such as prepaid interest charges or the first year of property taxes. Paying points is an attractive incentive that you also can use as a tax deduction. Most lenders limit the amount of closing costs you can pay, but this can make a difference for cash-poor buyers.

Pay the First 6 Months of Taxes

Offer to pay the first 6 months of taxes for the buyer. This can be a tremendous incentive, especially if the taxes in your area are higher.

Cooperate with Agents

The first few weeks that your For Sale by Owner sign is in the ground, you will receive several calls from agents who will try to convince you to list your home with them. To help elicit the interest of agents in your area, let each agent know that you are willing to cooperate with buyer's agents by paying them a 2.5 or 3 percent commission rate. A quick sale may make it worthwhile to pay the agent a commission. They will likely want you to sign an agreement. Be sure, however, that it specifies the amount the agent will be paid and that the agent is representing the buyer only and is not acting as a dual agent.

Increase Agent Commission

To provide an incentive to agents to show your house more, offer a 0.5 percent commission increase if the agent presents you with a contract within 30 days. Most agents will work very hard to earn the additional commission.

Do You Need an Agent?

At what point do you realize that despite your best efforts, you need to hire a real estate agent to sell your property? It depends on your schedule and energy level. But if you are frustrated and ready to throw in the towel after months and months of trying to sell your home, it may be time to call in a professional real estate expert to help the sale move more quickly or at least to take the pressure off you and put it squarely on him or her.

The NAR cites that between 85 and 95 percent of all homes are sold with the help of an agent, depending on the neighborhood. If you decide to list with an agent, you may ask to exclude the names of buyers who have already seen your home via open houses or showings in the written contract. That way if a buyer who had seen your home before you listed with a real estate agent comes back with an offer, he or she can be treated the same as he or she would have if the home sold by owner and you will not have to pay a commission.

> "Going from selling by owner to hiring a realtor is a progression. First a seller will try to sell by owner. If the home does not sell, then he or she will sign up with a flat-fee service realtor. If the home does not sell, then the seller will list with a full-service agent. But it can also go in reverse. We have several clients who, for one reason or another, canceled their listing with an agent and decided to try to sell their home by owner."
>
> Professional Realtor
> Flat Fee Listing Company

Remember, there are no guarantees that a real estate agent will be able to sell your home quickly either, regardless of his or her sales pitch. If the agent had a buyer waiting in the wings, why did the agent not bring him or her through when the home was FSBO?

Also, the fact that you are listing with a real estate agent does not mean that you cannot sell your home by owner again. You can sign a 60- to 90-day listing agreement, and if after that time you feel you can get better results on your own, you can always go back to being an FSBO.

Tip

Before listing your home with a real estate agent, read the fine print carefully. There are often covenants stating that you cannot list with another agent for 6 to 12 months after ending the agreement. There also might be language stating that if you sell to a buyer who may have walked through your home while listed with the agent, you will owe the real estate company and the agent a full commission. The reasoning is that because they brought the buyer to the property, they should be properly compensated for the lead.

If you are considering listing with a real estate agent, be aware of the limitations you may be signing away.

Free Forms and Checklists

Visit Socrates.com and register to receive a variety of useful FREE forms, letters and checklists. See page iv for details on how to register (you will need the 7-digit registration code provided on the enclosed CD).

9

. . . . . .

Selling by Auction

Auctioning Your Home

These days, auctioning a home is not necessarily a measure of desperation. A voluntary auction is not the same as a foreclosure. The auction format works well for many situations, including:

- Unique properties with a market value that is difficult to determine—these include trophy homes, mansions and land.

- Properties that would attract a small but geographically dispersed buying pool—building a customized marketing plan to educate potential buyers brings them together for the single sales event.

- Offering multiple properties at one time—an owner selling a group of properties may wish to sell them all at once. For example, the owner of a group of several condominium units may wish to sell all the units at once.

- Sellers who need a shortened selling timeline—owners may want to avoid a prolonged and costly cycle of showings, negotiations and deal-killing contingencies.

- Sellers who need a specific date of sale—this can apply to sellers looking to clear the books by year's end or looking to sell before expensive carrying costs erode value.

- In the rare instance when a home has not sold by traditional methods and the owner is ready to sell.

Other advantages of selling by auction include:

- Buyers come prepared to buy. Lookers are eliminated because most often bidders must qualify through a deposit of a certified or cashier's check.

- Auction brings interested buyers to a point of decision. Buyers feel that if all the properties are sold before the auction ends, it represents their last chance to purchase a desired property.

- Sellers get maximum exposure for their properties. The marketing strategy differs from conventional advertising. It is more concentrated and, therefore, more intense and visible.

- High carrying costs are avoided. Through auctions, the seller is in control and knows that if properly priced, his or her property will sell on a certain date, which is usually within 45-60 days from the auction listing. By selling quickly, the seller is able to avoid high carrying costs, such as insurance, real estate taxes, security and maintenance and is also able to benefit from the use of the monies to reinvest in other real estate or investment opportunities.

Additional benefits include:

- It offers the seller another option.
- It creates competition among buyers. The auction price can exceed the price of a negotiated sale. An auction generates excitement and heightens buyer interest.
- It requires that potential buyers prequalify for loans. Prequalified buyers accelerate sales and the property sometimes can be sold within 6 weeks of listing.
- Auction is a true free market form. The highest bidding buyer pays the lowest price a seller will accept.
- It allows the seller to know exactly when the property will sell.
- It enables the seller to set the terms and conditions of the sale, maintain control of the property throughout the auction, depending on auction type and actively participate in the sale process.
- It reduces the time that the property is on the market.
- It eliminates numerous and unscheduled showings.
- It removes the seller from the negotiation process.
- It facilitates an aggressive marketing program that increases potential in and awareness of a property.

As you can see, the home auctions conducted today offer sellers many benefits without the stigma attached to home auctions of the past. Various auction formats are available for sellers, allowing them to choose the auction type that best suits their needs and reap the greatest rewards.

The Auction Industry

The auction industry in the United States consists of approximately 35,000 full-time auctioneers with an estimated 24,000 of them selling real estate at some time. Approximately 1,000 regional and national firms specialize in real estate and market more than 70 percent of all real estate sold at auction. In 1980, more than $50 billion in real and personal assets were sold using the auction method of marketing. Real property made up 20 percent of this amount. By the end of 1998, more than $49.5 billion in real property was sold using the auction method of marketing. Sales of all categories of real property continue to grow and are estimated to exceed $60 billion, including public and private sector transactions in all real estate categories.

Until recently, auctions were viewed as distress sales, a means for a seller to find a buyer before the property was foreclosed on by a lender. While the vast majority of real estate auctions are distress sales, they are not the only sales. Valuable items, including real estate, are auctioned every day by owners who are not in financial distress. The auction method is the best way to sell a property in an aboveboard manner with nothing hidden.

It is important to note that not all property auctions result in a successful sale. If the minimum bid is not reached, if the winning bidder does not have the proper documentation or down payment, or if the property does not attract enough interested buyers, the auction may end suddenly without securing a buyer.

Why Conduct an Auction?

If you are in a hurry to sell or perhaps selling an estate you inherited, an auction affords you the opportunity to sell a property that you cannot or may not want to spend a lot of time marketing. Usually, properties sold at auction are sold in as-is condition. Homes are sold on a cash-sale basis. The seller does not offer financing. The buyer is usually required to put 10 percent down in the form of cash or certified check at the time of the sale, with the remaining balance paid in full within 48 hours. This requires the buyer to obtain financing in advance.

Property Sold As-Is

The contract of sale that a buyer signs to purchase a property at an auction is different from the contract of sale the buyer may sign for other property sales. There are several factors in an auction that are different from a sale by a private party or a real estate agent transaction. In an auction situation, a trustee or substitute trustee is charged with selling the property. Usually the property will be sold as-is with no warranties. The buyer pays all closing costs and usually does not have the right of inspection for further negotiation after the sale.

A property sale conducted through a private party or real estate agent designates assigned closing costs to the seller and the buyer. The buyer also has the right to inspect the premises prior to the negotiation of the sale.

If you are unfamiliar with how auctions work, it is advisable to tag along with someone who is knowledgeable with the process to learn and become comfortable with the terminology and procedures.

Types of Auctions

There are many different types of auctions. Determining which type of auction is best for your property and situation should be discussed with the auctioneer.

Public Auction

Interested bidders gather at a specific location at a designated time and openly bid against one another for the purchase of the property. The bidder with the highest bid ultimately wins the property.

Sealed Bid Auction

Bidders get one chance to submit a bid by a specified date and may never know the amount of the winning bid. The bidders submit their bids by mail in a sealed envelope. On the deadline date, the envelopes are unsealed and bids are compared. The highest or best offer, as determined by the seller, typically is accepted within 48 to 72 hours after the deadline. After the bid deadline, the seller may invite the top several bidders to submit a best and final offer (BAFO).

Absolute Auction

The property is sold to the highest bidder, no matter how low the price, even if the winning bid is below the seller's minimum desired price. The property absolutely will be sold regardless of the bid. This type of auction also is referred to as auction without reserve. Once a bid is made, there is an acceptance of the offer, and the seller is bound to complete the sale. The bidder also is bound by the acceptance of the offer to sell. To negate a binding contract, the seller must withdraw the offer to sell before the first bid is received. This is a popular auction method for selling private residential property.

Reserve Bid Auction

The seller sets a minimum price for the property; the property is sold only if the highest bidder meets or exceeds the reserve price. The highest bidder must be told of the seller's acceptance or rejection of his or her bid within 48 hours. This is also a popular auction method for selling private residential property. The advertising can state the specific reserve price or that the seller reserves the right to accept or reject the final bid.

Spot Bid Auction

Buyers put their bids in writing. The bids are collected, and the auctioneer determines who the highest bidder is. Each bidder gets only one chance to make a bid, so he or she is forced to bid his or her top price. This type of auction is very similar to a reserve bid auction.

Dutch Auction

In a Dutch auction, the auctioneer starts the bidding at the highest price and continues to lower the price until someone bids. The first bidder who calls out wins the bid. Another bidder can advance the bid, however, resulting in a blending of the Dutch–descending–system with the English–ascending–system. A Dutch auction often is conducted with a minimum reserve amount and may also be advertised as auction with reserve. In an auction with reserve, the seller does not have an obligation to accept an offer below the reserve price. If, however, the reserve price is met or exceeded and the seller refuses to accept the qualifying bid, the auctioneer still earns the commission because he or she found a qualified buyer who was willing to pay above the reserve amount.

Hybrid Auction

This is similar to an absolute auction with a minimum opening bid. The seller reserves the right not to accept any bids that do not reach the stated minimum opening bid. Once a bid has been received that meets or exceeds the minimum opening amount, the auction reverts to an absolute auction and the seller is obligated to sell the property.

Weekend Auction

The name of this auction indicates exactly when the auction will take place—over the weekend. The home is open to preview on Friday or Saturday and the auction is conducted on Sunday. The auction may be shortened to allow previewing on Friday only, with the auction beginning on Saturday.

Making the Auction Decision

There are a number of factors to review before making the decision to take your property to auction.

The Market Environment

Do some research into how real estate auctions are accepted by buyers in your community. If your geographic area has not fully embraced auctions as a viable selling alternative, it may be difficult to attract enough buyers to make the sale competitive. Also, look objectively at your property. A property that has been available for sale for a long period of time, by owner or with a real estate agent, and that has experienced several price reductions, may not do well in an auction. Prospective buyers may view the property as overpriced or assume that the seller may be desperate.

The Sales Price

A market analysis comparing sales prices of similar properties by auction should be conducted to determine an estimated sales price. Any auction house you interview should be able to provide a list of properties that sold by auction, the auction price and the listed or appraised valued of the properties. An auctioneer can provide you with best- and worst-case scenarios for bidding. The type of auction method you choose also can affect the sales price of the property.

Timing is also a factor when determining the potential sales price. If the property is seasonal, such as a summer retreat home or winter mountain home, consider scheduling an auction during the optimal selling time. Timing also may be related to economic factors, such as changing interest rates or employment rates. Higher interest or unemployment rates or a struggling economy will affect your potential gross sales estimates.

General market factors also should be considered. How many homes are available for sale in your immediate area? If you are attempting to sell in a buyers' market, your overall competition will be greater, potentially hurting your ability to achieve your maximum sales potential.

Holding Periods

The holding period is the period during which the property is being made ready for auction and prior to the close. Holding periods include marketing time, the auction event itself and closing procedures. The holding period ranges from as little as 30 days to as long as 6 months.

Marketing

The marketing period is the span of time between the signing of the contract and the conducting of the sale. Allocate time during this period to prepare the property for sale, especially if improvements are required. The time to market the property is also built into this period. Allow 4 to 8 weeks to develop and distribute marketing materials and allow prospective buyers to view the property.

The Auction Event

The auction includes the auction day and all setup and tear-down of staging materials related to the auction. Build in 2 or 3 days for this time period.

Closing

The time it takes to close the transaction after the auction has taken place is called the closing period. The amount of time depends on the property, the market and document preparation. A closing date may be scheduled as quickly as 2 weeks or as long as 3 months. Some auction firms may make same-day closing available for prequalified buyers.

Holding Costs of Property

Holding costs are all costs associated with the property during the holding period. These costs may include insurance, interest, taxes, security or caretaking fees, association fees, liens and management fees.

The longer the holding period the greater your costs will be. Determine what the monthly holding fees will be and then multiply that number by the total number of months you may be holding the property. Expect to build the following fees into your budget:

Monthly Expenses for Property	Monthly Holding Costs	3-Month Holding Costs
Insurance	$ 75	$225
Association/Management fee	$150	$450
Taxes	$200	$600
Maintenance	$ 50	$150
Miscellaneous	$ 50	$150
Total Costs	$ 525	$1,575

Current Market Value of the Property

A CMA should be conducted for homes available for auction just as a CMA is conducted for a home sold by owner or through a real estate agent. Compare similar properties that have recently sold to ensure that your property is being offered at a fair price.

Estimated Marketing Costs

Advertising, promotion and public relations are some of the marketing costs attached to the sale. How much marketing is the auction house proposing to coordinate for your property? Estimate how much money will be needed to promote your auction effectively. Depending on the arrangement with the auctioneer, these costs also may be deducted from the gross proceeds from the sale of the property.

Selecting a Professional Auctioneer

Most states require professional auctioneers to be bonded or have a license to sell real estate at auction. The degree of licensure varies from state to state; a few auction-license states do not require an examination to obtain a license. The nonexamination states may require only that the auctioneer meet fee and bond requirements. It is recommended that you select an auctioneer who is a member of the National Auctioneers Association (NAA).

The NAA is the professional organization for practicing auctioneers, their associates, affiliated businesses and other related professionals. Membership in the NAA is voluntary and carries with it a requirement of professional commitment to other professionals, clients, customers and the public at large that extends beyond that of laws and professional regulations.

Guidelines to Choosing an Auctioneer

Experience

Not all firms have experience selling residential property. The upward trend in auction marketing is toward specialization by type of property. Research the types of properties an auction marketing firm has experience with and select a firm that has experience with your type of property.

Advertising Capabilities

Review the company's own promotional brochures for clarity and attractiveness. Ask to see typical marketing materials and advertising schedules for previous clients. A successful marketing plan includes multimedia promotions utilizing advertising, press relations and media.

Is the Company Responsive to Your Calls?

Do they contact you promptly or do you consistently receive a recording stating that they are unavailable?

Check the Better Business Bureau

Is the company in good standing with the state? Have complaints been lodged against the company?

Attend Several Auctions Run by the Company

Consider attending auctions that are being conducted by different auction companies and then compare how well-organized and well-attended each auction was.

Check Fees and Services

Ask for a list of services and fees from each auction house you approach.

Length of Time the Auction Company Has Been in Business

Inquire how long the company has been in business. Investigate the length of service of key employees.

Administrative Support

Inquire about the administrative resources needed to conduct a successful auction. Does the auction house have enough experienced staff to create and execute a marketing proposal and to run a smooth auction?

The Role of the Auctioneer

The role of the auctioneer is an important one. A good auctioneer will provide full disclosure about the property to help avoid any potential conflicts. Full disclosure includes the auctioneer notifying the owner if the auctioneer is interested in purchasing the property. The auctioneer plays the role of impartial advocate if family members are competing to purchase the property and does not improperly disclose confidential information obtained in the course of the professional service to a client.

An auctioneer has an obligation to conduct business in a professional manner and should not accept an auction if his or her previous experience is not sufficient to complete the auction competently. The auctioneer will supply a written contract summarizing the responsibilities of both parties that include the following items: ownership; description of the property; type, date and location of auction; seller's legal right to sell; liens and encumbrances, if any; bulk sales law compliance, if applicable; default to buyer or seller; the buyer's premium; real estate commission, if any; and the handling of refunds received and controlled by the auction firm and auctioneer's fees.

In some areas of the country, a buyer's premium or commission on the sale of real property is common, while in others it is not. If a buyer's premium is to be used as part or all of the compensation to the auctioneer, this information should be included in the written contract.

The written contact should also include: duties and obligations of the parties; services to be provided by auctioneer; insurance coverage relating to liability, theft and casualty loss; and use of a buyer's premium.

Auctioneer's Fees

A professional auctioneer may charge up to 10 percent of the home's final sales price; however, rates are usually negotiable.

In some parts of the country the auctioneer's fee is paid by the buyer and is called a buyer's premium. To cover the auctioneer's commission, the seller will add a buyer's fee of up to 15 percent to the sales price. In other areas, the seller will pay the fee by adding an agreed upon percentage to the opening bid to cover the commission.

If a real estate agent or agent brings a buyer to the auction and the deal closes, the auction house will pay the agent a negotiable commission, generally ranging around 2.5 percent. The agent must, however, register the client with the auction house before the sale.

Advertising Your Auction—Bidders Wanted

Advertising is vital to conducting a successful auction because you need crowds of people to do the bidding. Before a marketing program can be implemented, a total promotion budget should be developed. This budget details how monies will be allocated for each marketing activity. Budgets are generally broken down by media, time periods–in weeks–and even by markets. Most auction houses pass all advertising costs directly on to the seller, so it is necessary to gain the approval of the seller before spending promotion dollars.

There is no set advertising budget amount to spend. However, an allotment of 10 percent of the projected sales price can be used as a preliminary guide. The amount spent on advertising should be proportionate to the minimum bid acceptance amount and should be considered when developing an overall auction budget.

A comprehensive marketing plan should be developed as soon as possible. It may take up to 6 weeks to develop an information brochure, coordinate advertisements in local newspapers, post a picture of the property on the auctioneer's Web site–or create an independent Web site–and send mailers to prospective buyers.

Typical Promotion Schedule

Week 1

- Contact the public relations company, reserve space with local papers and magazines; sign insertion orders.
- Collect photographs of property; begin drafting brochure copy.
- Order mailing lists; order signs.

Week 2

- Post a picture and description of the property on the auctioneer's Web site.
- Send photos to the public relations team.
- Create and design ads and send to papers and magazines with purchase order.
- Send final brochure copy to auctioneer.

Week 3

- Approve final brochure copy and send to printer.
- Mail postcards or fliers to core list and surrounding neighbors.
- Approve press release and send to media.

Week 4

- Prepare media kit.
- Send information to agents about auction.
- Invite agents for a preview of the home.

Week 5

- Conduct media tour; generate interest.
- Hold the first open house.

Week 6

- Prepare buyer folders.
- Conduct the auction.

What to Include in the Advertisement

Include the following information on all sales literature and advertisements:

- date, time and place of sale
- a short description of the property
- a picture, if available
- the auctioneer's name, address, phone number and Web site
- terms of the sale
- the type of auction—absolute, Dutch, etc.
- the opening bid or minimum opening bid

Tip
Some auction companies prefer that the reserve price be published on the promotional materials. It may be stated as a minimum opening bid. Other companies will only want the opening bid to be publicized if it is significantly less–50-70 percent–than the property's market value in order for it to make an impact and attract buyers.

Discounts on Other Socrates Products

In addition to a variety of free forms and checklists, you will find special offers on a variety of Socrates products. Visit **www.socrates. com/books/ForSaleByOwner.aspx** for more information.

10
· · · · · ·
Basic Principles of Law When Selling

Fair Housing Act

As discussed in Chapter Four, the Fair Housing Act prohibits discrimination by direct providers of housing, such as landlords and real estate companies, as well as other entities, such as municipalities, banks or other lending institutions and homeowners insurance companies whose discriminatory practices make housing unavailable to persons because of:

- race or color
- religion
- sex
- national origin
- familial status
- disability

The Fair Housing Act also provides procedures for handling individual complaints of discrimination. Individuals who believe that they have been victims of an illegal housing practice may file a complaint with the Department of Housing and Urban Development (HUD) or file their own lawsuit in federal or state court.

Placing Earnest Money into Escrow

Money deposited with a contract is referred to as the deposit or earnest money and should be held in an escrow or trust account by the attorney or in a separate escrow account by the title company. The money cannot be touched until the closing takes place or the contract is canceled. The account should also be interest bearing.

The following is an example of an agreement to provide escrow services:

ESCROW AGREEMENT

For Earnest Money, Binders and Other Deposits

Agreement between:

_____

(Seller)

_____

(Buyer) and

_____

(Escrow Agent)

Simultaneously with the making of this agreement, Seller and Buyer have entered into a contract (the Contract), by which Seller will sell to Buyer the following property:

Street address:_____

City: _____ County: _____ State: ___ Zip Code: _____

The closing will take place at such time and place as Seller and Buyer may jointly designate in writing. Pursuant to the Contract, Buyer must deposit:

_____ Dollars ($_____) as down payment to be held in escrow by Escrow Agent, or

_____ Dollars ($_____) as earnest money deposit to be held in escrow by Escrow Agent.

The _____ Dollars ($_____) down payment or earnest money referred to above has been paid by Buyer to Escrow Agent. Escrow Agent acknowledges receipt of _____ Dollars ($_____) from Buyer by check, subject to collection.

If the closing takes place under the Contract, Escrow Agent at the time of closing shall pay the amount deposited with Agent to Seller in accordance with Seller's written instructions.

If no closing takes place under the Contract, Escrow Agent shall continue to hold the amount deposited until receipt of written authorization for its disposition signed by both Buyer and Seller. If there is any dispute as to whom Escrow Agent is to deliver the amount deposited, Escrow Agent shall hold the sum until the parties' rights are finally determined in an appropriate action or proceeding or until a court orders Escrow Agent to deposit the down payment or earnest money with it.

Escrow Agent assumes no liability except that of a stakeholder. Escrow Agent's duties are limited to those specifically set out in this agreement. Escrow Agent shall incur no liability to anyone except for willful misconduct or gross negligence so long as the Escrow Agent acts in good faith. Seller and Buyer release Escrow Agent from any act done or omitted in good faith in the performance of Escrow Agent's duties.

Special provisions:

_____

_____

_____

Signed in the presence of:

_____

_____

_____

_____

Seller

_____

Witness

_____

Date

_____

Buyer

_____

Witness

_____

Date

Tax and Estate Planning

If you sold your primary home, you may be able to exclude up to $250,000 of gain–$500,000 for married taxpayers filing jointly–from your federal tax return. This exclusion is allowed each time that you sell your primary home, but generally no more frequently than once every 2 years.

To be eligible for this exclusion, your home must have been owned by you and used as your main residence for a period of at least 2 out of the 5 years prior to its sale. The 2 years may consist of 24 full months or 730 days. Short absences, such as for a summer vacation, count as periods of use. Longer breaks, such as a 1-year sabbatical, do not.

To qualify, you also must not have excluded a gain on another home sold during the 2 years before the current sale. If you and your spouse file a joint return for the year of the sale, you can exclude the gain if either of you qualify for the exclusion. But both of you would have to meet the use test to claim the $500,000 maximum amount.

If you do not meet the ownership and use tests, you may be allowed to exclude a reduced maximum amount of the gain realized on the sale of your home if you sold your home due to health reasons, a change in place of employment or certain unforeseen circumstances. Unforeseen circumstances include, for example, divorce or legal separation, natural or man-made disaster resulting in a casualty to your home or an involuntary conversion of your home.

If you can exclude all the gain from the sale of your home, you do not report any of that gain on your federal tax return. If you cannot exclude all the gain from the sale of your home, use Schedule D, Capital Gains or Losses of Form 1040 to report it.

You can also find more information on the following at **www.irs.gov**:

> Publication 523, Selling Your Home
>
> Schedule D, Capital Gains and Losses
>
> Tax Topic 701—Sale of Your Home
>
> Publication 3, Armed Forces Tax Guide
>
> Highlights: Military Family Tax Relief Act
>
> Subscribe to IRS Tax Tips

The Final Walk-Through

The day before or the day of the closing, the buyers will want to tour and inspect the premises one more time. This inspection is referred to as the final walk-through. The buyers want to ensure that you have made the repairs agreed on from the inspection punch list and that you are leaving the home in good condition. The buyers also will inspect all heating, cooling and plumbing systems and make sure that any appliances they have purchased with the home are on the premises and are in working condition.

In the event that a repair was not made before the final inspection or an appliance is missing, the buyers may demand that payment–two or three times the cost of the repair or appliance–be held in escrow until the repair is satisfactorily made. The escrow amount will be withheld from the payout to the seller and returned once the seller shows proof of repair.

Final Walk-Through Checklist

The final walk-through should be done anywhere from 24 to 72 hours before closing. It is best to do it after the sellers have moved but before closing. Do not put off this inspection because if problems still exist, you will need time to get them corrected before closing.

If possible, the home inspector who suggested that the repairs be made should accompany you and the buyer on the walk-through to verify that repairs have been made. The final walk-through is not the time to do a home inspection. It is simply an opportunity to make sure that the home is in the same condition it was in when the contract was signed.

Have items been damaged during the move? Inspect floors for rips or gouges. Look at the walls, especially around door frames that large furniture and appliances might have been moved through.

Most offers to purchase include wording that states that all major systems in the home must be working at the time of closing, so it is fine to do a quick test of appliances and other items, such as the furnace and air conditioning. Those items should have been checked during the home inspection, but there is always a chance that they have quit working since that date.

Make sure all items you agreed to leave are still there. Likewise, make sure all items you agreed to remove have been removed. If the condition of the home has changed since the offer to purchase, have the problems fixed before the deed changes hands.

If necessary, repair or replacement funds can be negotiated, deposited into an attorney's trust fund and then drawn on to bring the home back into the condition that it was in on your contract date. If you do not use an attorney to close in your state, ask your real estate agent for advice on how to proceed. A buyer may request a hold back of an amount that exceeds the estimate for making repairs. An alternative is to negotiate a flat amount to be paid at closing. If damage is excessive, it might be advisable to delay closing until repairs are made.

The following is an example of a standard final walk-through checklist:

Present and in good working order
Light fixtures
Dining room chandelier, kitchen lights, living/dining room sconces
Ceiling fan remotes: circle all that apply :   Bedroom 1, Bedroom 2, Bedroom 3, Bedroom 4, Family Room, Kitchen
Rugs clean and stain-free
Chimney serviced and cleaned on:
Gas fireplace key received
Furnace serviced, cleaned and filter changed on:
Air conditioner serviced, cleaned and filter changed on:

	Water softener in working condition
	Hot water heater in working condition
	Humidifier in working condition
	Wood floors cleaned or buffed
	Kitchen
	Oven/range in working condition
	Microwave in working condition
	Dishwasher in working condition
	Garbage disposal in working condition
	Washing machine in working condition
	Dryer in working condition
	Draperies and blinds in place
	Home is in broom-clean condition
	Family room
	Bedroom
	Living room
	Basement
	Bathrooms
	All window and door screens accounted for
	All storm windows accounted for
	Garage remote controllers received # _____
	Keys for all locks received
	Mailbox key
	Codes for the alarm system
	Access card or key to garage or parking area, pool, exercise facility or club room
	Other work completed per inspection:
	Notes: Still needs repair/new damage

Closing the Deal

The closing is when the buyer pays the seller for the home, and the seller in turn hands the deed to the property over to the buyer. The closing of a transaction is a formal process that may take place at a bank, the title company's office, a real estate office or a lawyer's office. Where the transaction takes place is not as important as the event itself.

There is not much work for the seller to do at closing other than sign the forms prepared by the attorney or closing agent. Most of the reviewing of paperwork falls on the buyer. The buyer must review both the seller's documents and loan document and sign or initial almost every sheet. Besides the various disclosure forms you may have to sign:

- the RESPA (Real Estate Settlement Procedures Act) HUD-1 statement, which outlines who provides the money and from which sources and details how the money gets paid out

- a disclosure statement regarding any construction contracts or any agreements entered into during the past 3 to 6 months for work already done or to be done—this certifies that all outstanding obligations to contractors for work performed, or to be performed, have been paid and that there are no liens on the property

- a disclosure statement stating who resides on the property if it is not the buyer or seller or if the property is leased by tenants

- a statement about any other events that could affect title to the property, such as lawsuits, wills or judgments

- IRS Form 1099, which relates to the sale of the property—the seller provides the closing agent with his or her Social Security number and IRS Form 1099 will be sent to the IRS. This form will be used to cross-check your IRS tax return with documentation signed by the title company regarding the sale of the property and the sale price.

Most documents must be signed and notarized. The seller and buyer receive copies of all forms for safekeeping.

Must I Hire a Lawyer?

A lawyer is not required to complete the sale. The seller may save the attorney fees by doing all the ordering of the required documents, submitting applications and paying taxes and fees. Hiring a real estate attorney to make sure all requirements have been satisfied before closing will make the closing process easier. In many areas, lawyers are not introduced into the sale unless there is a dispute or issue between the seller and buyer that cannot be resolved.

The Closing

Closing, also referred to as settlement, is the procedure in which you relinquish any claim to the property and the new owners take possession. The buyer generally takes possession of the property when all loan agreements are signed and the seller hands over the keys.

What to Bring to the Closing

There are many small and seemingly inconsequential details that the seller and buyer must take care of before a real estate transaction is completed. When you attend a closing, make sure you bring:

- a picture ID to prove that you are who you say you are—it must be a picture ID. A driver's license or passport will suffice.
- your checkbook in the event that the buyer reopens negotiations without warning
- sense of humor in the event the buyer reopens negotiations at the eleventh hour

Along with the photo ID and checkbook, you will also be asked to produce several other documents to verify that fees have been paid, repairs have been made and insurance policies have been procured. A short list of details you will need to finalize before the sale is completed follows. Who pays the fees or takes care of each detail has already been agreed upon in writing to avoid any disputes that may delay a sale.

Seller's Checklist—What to Take to the Closing

The following is a list of the various items you should take with you to the closing. This information will be turned over to the buyer.

What to Take

____ List of service people you use including phone numbers

 ____ Lawn service

 ____ Repairs: general, appliances, etc.

 ____ Heating/Air conditioning

____ Exterminator

____ All known keys to your home

____ Garage door opener(s)

____ A list of all service contracts in effect

____ All appliance service manuals

____ Blueprints, surveys and any other documentation on the house

____ Any information that may be helpful to the new buyer

What to Expect

- signing an unending stack of documents—deed, bill of sale for personal property, closing statement, etc.
- minor glitches or disagreements—rarely does a closing go without a hitch, but most can be worked out

- to receive a check from the proceeds of the sale
- confirmation that agreed repairs have been made and paid for—If not, monies will be escrowed to cover them
- a no-lien affidavit showing that all bills have been paid except for those known and agreed to by both parties

The Buyer

If the sales contract contained contingencies the buyer needed to satisfy in order to complete the sale–financial, attorney approval or inspections–the seller should verify that all contingencies have been met.

Municipal Inspections

In some areas, the local building inspector must visit the property, inspect the home and issue a certificate permitting the sale of the home. Without the inspection certificate, the owner will not be able to transfer the property to the buyer. If the inspector finds building code violations, these violations must be corrected prior to closing. The home must be reinspected and the seller must obtain the certificate needed for closing.

Repairs Completed

Repairs to fixtures or mechanical systems as requested by the buyer and agreed to by the seller must be made prior to the closing. The seller should provide proof the item has been repaired or inspected to the buyer's satisfaction. The items included are limited to the punch list provided by the buyer as a result of the home inspection. If, for example, the buyer requested the furnace be inspected by a certified HVAC company, the seller should be able to produce a dated receipt indicating that the request has been honored. If windows needed work, the seller must produce documentation showing that the cracked window panes have been repaired.

If the requested repairs have still not been made at the time of closing, the buyer may request an amount of money be held in reserve or out of escrow until repairs are made to satisfaction. This means an agreed upon amount of money will be held back from the seller until proof that repairs have been made and paid for by the seller is presented. In some cases, the buyer will agree to make the corrections and deduct the cost from the reserve. Once all repairs have been made, the attorney or escrow holding company will return the balance of the reserve to the seller.

Transfer Taxes

Transfer or excise taxes are fees that the buyer or seller–depending on what is customary in your area–must pay to the city, state and county when the seller transfers ownership of the home to the buyer. In some areas, it is a straight percentage of the sale price of the home and is payable to the state. In other areas, the state, county and city have different taxing amounts, and the buyer or seller pays the required tax to each level of government and then provides proof of payment at the time of closing. In some areas, they are called transfer stamps.

This is because proof of payment is provided in the form of stamps, which are the same size as a U.S. Postal Service stamp, positioned on the certificate of payment.

Plat of Survey

A survey, also known as a plat of survey, completed within 90 days from the date of closing may be required by the lender. The seller usually orders a survey of the property. In states where surveys are not commonly ordered with each sale, the existing survey is provided by the seller.

Title Insurance

In most states, the seller must prove he or she has good, or clear, title to the property by providing the buyer with a title insurance commitment. The commitment is issued by a title insurance company that tracks all prior owners as far back as when the property was first purchased from the government and looks for matters such as liens that may affect the property. In many cases, the seller is responsible for obtaining and paying for the title commitment. The cost of title insurance is based on the cost of your home. A copy of the policy should be presented to the buyer at the time of closing. In some states, a lender may require that the buyer also purchase a title insurance policy before financing can be completed. The buyer should check lender requirements. The title insurance policy purchased by the seller might be considered acceptable as proof that the property has a clear title and no outstanding claims.

All Liens Satisfied

All tax or building liens should be cleared or paid up at the time of closing. The seller should provide proof of lien discharge at the time of closing.

Pest Inspections

Some states require termite or pest inspections to be completed prior to settlement. A certificate indicating that there is no evidence of pest infestation should be provided to the buyer at the closing.

Paid Assessment Letter

If you live in a condominium or co-op or are part of a homeowners' association, you must be able to present a letter from the board of directors stating that you have paid all of your assessments to the association through the date of closing. If the seller cannot produce proof that dues have been paid, the buyer may hold back a portion of the escrow to pay any fines or back dues owed.

Waiver of Right of First Refusal

Most condominium and co-op associations maintain the right of first refusal. This means they have the right to purchase the unit before you sell it to a buyer. If you are subject to this provision, you must be able to produce a letter stating that the association has been granted the right of first refusal and is waiving its right to purchase the home or unit.

Insurance Certificate

If you live in a condominium or co-op, you must provide a certificate of insurance from the company that insures your building. This certificate will name the buyer and his or her lender as insured under the policy. If you are selling a single family home or town home, the buyer's lender will require proof of insurance before the sale can be completed. The lender wants to be assured that in the event the home burns down or is damaged in any way, the insurance policy will cover the amount borrowed and the mortgage can be paid off by the owner.

Water Certificate

Some municipalities require that you produce a copy of your paid water bill at closing.

Loan Payoff Letter

If you have a mortgage, line of credit or equity line of credit on the home you will need a letter from your lender stating a payoff amount calculated up to the date of closing. At the time you sell your home, you will be required to pay off each lender.

Utilities

Contact each utility company, notify them of your intent to move and request that they schedule a final meter reading date. If you are moving out of the local area, you may be required to pay the amount before the closing date. If you are moving locally and intend to hook up again with service providers, you may be able to continue paying your bill as you normally would each month. Inquire how each service provider prefers to handle the final bills. Contact the telephone, gas, electric, water, garbage pickup, alarm, sewer and cable companies.

Prorated Taxes Paid

Some taxing municipalities require residents to pay their tax bill in arrears—the 2004 tax bill is paid in 2005. Others require residents to prepay their taxes for future payments—2005 taxes are collected on 2004 escrow payments. Still others send tax bills to residents in 6-month amounts as they become due—the January through May bill is due March 1, for example. Check with your local municipality. If you prepay your taxes, you will receive a check equaling the amount you have already put in at the time of closing. The buyer will need to replace that money by putting the tax amount due at the time of closing into escrow. If your taxes are due in arrears, any money the seller has put into escrow will remain in the account for the next tax installment.

Taking Possession

Taking possession of a property takes place when the seller hands over all keys to the home to the buyer after all the paperwork has been signed.

Movers

Arrange for movers at least 2 months in advance of the closing, especially if you are planning on moving the first or last day of the month. The week before the move, confirm the time and date of your move with the moving company.

Mail

Notify each creditor directly about your address change. Submit a change of address form 2 to 4 weeks before moving. It may take the post office several weeks to put the change into effect. Second- and third-class mail is not automatically forwarded; that means magazines, newspapers and newsletters will not automatically be rerouted to your new address. Contact each publisher separately with your new address. The post office provides a change of address kit that is free of charge, comprehensive and helpful. The kit includes checklists, postcards and other helpful tips to help make moving easier. Visit your local post office to request a kit.

Closing Costs

Knowing in advance the types of fees a seller must pay to complete the transfer of property to the new owner will eliminate surprises and disputes that may occur during the closing. The company conducting the closing, or your attorney, will provide a settlement costs closing sheet to you before the day of closing.

What the Seller Typically Pays

The seller typically pays for the following:

- transfer, excise or real estate tax
- title insurance policy
- recording fees
- prorated portion of taxes
- other miscellaneous charges

In some instances, the seller may be required to provide a certificate of compliance with local regulations regarding a septic or well system.

What the Buyer Typically Pays

The buyer typically pays for the following:

- home inspection fee
- recording fees
- prorated portion of taxes
- paid up certificate of insurance
- in some areas, the transfer or excise tax
- other miscellaneous charges

The Seller's Closing Statement

Estimated Seller's Closing Statement	
Seller:	John and Jane Doe
Buyer:	Jim and Jill Smith
Property:	123 Main Street, Anytown, USA
Date of closing:	December 15
Credits to Seller:	$
Purchase price	$500,500
Total:	$500,500
Credits to Buyer and Seller's Expenses:	
Earnest money	$10,000
Payoff first mortgage	$145,000
Payoff line of credit	$40,000
Overnight delivery charge	$55
Recording fee: Deed, mortgage and releases	$164
State transfer tax	$565.50
County transfer tax	$282.75
Village transfer tax	$1,296.50
Final water bill	$50
Attorney's fee	$500
Agency closing fee	$700
Recording fee: Mortgage	$75
Association fee:	$50
Owners title insurance policy	$1,283.25
EPL endorsement	$100
Location endorsement	$100
Real estate tax credit (Jan. 1-Dec. 15)	$7,231.57
Subtotal of Buyer's credits and Seller's expenses:	$207,453.57
Total due to Seller after credits and expenses paid	$293,046.43

Other costs that the seller is responsible for include:	
Cost of home warranty policy	$
Other credits given to buyers	$
FHA fees and costs paid for the buyer	$
Approved:	

_____   _____

Seller   Buyer

_____   _____

Seller   Buyer

Free Forms and Checklists

Visit Socrates.com and register to receive a variety of useful FREE forms, letters and checklists. See page iv for details on how to register (you will need the 7-digit registration code provided on the enclosed CD).

11
. . . . . .
Resources

Associations

American Society of Appraisers (ASA)

ASA is a professional society of persons involved in the appraisal of both real estate and personal property.

American Society of Appraisers
555 Herndon Parkway, Suite 125
Herndon, VA 20170
Phone: 1.703.478.2228
Fax: 1.703.742.8471
www.appraisers.org

American Society of Home Inspectors® (ASHI)

ASHI is a professional organization for home inspectors and those who determine the physical condition of homes.

American Society of Home Inspectors
932 Lee Street, Suite 101
Des Plaines, IL 60016
Phone: 1.800.743.ASHI (800.743.2744)
Fax: 1.847.759.1620
www.ashi.org

National Association of Independent Fee Appraisers (NAIFA)

NAIFA is an organization of real estate appraisers; it offers professional licensure to qualified persons.

National Association of Independent Fee Appraisers
401 N. Michigan Avenue, Suite 2200
Chicago, IL 60611
Phone: 1.312.321.6830
Fax: 1.312.673.6652
www.naifa.com

National Association of Real Estate Brokers (NAREB)

NAREB is a national trade association that brings together African Americans professionally employed in the real estate industry to promote the meaningful exchange of ideas. Members include not only real estate brokers but also appraisers, property managers and other interested real estate professionals.

National Association of Real Estate Brokers
9831 Greenbelt Road
Lanham, MD 20706
Phone: 1.301.552.9340
FAX: 1.301.552.9216
www.nareb.com

National Association of Realtors® (NAR)

NAR is dedicated to the betterment of the real estate industry through education and legislation. It also sets high ethical and professional standards for its members. Founded in 1908, it currently has more than 750,000 members.

National Association of Realtors
430 N. Michigan Avenue
Chicago, IL 60611
Phone: 1.800.874.6500
www.realtor.org

Office of Interstate Land Sales Registration

The Office of Interstate Land Sales Registration is an agency of the U.S. Department of Housing and Urban Development (HUD) that is responsible for enforcing the Interstate Land Sales Full Disclosure Act.

U.S. Department of Housing and Urban Development
451 7th Street SW
Washington, DC 20410
Phone: 1.202.708.1112
TTY: 1.202.708.1455
www.hud.gov

American Bar Association (ABA)

The ABA is the world's largest voluntary professional association. With more than 400,000 members, the ABA provides law school accreditation, continuing legal education, information about the law, programs to assist lawyers and judges in their work, and initiatives to improve the legal system for the public.

American Bar Association
321 N. Clark Street
Chicago, IL 60610
Phone: 1.312.988.5000

American Bar Association
740 15th St. NW
Washington, DC 20005
Phone: 1.202.662.1000
www.abanet.org

Appraisers

Appraisers Association of America

Appraisers Association of America keeps members updated regarding related industry financial developments, such as sales trends, market pricing, domestic and foreign competition, etc.

Appraisers Association of America Inc.
386 Park Avenue S, Suite 2000
New York, NY 10016
Phone: 1.212.889.5404
www.appraisersassoc.org

Home Inspectors

American Institute of Inspectors®

The American Institute of Inspectors is a nonprofit organization that serves the needs of residential and commercial building inspectors.

The American Institute of Inspectors
1421 Esplanade Avenue, Suite 7
Klamath Falls, OR 97601
Phone: 1.800.877.4770
www.inspection.org

National Association of Certified Home Inspectors

The National Association of Certified Home Inspectors is a nonprofit organization helping home inspectors achieve financial success and maintain inspection excellence.

National Association of Certified Home Inspectors
P.O. Box 987
Valley Forge, PA 19482
Phone: 1.650.429.2057
www.nachi.org

Mortgage Providers

Fannie Mae

Fannie Mae provides financial products and services that make it possible for low-, moderate- and middle-income families to buy homes of their own.

Fannie Mae
3900 Wisconsin Avenue NW
Washington, DC 20016
Phone: 1.202.752.7000
www.fanniemae.com

U.S. Department of Housing and Urban Development (HUD)

The Office of Housing and Urban Development provides vital public services through its nationally administered programs. It oversees the Federal Housing Administration (FHA), the largest mortgage insurer in the world and regulates housing industry businesses.

U.S. Department of Housing and Urban Development
451 7th Street SW
Washington, DC 20410
Phone: 1.202.708.1112
TTY: 1.202.708.1455
www.hud.gov

Federal Housing Administration (FHA)

FHA provides mortgage insurance on loans made by FHA-approved lenders throughout the United States and its territories. FHA insures mortgages on single family and multi-family homes. The FHA falls under the direction of HUD.

Federal Housing Administration
451 7th Street SW
Washington, DC 20410
Phone: 1.202.708.1112
TTY: 1.202.708.1455
www.hud.gov

Department of Veterans Affairs (VA)

About a quarter of the nation's population–approximately 70 million people–are potentially eligible for VA benefits and services because they are veterans, family members of veterans or survivors of veterans.

Department of Veterans Affairs
810 Vermont Avenue NW
Washington, DC 20420
Phone: 1.800.827.1000
www.va.gov

Title Insurance and Escrow Agencies

American Escrow Association (AEA)

AEA is the national association of real estate settlement agents.

American Escrow Association
211 N. Union Street, Suite 100
Alexandria, VA 22314
Phone: 1.703.519.1240
www.a-e-a.org

American Land Title Associations (ALTA)

Founded in 1907, ALTA is the national trade association and voice of the abstract and title insurance industry. ALTA members search, review and insure land titles to protect home buyers and mortgage lenders who invest in real estate.

American Land Title Association
1828 L Street NW, Suite 705
Washington, DC 20036
Phone: 1.800.787.ALTA
Fax: 1.888.FAX.ALTA
www.alta.org

Online Resources

For Sale by Owner Web Sites

www.buyowner.com

Since 1984, Buy Owner has been a pioneer in the real estate industry and has helped buyers and sellers of real estate save thousands of dollars in real estate commissions.

www.agentdirectmls.com

AgentDirectMLS.com allows sellers to list their homes on the local Multiple Listing Service database and **www.realtor.com** for a one-time fee.

www.forsalebyowner.com

Since 1997, ForSaleByOwner.com has helped home owners save billions of dollars in real estate commissions. It is among the top five most visited real estate sites in the world and the largest FSBO homes for sale site.

www.fsbo.com

Established in 1994, FSBO.com has been saving buyers and sellers thousands in commissions for more than a decade.

www.homesbyowner.com

HomesByOwner.com lists FSBO properties in more than 370 metro areas in the United States. HomesByOwner.com has teamed with more than a hundred affiliates in local markets around the United States to provide the best FSBO advertising for property owners.

www.owners.com

Owners.com is the Largest FSBO site in America, serving more than 5 million self-directed real estate buyers and sellers.

www.virtualfsbo.com

VirtualFSBO.com is a free site for buying and selling houses that also provides useful sales tips.

www.flatfeelisting.com

FlatFeeListing.com lists your property in your local area real estate MLS database.

www.byowner.com

ByOwner.com helps homeowners sell their homes without real estate agent fees.

www.fsbosupport.com

FSBOSupport.com advertises itself as America's most affordable and fastest MLS network.

www.militarybyowner.com

MilitaryByOwner.com advertises homes for sale by owner or for rent near U.S. military bases.

www.sellyourhomeyourself.com

SellYourHomeYourself.com advertises that it provides all the resources you need to sell a home yourself.

www.homegain.com

Affiliated with the NAR, HomeGain helps sellers and buyers find local real estate agents, homes for sale and more.

www.yourcityfsbo.com

YourCityFSBO.com contains information and tips for both the FSBO buyer and FSBO seller.

www.ebay.com

Sell anything by auction, including real estate on eBay®.

www.fiftystatesfsbo.com

Designed by real estate professionals, Fifty States For Sale By Owner claims to offer everything you need to successfully sell by owner.

www.mobilehomesbuyowner.com

Mobile Homes Buy Owner connects buyers and sellers of mobile homes and has mobile home listings with photos and descriptions.

FSBO Advertising Companies

www.realestate.yahoo.com

Yahoo!® Real Estate posts your ad nationwide to reach the Internet's largest classified audience.

www.propertysites.com

PropertySites℠ advertises your home and provides tips for advertising, showing and selling it.

www.fsbonetwork.com

FSBONetwork.com is the official organization of FSBO publications.

www.fsboadvertisingservice.com

FSBOAdvertising™ lists real estate classified ads offering sellers and buyers an efficient tool for finding and buying real estate directly from the owners.

www.onlinerealtysales.com

OnlineRealtySales.com offers online real estate listings that generate more than 5.8 million hits per month.

www.saveonmls.com

SaveOnMLS® is an online listing that markets more than $100 million of properties each year.

Tips and General Resources

www.fsbotips.com

FSBO Tips advises real estate sellers and buyers how to save money by eliminating unnecessary fees and commissions.

www.33tips.com

This site lists 33 things you can do to immediately improve the marketability of your home.

www.audrie.com

Audrie.com offers tips on selling your own home.

www.realestateabc.com

This site provides tips, reports and analysis about home selling across the United States.

School Reports

www.homefair.com

This site rates local schools in different areas around the country.

Appendix A

· · · · · ·

Moving

A local move may cost a few hundred dollars, while a long-distance move may cost several thousand dollars. When figuring the cost of a move and hiring a mover, it is recommended that you obtain a minimum of three quotes from reputable moving companies. It is also a good idea to inquire about replacement insurance for lost and stolen items.

Tip
Planning a move with children is more challenging. Make your travel arrangements well in advance and aim to make the trip as stress free as possible. If flying, try to book a direct flight. If driving, estimate how far you will get each day and book accommodations in advance. Plan sightseeing stops along the way to break up travel time. Try to pack younger children's belongings last and unpack them first to minimize the disruption of a move for them.

Moving Checklist

Careful preplanning is essential to a successful move. Start by making a plan for packing—which rooms get packed first, next and last.

Use the following checklist to help you and your loved ones have the smoothest move possible:

_____ Set up appointments for important services such as telephone and cable television hookups and Internet access to be installed prior to arriving in your new home.

_____ Assign every family member a sorting, packing and moving day job–or two–to increase efficiency and ensure that everyone feels as though they are part of the process.

_____ If you have young children, plan ahead of time how you will keep them safe and occupied on moving day.

_____ Keep pets safe and out of the way on moving day when doors are open and moving trucks are in the driveway. If you are moving a long distance, think about how best to transport them to their new home.

_____ Keep all essential records in a secure folder that is not packed away but goes with you, especially anything needed for children's enrollment in their new schools, including birth certificates and medical, dental and school records.

_____ Identify irreplaceable family keepsakes that can easily be carried—baby books, photographs, art projects, etc. Take them with you in the car or on the plane.

_____ Pack a bag, box or suitcase with the necessities you will need to unpack immediately when you arrive in your new home—toilet paper, soap, shampoo, bath towels, paper towels, shower curtain, etc. Carry it with you in the car or on the plane. It will be easier than having to run out and buy these things upon arrival.

_____ Make sure every family member has an overnight bag of clothing, special favorites–toy, blanket, CD–things to read or do en route to the new home, favorite snacks, toothbrushes and toothpaste. These are considered essentials for getting to the new home, getting through the first night and tackling unpacking in the morning.

_____ Develop a contingency plan for sleeping in your new home the first night, especially if you arrive before your beds do. Plan on taking sleeping bags or air mattresses with you or make a hotel reservation that can be canceled if not needed.

_____ Locate nearby restaurants and supermarkets in your new community. Assign one member of the family to stock up on groceries or order takeout to keep everyone fed.

_____ Number each box and identify the contents of each. Group items packed in each box by room. This will help you identify which box contains an item you need immediately and you will know quickly if a box is missing. If a box does get lost, you will have a detailed list of all items included in it to provide to the insurance company.

_____ Do not pack chemicals or hazardous cleaning supplies in boxes to be transported on a moving truck. Heat, cold and damage to containers may cause leaking. Give away extra cleaning supplies or leave them for the new owners to use or safely dispose of.

Moving Timeline

1 Month before Moving

_____ Fill out change of address order form for post office.

_____ Fill out an IRS change of address form.

_____ Notify credit card and other financial service companies of your new address.

_____ Notify magazine subscription companies of your change of address.

_____ Make arrangements with a moving company or reserve a rental truck.

_____ Make travel arrangements with airlines, buses, car rental agencies and hotels, if necessary.

_____ Transfer memberships in churches, clubs and civic organizations.

_____ Obtain medical and dental records, X-rays and prescription histories. Ask your doctor and dentist for referrals and to transfer prescriptions.

_____ Set up new bank accounts.

_____ Check into the laws and requirements of your new location regarding home-based businesses, professional tests, business licenses and any special laws that might be applicable to you.

_____ Take inventory of your belongings before packing, in the event you need to file an insurance claim later. If possible, take pictures or videotape your belongings. Record serial numbers of electronic equipment.

_____ Make arrangements for transporting pets.

_____ Start using up food items, so that there is less left to pack and possibly spoil.

1 to 2 Weeks before Moving

_____ Switch utility services to new address. Inform electric, disposal, water, newspaper, telephone and cable companies of your move.

_____ Arrange for help on moving day.

_____ Confirm travel reservations.

_____ Reserve elevator if moving from an apartment.

_____ Have appliances serviced for moving.

_____ Clean rugs and clothing and have them wrapped for moving.

_____ Plan ahead for special needs of infants.

_____ Close bank accounts and have your funds transferred to your new bank. Before closing, be sure there are no outstanding checks or automatic payments that have not been processed.

_____ Collect valuables from safe-deposit boxes. Make copies of any important documents before mailing or hand carry them to your new address.

_____ Check with your insurance agent to ensure that you will be covered through your homeowners' or renters' policy during the move.

_____ Defrost the freezer and refrigerator. Place deodorizer inside each to control odors.

_____ Give a close friend or relative your travel route and schedule so you may be reached if needed.

On Moving Day

_____ Double-check closets, drawers, shelves, attic and garage to be sure they are empty.

_____ Carry important documents, currency and jewelry yourself or use registered mail.

_____ Carry traveler's checks for quick, available funds.

_____ When the moving truck arrives, you will be required to pay for the move before the workers start unloading the truck. Make sure you have a cashier's check for the exact amount made out to the moving company. Most movers do not like to handle that much cash and will not accept personal checks.

Arriving at New Home

_____ Renew your driver's license, auto registrations and tags within 30 days. Also, register bikes and pets with the municipality.

_____ Shop around for new insurance policies, especially auto coverage.

_____ Revise your will and other legal papers to avoid longer probate and higher legal fees.

_____ Locate the hospitals, police stations, veterinarian and fire stations near your home.

Miscellaneous Packing Tips

- Keep the following supplies handy for packing: boxes, marking pen, bubble wrap, newspaper and tissue, tape, scissors and tape measure.

- Use strong boxes and containers that can be tightly secured. Purchase special boxes for dishes, wardrobe and other special items.

- Pack audio and video equipment in the original boxes. Label cables and tighten transit screws. If you remove screws, tape them to the objects they are removed from.

- Avoid loading more than 50 pounds into one box.

- Label each box and indicate the following: (a) which room it should go in, (b) whether it is fragile and (c) if it should be loaded last so it will be unloaded first.

- Cushion contents with packing material. Save room by using towels and blankets to wrap fragile items.

- Pack books tightly on end in small boxes. If they are musty smelling, sprinkle talcum powder between the pages and wrap them before packing. Leave them stored for a couple of months to eliminate the smell.

- Have rugs and draperies cleaned before moving and leave them in wrappings for the move.

- Pack medicines in a leak-proof container.

- Carry all valuables with you.

• Check with your local U.S. Department of Agriculture branch for regulations regarding moving plants from one state to another. Many states have restrictions on bringing certain plants into the state to prevent importing insects or other pests that can destroy valuable cash crops.

Tips for Moving Pets

The following are tips for moving your pets to their new home:

• Cats and dogs can be taken in your car. If your pets travel with you, remember to take along food, water and a leash for letting your pet out of the car. Keep a number of plastic bags to clean up after your pet.

• Put a blanket or sheet over the seats to keep your car clean.

• Animals can get carsick and will require frequent stops along the way. Also, check ahead to see if the hotel where you are staying allows pets. Depending on the animal's age, temperament and size, it might be better to have it shipped by air. Be sure to check if your destination has any local requirements or restrictions on animals. Some vets may prescribe a light sedative to keep pets calm during the move.

• If you are shipping your pet by air, make sure to arrange for someone to meet your pet at the destination airport and take care of it until you arrive. A kennel can do this for you and keep your pet until you have completed your move.

If you are flying to your new destination, your cat or dog can ride in the baggage compartment. You may need the following items:

• Health certificate—obtain this from your veterinarian.

• Pet container—the airline might have a special container available, or you can use your own as long as it complies with airline regulations.

• Tranquilizers—your vet can provide tranquilizers to give to your pet immediately before going to the airport.

• Your scent—your pet can be comforted by having a piece of cloth with your scent on it.

Tips for Successfully Moving Houseplants

Two weeks before you move, prune your plants to facilitate packing. Consult a florist or a plant book for instructions.

One week before you move, place your plants in a black plastic bag along with a bug/pest strip, conventional flea collar or bug powder. Close the bag and place it in a cool area overnight to kill any pests on the plant or in the soil. You also may add dish soap to the soil and water. The liquid dish soap will not harm the plant but will kill any bugs burrowed in the soil.

One day before you move, place the plants in cardboard containers. Hold them in place with dampened newspaper or packing paper. Use paper to cushion the leaves and place a final layer of wet paper on top to keep them moist. If you must leave your plants behind, then take cuttings. Put them in a plastic bag with wet paper towels around them.

On the day of your move set the boxes aside and mark "DO NOT LOAD" so they will not be taken on the moving van. Close the boxes and punch air holes in the top before loading them into your car.

Park your car in a shaded area in the summer and a sunny spot in the winter. Upon arrival, unpack the plants as soon as possible. Remove plants through the bottom of the box to avoid breaking the stems. Do not expose the plants to much sunlight at first. Let them gradually become accustomed to more light.

Hiring a Moving Company

Consumer complaints against moving companies have been rising. The following are some tips that can help your move go smoothly:

- Get a binding estimate from the moving company. Make sure the amount is written in the contract.
- Inquire about their on-time record and check for complaints with the local Better Business Bureau or consumer complaints department.
- Movers are limited by law regarding what they can reimburse you for lost or damaged goods. To cover potential damage, check your existing homeowners' or renters' policy. Most movers offer separate insurance to cover lost or damaged items. Inquire about the costs, the length of coverage and deductibles.
- Ask about expected gratuities.
- Make sure the contract includes a guarantee of how many hours the job will take; allow an overrun of no more than 10 percent.
- Be sure that all charges are listed on the contract.
- Inform the moving company of how many stairs are at your new home.
- Watch loading and unloading and examine all items carefully before signing a receipt.
- Document an inventory of your belongings before you pack.

Glossary

· · · · · ·

A
· · · ·

abstract of title A summary of the documents registered in any local land registry office that affect ownership (title) of a house or condominium.

accelerated depreciation Depreciation is a reduction in the value of a property resulting from the passage of time or changes in economic circumstances. Homeowners in recent years have come to think that property can only become more valuable (i.e., appreciate) but property does depreciate. For example, even though it may be well maintained, a property that is located in an area that becomes a hopeless slum or is beside the planned route for an expressway can depreciate. Depreciation may be used as a tax reduction. If a property loses its value quickly, this depreciation may be speeded-up and claimed in the first few years of ownership; the depreciation deduction then decreases later in the property's life. Any income tax expert can provide details. Another term for depreciation is writing down.

acceptance A positive (and voluntary) response to an offer or counteroffer for a property that sets out price and terms. This positive response creates a binding agreement between the buyer and seller. Acceptance may be conditional (i.e., based on certain events taking place). For example, in buying a new residence, the buyer may make his or her offer conditional on the sale of his or her current home within a certain number of months.

access The right to enter a property. This may be restricted to certain times and to certain categories of people (e.g., those who read gas or electric meters or deliver the mail).

access right The right of an owner to enter or leave a property; this right may be expressed or implied.

accessible/accessibility The ease (or not) by which one may reach a property.

accessory building A structure on a property (e.g., a garage, a garden shed) that serves a specific purpose for the home or main building.

accredited assessment evaluator (AEE) A property evaluator who has met the requirements of the International Association of Assessing Officers.

accredited land consultant (ALC) A person who has met the requirements of the Realtors Land Institute to be an advisor in marketing real estate.

accredited residential manager (ARM) A person who has satisfied the requirements of the Institute of Real Estate Management (IREM), allowing him or her to manage residential properties.

acquisition The act of taking title to a property.

acquisition cost The cost to the buyer of obtaining title to any property, outside of the actual purchase price. These costs can include escrow fees, title insurance, lender's fees and interest, legal fees, and land transfer fees.

acre A land area that is equal to 43,560 square feet. Property, particularly farm property, is often described in acres.

actual age The years a building has been in existence (i.e., its chronological age). Its effective age is a more subjective judgment; it reflects the condition of the building (i.e., how well it has been maintained). Two houses on the same street may both have been constructed 50 years ago (i.e., their actual age), but one, because of upkeep and renovation, may look almost new, whereas the other, because of neglect, may look much older than its chronological age (i.e., its effective age).

actual authority The power a real estate agent, broker, or other representative may or may not have to bind a buyer or seller to an agreement.

actual possession When the owner of a property occupies it on a continuing day-to-day basis.

addendum Something added to a document (e.g., lease, contract, purchase agreement) that then forms part of it. May be used to add some provision to the original document or to clarify some aspect of that original document.

adjacent/adjoining land A term that may have a different meaning in different locales. In general, it refers to land that is located very near a particular piece of property, sometimes abutting it (i.e., sharing the same boundary).

adjusted sales price A way of deciding what the price of a property should be according to the following method: taking the price of a comparable property that has recently been sold, adding the value of any recent improvements to the subject property not matched by the comparable property, and subtracting the value of any improvements or features in the comparable property not matched by the subject property.

adjustments Anything that, at closing, changes the value of the property (e.g., taxes overpaid or underpaid by the seller, fuel for several months stored on the premises and provided to the buyer, rent collected from tenants for the following month). A statement of adjustments is presented by the closing officer to the buyer or seller.

aesthetic value The value that is added to the price of a property by its overall physical appearance and presentation. A beautifully landscaped house may be worth more to a potential buyer than the same house in the same neighborhood that is less pleasing in appearance.

affidavit of title The seller's statement that the title (i.e., proof of ownership) is valid, can be sold, and is subject to no defects except those set out in the agreement of sale.

affirmative fair housing marketing plan A plan that is sponsored by the U.S. Department of Housing and Urban Development (HUD) to foster the integration of different races in new housing projects. Such a plan must be presented by a developer before a project is eligible for certain U.S. government grants.

agent Anyone (albeit usually a real estate agent) who is authorized by a buyer or seller of property to act on that person's behalf in any dealings with third parties. The third party may rely on the agreement and assurances of the agent as being binding on the person represented.

agreement of sale Also called purchase agreement, agreement of purchase and sale, land agreement, etc. A legal contract in which the buyer agrees to buy and the seller agrees to sell a specific property. The agreement of sale contains all the terms and conditions of the transaction and is signed by both parties. These documents are essentially the same but differ slightly from state to state.

amenities Improvements to a property (other than necessities) that increase its desirability and enhance its value such as a swimming pool, central air conditioning, a patio or deck, or nearby attractions such as highways, good schools or public transportation.

American Society of Appraisers (ASA) A professional society composed of persons involved in the appraisal of both real estate and personal property.

American Society of Home Inspectors (ASHI) Specialists in the inspection of and determination of the physical condition of homes.

American Society of Real Estate Counselors (ASREC) Individuals who specialize in helping people to buy and sell homes.

annual percentage rate (APR) The total cost of a loan (i.e., of borrowing the money to buy a property) in any given year expressed as a percentage of a loan amount (e.g., 6.5 percent). It includes compounded interest. The lender (i.e., the institution or person that holds the mortgage) is required by the Federal Truth-in-Lending Act to disclose the APR to the borrower.

AO (accepted offer) An acronym (i.e., abbreviation) used by real estate agents to indicate that the buyer's offer to purchase has been accepted by the seller or by the agent on behalf of the seller.

application fees The fees that a lender charges an applicant to apply for a mortgage. These fees usually include the costs of a property appraisal and a credit report (from one of the three main U.S. credit agencies) and they often are not returned to the applicant even if the mortgage loan is not approved.

appointments Decorative touches (i.e., fresh paint in a house, new blinds in a condominium) that may affect the value of a property.

appraisal An estimate of the value of a property on a certain date, usually provided by a qualified appraiser, after both an inspection of the property and a comparison of that property with other comparable properties that have recently been sold.

appraisal principles Factors that a qualified appraiser will consider in making an appraisal. These include the value (as determined by recent sale) of comparable properties, the appraised property's location, the level of competition in the current sales market, the current supply of comparable properties, and current market interest in such properties (i.e., supply and demand).

appraisal process In a particular market, appraisers try to use a standardized approach (i.e., to use the same appraisal principles) to ensure consistency and accuracy.

appraisal report A document, issued by an appraiser to the seller (or buyer), that documents the factors the appraiser has used to arrive at the appraisal amount. It also sets out the positive and negative aspects of a property, so that the client can understand the appraiser's thinking. Finally, it sets out the appraiser's valuation.

appraiser A professional who is trained to assess the value of commercial or residential property.

appreciation The increase in value of a property over time. This increase can be the result of many factors, such as inflation, increased demand for property resulting from low interest rates, the condition of the market, or the gentrification of a particular area.

approved attorney Any lawyer who is acceptable to title companies. This is usually any lawyer who can complete transactions having to do with title insurance (i.e., is capable of rendering opinions about the validity of title).

appurtenance A right, or entitlement, that is included within the ownership of a property and passes to the new owner when the title passes. An easement is one example: the new owner may be entitled to use a driveway to a garage on the previous owner's property even though that driveway is partially built on a neighbor's property.

as is/as is agreement The situation in which a property is accepted by the buyer (or tenant) in the condition existing at the time of the sale or lease; the seller (or lessor) is released from any liability after closing. Most agreements of sale contain such a provision.

asking price The amount at which a property is offered, by a seller, for sale. This price may change as a result of negotiations between the buyer and seller. In a tight market, a good property in a desirable location may bring more than the initial asking price as a result of bidding by numerous potential buyers.

assessment Estimating the value of land or other property for tax purposes. It can also refer to the means by which a municipality raises taxes, or to the fees that a condominium association charges owners for basic (and common) services such as upkeep and maintenance or utility fees such as gas or oil for heating.

assessor Also called the tax assessor. The person who is employed by a municipality to estimate the value of properties to provide a basis for the municipality to levy real estate taxes.

associate agent An otherwise qualified real estate agent or agent who is working for or with another agent.

assumable mortgage A mortgage that can be taken over (i.e., assumed) by the buyer from the seller when a property is sold. If interest rates are high, a low-rate assumable mortgage can be a great selling point for a property. However, this is not necessarily a common provision in mortgages. Buyers and sellers should always determine whether the mortgage contract contains such a clause.

assumption fee The amount the lender charges the person who is taking over an assumable mortgage. There is almost always such a fee, and buyers should always inquire as to its amount.

assumption of mortgage The formal agreement whereby one takes on the responsibilities of an assumable mortgage.

attestation/attestation clause A statement by a witness to the finalization (i.e., closing) of a deed or mortgage that the document was properly execute, and that the persons signing the document were aware of what they were doing (i.e., they understood the contents and responsibilities of the document). Such witnessing is required by various states.

attorney's opinion of title A statement of a lawyer's conclusions about the legal condition of title to (i.e., ownership of) a property that is issued after the lawyer's investigation of that title.

auction Selling property to the highest bidder at a public sale. Auctions are often used to sell property that has been foreclosed on or property that has failed to sell in the marketplace.

auctioneer A professional who sells property at public auctions. Depending on local laws, this can be either a real estate agent or a licensed auctioneer. The auctioneer is usually paid a percentage of the final sale price of each property being auctioned.

authorization to sell The contract between a seller and a real estate agent that allows the agent to sell a property. It also sets out the rights and obligations of the seller and agent. Some such agreements involve a time limit, after which both sides are allowed to terminate the agreement.

B

back-title letter/certificate In states in which lawyers are required to examine title for title insurance purposes, this document is given to the attorney by the title insurance company to certify the condition of a title as of a certain date.

backup contract A secondary offer (from a potential buyer) for a property on which an offer from another buyer has already been made. This contract will come into effect if the first offer is not accepted or is withdrawn.

bathroom A room in a house or in an apartment or condominium unit that contains a toilet, a sink, and either a bathtub or a bathtub and shower combination. A room that contains these facilities but has only a shower and no tub is called a three-quarters bath. If the room contains only a toilet and sink, it is called a half bath.

bedroom community An area that includes mainly housing (residential or rental) and very few businesses. The term usually refers to a commuter town or suburb whose residents work in the central city or a in more economically diverse suburb.

benchmark A permanent feature of land, such as a creek, protrusion of stone, or long-standing grove of trees, that is used as a point of reference by a land surveyor.

betterment Any improvement of real estate that leads to an increase in its value. Landscaping, renovation, and improvements in outbuildings (e.g., a garage) are all forms of betterment.

bilateral/reciprocal contract Any contract in which the parties (e.g., the buyer and seller in a real estate contract) make each other promises.

bi-level Premises that are on two levels; commonly refers to a house but can also refer to an apartment or condominium unit. Also called split level.

blighted area Any area in which the buildings, and sometimes the infrastructure, have been allowed to decay. As a result, property has depreciated.

block A square or rectangular area in a city that is enclosed by streets or, in some states, part of the legal description of a subdivision (e.g., lot 1, block 3, tract 6).

board The elected managers of a condominium association.

boilerplate A slang term for a standard provision that usually appears in all similar contracts, such as the embargo against wild animals that is contained in virtually any lease for an apartment.

bona fide (Latin: in good faith) Without any kind of deceit.

borrower (mortgagor) A person who receives money from a lender to buy property, in exchange for a written promise to repay that money with interest. The borrower also accepts the lender's lien on that property until the debt is paid in full.

boundary The legally determined edge or limit of a property.

breach of contract In law, the failure to live up to the terms of any contract.

breezeway In a house with no garage, a canopy that extends from the house over a driveway, creating protection from the weather for an automobile and for people going to and from the automobile and the house.

bridge loan/financing A form of interim loan that is most commonly used when a buyer has bought a new house or condominium unit but has yet to sell his or her current residence. Thus, he or she may lack the funds necessary to make the down payment on the new residence or to pay two mortgages simultaneously. The bridge loan usually covers the down payment on the new premises and the monthly mortgage payment for a stated number of months. The bridge loan customarily ends when the buyer has sold the old premises and has the funds to pay off the lender.

broker Refers to two kinds of brokers: a mortgage broker, who brings potential borrowers together with potential lenders; and a real estate broker, who brings buyers together with sellers. Real estate broker is a professional designation; it requires training and licensing.

brokerage The act by brokers of bringing together principals (e.g., buyer and seller, landlord and tenant) in return for a fee, often a percentage of a transaction's value (5 percent to 10 percent).

building code Regulations that are established and enforced by a municipality to guarantee standards and quality of construction.

building line/setback The minimum distance from a property line or boundary that a building may be constructed; this is established by agreement or by municipal ordinances.

built-ins Items that are not part of the actual construction of a building but are not readily movable, such as stoves, microwaves, dishwashers, ovens, or furniture that has been fixed to the building in some way , such as bookcases or a hideaway bed.

buy-back agreement A contract between a buyer and a seller in which the seller agrees to buy the property back from the buyer if a certain event occurs within a set period. The price of such a buy-back is usually set out in the contract.

buy down The payment of extra money on a loan, such as the payment of additional principal when making a monthly mortgage payment, to reduce the interest rate and/or the life of the loan.

buyer's agent/broker A real estate agent who represents the potential buyer. Agents commonly represent the seller, but potential buyers increasingly are engaging real estate agents to watch out for their interests also.

buyer's market A market in which there is more property for sale than there are buyers available to purchase it. This situation usually causes the value of available property to decrease. It most commonly occurs in over-built markets or when a poor economy results in few buyers being present in the marketplace.

buy-sell offer An offer by one owner to buy out the interests of another owner or partner.

by-laws Rules and regulations enacted by a governing body. The term commonly refers to the rules of a condominium management board, which usually are agreed to by a poll of the condominium-unit owners.

C

cancellation clause A clause in a contract, such as a mortgage, that sets forth the conditions under which each party may cancel or terminate the agreement.

capital expenditure/improvement Money that is spent to improve a property and thus enhance its value, excluding repairs. Such expenditures may include building a new garage and adding a room to a house.

capital gain An increase in the value of capital property (i.e., property other than a principal residence) on which tax is payable, usually upon sale of the property.

capital loss A decrease in the value of capital property (i.e., property other than a principal residence), which the owner may use against capital gains or against regular income when paying his or her taxes, depending on the tax rules.

cash sale The sale of a property for cash; no mortgage or other financing is involved.

caveat emptor (Latin: let the buyer beware) A legal maxim suggesting that the buyer of any property takes a risk regarding the condition of the property and, that it is the responsibility of the buyer to determine the condition before the purchase is completed. Many states now have laws that place more responsibility for disclosure on the seller and the real estate agent. Potential buyers should always check on their rights with their real estate agent.

CC&Rs Abbreviated term for covenants, conditions and restrictions, which are the obligations of any real estate contract.

certificate of eligibility A document issued by the U.S. Department of Veteran's Affairs (VA) that allows qualified veterans to apply for either subsidized or guaranteed housing loans.

certificate of insurance Issued by an insurance company, this document sets out the particulars of the coverage that is being provided for a specific property.

certificate of occupancy A document issued by a local municipality certifying that a particular dwelling is in proper condition for human occupation (i.e., that it complies with local building and safety by-laws).

certificate of reasonable value (CRV) A document issued by the U.S. Department of Veteran's Affairs (VA) that sets out the market value, based on an appraisal, of a certain property. It purpose is to establish the maximum principal that will be available on a VA mortgage on that property.

certificate of sale A certificate issued at a court sale that entitles the buyer to a deed to a particular property.

certificate of satisfaction A document provided by a lender and subsequently registered on a title certifying that a mortgage has been paid out and that the property has been released to the buyer (i.e., it has no claims against it).

certificate of title A written opinion by a lawyer as to the validity of a person's claim to ownership of a particular property; such opinions may also be issued through a title.

certified copy A declaration, usually by the holder of the original document or by a lawyer, that the copy is a true (i.e., exact) copy of the original.

certified general appraiser Someone who is licensed, after training, to appraise the value of property (qualification requirements can vary, depending on the particular jurisdiction).

certified home inspector (CHI) Someone who is licensed, after training, to inspect and report on the physical condition of property (qualification requirements may vary, depending on the particular jurisdiction).

certified residential appraiser (CRA) Someone who has met the licensing requirements to appraise the value of only and specifically residential property. See certified general appraiser.

certified residential broker (CRB) Someone who has met the requirements of the Realtors National Marketing Institute to be an agent or agent for residential properties. The Realtors National Marketing Institute is affiliated with the National Association of Realtors®.

certified residential specialist (CRS) Someone who has met the requirements of the Realtors National Marketing Institute, which is affiliated with the National Association of Realtors®. A CRS must have successfully completed an educational program, have an acceptable level of residential sales experience and already be a graduate of the Real Estate Institute.

chattel A word that is not used much in common speech but is often used in real estate documents to describe personal property that is part of the property but is not fixed to the land or to a building. This is different from a fixture, which is part of the land or building. A homeowner's dining room table and chairs are a form of chattel; the chandelier above the table, which is secured to the ceiling, is a fixture. Fixtures are commonly included in the sale of a property, whereas chattels usually are not unless they are itemized in the agreement of sale.

claim Any legal right that one asserts against another person or institution: in real estate, often a formal request for some right that the claimant feels he or she is due, such as a right of way; in insurance, the request by a person insured by an insurance company, to that company, to be paid on some aspect of his or her insurance policy.

clear title Property for which the title is free of competing claims, liens or mortgages. Also called free and clear.

client The customer or principal; that is, the person who hires a professional real estate agent or agent to work on his or her behalf.

closing The final procedure in any real estate transaction in which the parties to the transaction (or their representatives) meet to execute documents, exchange funds, and complete the sale (and, if a mortgage is involved, the loan). A closing typically takes place at the offices of a title company.

closing costs Expenses, usually those of the buyer, that are over and above the cost (i.e., the sale price) of the property itself, such as legal fees, mortgage application fees, taxes, appraisal fees, title registration fees, etc.

closing date The date set out in the agreement of sale on which the final real estate transaction (i.e., the closing) is to take place. On that date, the appropriate documents will be completed, the purchase price paid, and the transfer of title (i.e., ownership) recorded. Also known as completion date.

closing statement A document that lists the financial settlement between the buyer and seller of real estate, including the costs that each must pay at closing. This statement usually is circulated to the buyer and seller before the closing date. Also known as a HUD-I settlement statement.

cloud (on title) Any unresolved claim of ownership against all or part of a property that affects the owner's title to that property and the marketability of that title. This kind of claim is usually resolved in court.

code Laws or regulations that are drawn up (often by the government) to cover a particular aspect of life in a municipality or state (e.g., a building code, a traffic code).

code of ethics A set of rules governing the activity of members of the organization or profession that establishes them. Lawyers and real estate agents have their own codes of ethics.

commission The amount paid to a real estate agent or agent as compensation for services rendered in the purchase, sale, or rental of property. The amount is usually a percentage of the sales price or the total rental.

commission split The dividing-up of a commission when two or more real estate agents have been involved in the sale (or purchase) of property.

commitment/commitment letter A written promise, by a lender or insurance company, to make a loan or insure a loan for a specified amount and on specified terms.

common-area assessments A periodic charge (usually monthly) that is levied against owners in a condominium complex. These fees are used by the condominium owners' association to pay for the maintenance of common areas in the building. Some assessments also include fees for utilities such as central heating or air conditioning. Also known as common-element fees or assessments.

common areas/common elements Those portions of a condominium or cooperative that are intended for the use of all tenants, such as the lobby, a work-out room, a swimming pool, or a sun terrace. With rental properties, such as an apartment building, the term is often used to mean the same thing.

community association Any organization created by property owners in a particular area to represent them collectively in dealing with the government, planning bodies, developers, etc.

comparables A way of establishing the market value of a particular property in which another property that has recently been sold and is similar in location, size, condition and amenities to the property in question, is used as a guide to establishing the asking price.

concessions Any sacrifice (in price or terms) that is made by one person to persuade another to enter into a real estate contract. An example might be the seller of a house or condominium unit offering to include some of his or her furniture in the already announced sale price as an inducement to a potential buyer.

condition(s) Requirements in a real estate agreement to purchase that must be fulfilled before the agreement becomes firm and binding. If the conditions are not fulfilled, the agreement will usually be regarded as cancelled and any deposit will be returned to the buyer.

conditional offer/conditional sales contract An offer to purchase or sell a property that comes into effect only if certain conditions are fulfilled.

condominium A structure comprised of two or more units in which the units are individually owned but the remainder of the property (i.e., the land, buildings, and amenities) is owned in common. The maintenance of these common areas is supervised by the condominium corporation, in which each unit owner owns a share and has voting rights.

condominium board of directors An organization comprised of some of the unit owners in a condominium building or development, who are elected to their posts at specified intervals by all of the unit owners. The purpose of the condominium board is to govern relations between all the owners, to administer the rules and regulations (i.e., the by-laws) of the condominium and generally to manage the condominium's operations. The last function particularly comes into force when there is no on-site, full-time manager.

consideration Anything legal and of value that induces either the buyer or the seller to enter into a contract to purchase or sell.

consumer reporting agency or bureau The source to which lenders turn for the credit history of any applicant for a loan. Also called a credit bureau.

contiguous Sharing a common boundary.

contingency A condition that must be fulfilled before a contract can become firm and binding. For example, the sale of a house may depend on whether the potential buyer can obtain financing.

contingency fees Fees that are paid only if a particular event takes place in the future For example, a real estate agent's fees are usually payable only if that agent succeeds in selling or leasing a property.

contract An agreement between two or more persons (or entities) that creates (or modifies) a legal relationship. In real estate, a contract is usually an offer for property and an acceptance of that offer (e.g., an agreement of sale).

contract of sale The written agreement between the seller and buyer for the sale of a property. It includes all the terms and financial details of the transaction. Also known as contract or agreement of purchase and sale, offer to purchase, and contract of purchase.

conventional loan There are two meanings: 1.) a loan or mortgage with a fixed interest rate, fixed payments and a fixed term (i.e., life); and 2.) a mortgage or deed or trust not insured by the government.

convey To transfer title to a property to someone else.

conveyance The act of transferring title to (or other interest in) a property to someone else. Also, the document that effects that transfer; such documents include most instruments by which an interest in real estate is created, mortgaged or assigned.

co-op Abbreviated term for cooperative, a form of ownership in which the occupiers of individual units in a building have shares in the cooperative corporation that owns the entire property. Co-ops are still popular in large American cities, such as New York and Chicago, but condominiums are the more usual form of apartment ownership in most American cities and suburbs.

cooperating broker An broker who is not the main (listing) broker in any real estate transaction but has assisted in the transaction and is therefore entitled to share in the commission. Often, the cooperating broker is the one who has found the buyer.

cost approach An appraisal method in which a property's value is estimated by adding the cost of the property and the cost of improvements and subtracting depreciation.

counteroffer A response to an offer. If a prospective buyer makes an offer to purchase a property (i.e., offers a price for that property), the seller may do one of three things: 1.) accept the offer; 2.) reject the offer outright; or 3.) suggest an alternative. For example, the listed or advertised price of a condominium is $350,000 and the prospective buyer offers $325,000. The seller makes a counteroffer of $340,000. By suggesting this alternative, the seller is legally regarded as having rejected the buyer's original offer. The buyer in turn may also counteroffer (e.g., suggest a price of $330,000).

credit history/credit report A statement of debts and obligations, both current and past, and of the record of payment of such debts. The lender obtains a credit history for an applicant to assess the risk in making a loan to that applicant. The lender is interested in determining whether a potential applicant is likely (and willing) to make the payments on a mortgage, and believes that her or his past behavior as a borrower will be a good indication of future behavior.

credit limit The maximum amount that an individual can borrow to buy property. This amount is set by the lender after an examination of the individual's credit history/credit report.

credit rating/credit risk An evaluation of a person's ability to manage current and future debt.

cul-de-sac A French term for a dead end; that is, a street or alley that is open only at one end. In real estate, the term often applies to a dead-end street in a subdivision that ends in an area where cars can turn around. Such a street is often viewed by potential buyers as an advantage because it insures privacy.

D

date of appraisal The precise day, month or year on which an assessment of the value of a property is given.

date of registration The precise day, month or year on which an instrument (e.g., a mortgage lien) was registered on the title to a property.

debt-equity ratio A comparison of what is owed on a property with its equity (i.e., the current market value of the property less the amount owed on the mortgage or loan).

debt financing The purchase of a property using any kind of credit rather than paying cash.

declaration of restrictions A statement made by the developer of a new subdivision setting out the rules in effect throughout that subdivision.

deed The legal instrument by which title to (i.e., ownership of) property is conveyed from one owner to another when a sale occurs.

deed in trust A legal instrument that conveys title to a property to a trustee; it may include statements about the duties or responsibilities of the trustee.

deed of trust Used in many states in place of a mortgage. Property is transferred by the buyer or borrower to a trustee. The beneficiary is the lender, and the property is reconveyed to the buyer when the loan obligation is paid.

deed restrictions A clause (or clauses) in a deed that limits the use of the property in some way.

deferred maintenance This term refers to a property that has not been adequately maintained. Its condition, and therefore its value, is depreciating.

delivery Turning over any legal document, particularly a deed, to another party and in doing so making it legally nonrevocable.

Department of Housing and Urban Development (HUD) The federal agency that concentrates on housing programs and on the renewal of urban and suburban communities.

department of real estate That department of the state government that is responsible for the licensing and regulation of persons engaged in the real estate business. The individual who heads the department is normally called the real estate commissioner. Other names for this department, depending on the state, are the division of real estate and the real estate commission. There is such a department in each of the 50 states.

Department of Veterans' Affairs (VA) The federal government agency that administers benefits for American military veterans, including property loans and mortgage programs.

deposit Money that is paid up front by a buyer to guarantee that she or he will actually complete a transaction to buy a particular property—in effect, it is a guarantee to the seller that the seller may remove the property from the market (i.e., that the sale is "firm"). If the buyer later fails to complete the transaction, she or he generally loses the deposit. Also called earnest money.

depreciation The decrease in value of a property over time, which can also lead to a reduction in the owner's taxes (i.e., a capital loss).

designated real estate broker An individual who has a real estate broker's license and who is appointed by a corporation or institution to oversee all of its real estate activities.

detached single-family home A freestanding house; that is, a house that does not share walls with another house and is designed to house just one family. Most houses in the United States are of this type.

deterioration The effects of time and wear-and-tear on a property, or neglect of that property, which causes its value to decrease unless some action is taken to counteract and correct these effects.

direct costs Expenses incurred in the improvement of property that can be directly attributed to making that improvement, such as fees, labor, materials, and taxes. Also known as hard costs.

disclosed principal The announcement of the name of a potential buyer by a real estate agent or agent to a seller.

disclosure In some U.S. jurisdictions, the seller of a property must provide a written statement to the buyer listing those defects in the property of which the seller is aware. For example, the seller may know that the roof of the property needs to be replaced, but may be unaware that there is severe termite damage to the property. Also called vendor's disclosure.

disclosure statement A legal requirement in some jurisdictions that the lender issue a document to a potential borrower outlining the terms and conditions of the loan or mortgage.

discount real estate broker A real estate agent or broker who works for a commission that is less than that which is usual in a particular marketplace. Sometimes a broker who usually works for a standard commission (i.e., is not a discount real estate broker) accepts a reduced commission in order to secure a client or a listing.

documentary stamp/documentary tax stamp A levy charged by the local government for the registration of a deed or mortgage; the stamp shows the amount of transfer tax paid.

documentary transfer tax State tax on the sale of real estate, often calculated as a percentage of the sale price.

dog Slang term for property that, because of poor condition or poor location, is slow to sell.

down payment The amount of money that is provided by the buyer toward the total price of the property (not including fees, taxes or other costs). In general, the down payment plus the principal of the mortgage equals the purchase price. The down payment is customarily cash paid by the buyer from his or her own funds—as opposed to that part of the purchase price that is financed by a lender. A down payment amount that is common in the United States is 20 percent of the total purchase price. However, if the borrower agrees to insure this part of the mortgage, some lenders will accept a 10 percent down payment.

dual agency In general, dual agency is a breach of real estate brokerage rules. If a single real estate agent is representing both the buyer and the seller in a particular transaction, the agent must disclose this fact to both sides. Otherwise, the agent is involved in a conflict of interest that is not allowed by most real estate brokerages.

duplex A single building that includes two separate living units. Also, an apartment or condominium unit that has two floors.

duress A situation in which threatening or coercive action has been used to cause someone to enter into a contract. Such a contract is invalid and may be challenged in court.

dwelling Another word for a home, house, or other living unit. Can also refer to a building specifically designed for residential use.

E

earnest money see deposit.

easement The right of the owner of one property to use part of the land of another for a specific purpose. The property that enjoys the right in this arrangement is said to be in the dominant position; the other is said to be in the servient position.

economic depreciation A reduction in the value of a property that is caused by reasons aside from the condition of the property itself. For example, a shopping mall that is built across from a row of houses may result in traffic and noise that make the street a less desirable residential area, and the houses may decline in value.

effective age The age of a structure as estimated by its condition rather than by its actual chronological age. This estimate may take into account both renovation and maintenance.

egress The right to come and go across the land, public or private, of another, most often to a road.

eminent domain The government's right to acquire private property for public use by condemnation; the government must always pay fair compensation to the owner when it exercises this right.

encroachment Construction (usually of a wall or fence) that is located wholly or in part on an adjoining lot and to which the owner of the adjoining property has not agreed. If the encroachment goes unchallenged for a long period, it may result in a claim for adverse possession.

encumbrance Any right, lien or charge attached to and binding on a property. An encumbrance can affect the owner's ability or right to sell that property until such time as it is removed.

energy-efficient Containing features that reduce the use of electricity or heating fuel, such as effective insulation, double-glazed windows, skylights or a state-of-the-art furnace. The fact that a property is energy-efficient can be a selling point in its favor.

energy tax credits A tax write-off that is available to property owners who take steps to reduce energy consumption.

environment In appraising, a term used for the characteristics of the area around a particular property that may have an effect on the desirability or value of that property. For example, a golf course is more likely to enhance property value than is a strip mall.

Equal Credit Opportunity Act A U.S. law guaranteeing that people of all races, ages, genders and religions must have an equal chance to borrow money.

equitable title The assumed interest of a buyer in a property for which the buyer has entered into an agreement to purchase.

equity The market value of a property, less the debts of that property Likely debts include the principal and accumulated interest on the mortgage, unpaid taxes and a home equity loan.

equity buildup The increase over time of an owner's interest in a property (i.e., the difference between the market value of the property and the amount owed on the mortgage and any other outstanding liens). With most mortgages, the mortgage holder may accelerate the process of building equity by making an extra payment on the principal each month. In addition, property in desirable areas of major American cities has risen in value significantly in recent years, further increasing owners' equity.

equity loan A loan to a home or condominium owner that is secured by the lender against the equity the owner has built up in the property. Equity loans have become increasingly popular in recent years as a way of consolidating credit card debt (the interest rate on equity loans is usually far less than that charged by credit card companies) and tapping into what is often a large amount of money to use for home repairs and renovation or to fund some major expense such as an expensive vacation or a child's college education.

equity purchaser A person who buys the equity of another in a property, often by assuming (i.e., taking over) a mortgage that the borrower can no longer afford to pay.

escape clause A provision in a contract that allows one or more of the parties involved to end the contract if certain events occur. For example, a potential buyer of a house may stipulate in the sale agreement that the agreement comes into effect only if the buyer is able to sell her or his current residence by the anticipated closing date.

escrow In real estate, the delivery of a deed by the seller to a third party (i.e., the escrow agent), to be delivered to the buyer at a certain time, usually the closing date. In some states, all instruments having to do with the sale (including the funds) are delivered to the escrow agent for dispersal on the closing date.

escrow account A form of trust. This is the account in which the funds required to effect a closing are held.

escrow agent A third party who is independent of the buyer and seller (usually an agent), and who receives items to be held in escrow, holds them until transfer is allowed, and then delivers them.

escrow collections/deposit Money that is deposited with the escrow agent and held for future payments as required by the contract (e.g., taxes and insurance on the property). Also known as reserves.

escrow disbursements The act of paying out escrow funds as required by the real estate contract. Also known as escrow payments.

escrow reimbursement Returning to the borrower any excess funds that are present in an escrow account after all debts have been paid.

evaluation An analysis of the value of a property according to its potential uses rather than its actual market value.

evidence of title A document that establishes ownership to property, most commonly a deed.

exclusive listing/exclusive agency listing/exclusive right to sell A written contract in which a property owner grants a single real estate agent or brokerage the right to sell that property. The owner promises to pay a fee or commission if the property is sold within a specific period, regardless of whether the agent or brokerage is the direct cause of the sale. In turn, the agent or broker may make specific promises, such as to advertise the property, to conduct open-house viewings, and to list the property on the brokerage's Web site.

executed contract A real estate contract that has been signed by the parties to the contract, and is therefore complete, legal and in force.

exposure/market exposure The extent to which a property that is for sale has been presented to the public, and the effectiveness of that marketing.

F
....

face-lift A slang term for cosmetic changes to the appearance of a property, such as new paint that may improve the selling price.

Fair Credit Reporting Act A federal law that protects consumers by establishing procedures whereby they can correct errors on credit reports; it gives consumers specific rights in dealing with credit reporting agencies.

fair market value The price that is likely to be agreed on by a buyer and seller for a specific property at a specific time. This price is typically arrived at by considering the sales prices of comparable properties in the area, taking into consideration any special features of or upgrades to the property in question.

Fannie Mae A slang term for the U.S. Federal National Mortgage Association. This association purchases, sells, and guarantees both conventional and government (e.g., VA) mortgages. Fannie Mae is a corporation established by the U.S. Congress; it is the largest supplier in the country of mortgages to home buyers and owners.

Federal Fair Housing Law Article VIII of the U.S. Civil Rights Act, this law forbids discrimination in either the sale or rental of residential property because of race, color, sex, religion or nationality.

Federal Housing Administration (FHA) A federal agency (a division of the U.S. Department of Housing and Urban Development, or HUD) that purchases first mortgages, both conventional and federally insured, from members of the Federal Reserve System and the Federal Home Loan Bank system. It also sets standards for the underwriting of private mortgages and insures residential mortgages made by private lenders.

Federal National Mortgage Association (FNMA) see Fannie Mae.

Federal Savings and Loan Insurance Corporation (FSLC) A federally chartered institution that insures mortgages issued by savings and loan associations.

Federal Truth in Lending Act A U.S. federal law that requires lenders to disclose all the terms of a loan arrangement (e.g., a mortgage) to the borrower in a specific, understandable way.

fee appraiser Another term for a professional appraiser, that is, someone who appraises property in return for a fee.

FHA see Federal Housing Administration.

final value estimate The final statement of an appraiser, outlining the appraiser's valuation of a particular property. Often, this statement includes the appraiser's comments on the evaluation method(s) used.

financing The way in which a potential purchaser intends to make up the difference between the cash that she or he has on hand and the purchase price of a property (e.g., by obtaining a loan from a mortgage lender or borrowing the money from a bank).

firm commitment A promise from a lender to lend a potential borrower a specific amount of money (on specific terms) to be secured against a specific property—in other words, a promise by the lender to give the potential borrower a mortgage.

firm offer An offer from a potential buyer of a property to the owner of that property indicating that the buyer will not negotiate any changes to that offer. For example, if a buyer offers $300,000 for a residence and indicates that the offer is firm, he or she will not consider the seller's counteroffer.

firm price An indication that the seller will not enter into negotiations with any potential buyer to change the price at which a property is offered. The indication that a price is "firm" is often included in any announcement or advertisement of the sale of the property.

first lien Any registered legal claim against a property that comes first when proceeds from a sale are distributed. The order of liens is the order in which they were registered; however, some claims automatically jump to first place in the line, such as real estate taxes owed to the government.

first mortgage A mortgage that, when registered, is the first to be able to claim payment from any sale proceeds. Often, owners of property take out a second mortgage, usually to "tap" some of the equity in their property. Such mortgages are paid, on a sale, only after the first mortgage has been paid.

fixed expenses These are the certain costs of owning and operating a property. The cost of painting a house is not a fixed expense but the property tax on that house is.

fixture Personal property that is attached to real property; this is treated legally as real property while it is so attached. Fixtures, unless they are specifically exempted from an accepted offer to purchase, are regarded as part of the property when that property is bought or sold. Furniture is generally not a fixture (see chattel), with the exception of furniture that is built-in (e.g., a bookcase). A lamp is not a fixture, whereas track lighting that is attached to the ceiling is a fixture.

flagpole lot A term for the shape of a property when access to it is via a narrow roadway (i.e., the flag pole) and the usable land at the end of the roadway is the open area (i.e., the rectangular flag).

flip The practice whereby a property is purchased in the hope that it can be sold quickly for a higher price. Often refers to the practice whereby someone reserves (with a comparatively small reservation fee) a condominium unit in a condominium building that is being constructed (or being converted from apartments); by the time the property is ready, but before the purchaser has to go through a closing, the condominium has increased in value and the purchaser can sell it for a high price, having invested only the amount necessary to "reserve" the property.

floodplain The area of land that is adjacent to a body of water. This land is under water sometimes and dry at other times. Houses built on such land are usually constructed on some type of stilts that keep them above water during times of flooding.

floor area The total area of all floors in a building.

floor-area ratio (FAR) The total area of the floor of a building compared with the total area of the land on which it stands. Minimum and maximum FARs are usually determined by local building bylaws and are described in local zoning restrictions.

floor plan A layout drawing of a building (or portion of a building) showing the size and the purpose of each room. Usually provided (by the seller's agent) to any potential buyer of the property. Floor plans may be quite specific, including doors, windows, stairways and other features.

for sale by owner (FSBO) The situation when a seller tries to find a buyer on his or her own, without using a real estate agent or agent.

G
.....

grandfather clause An exemption. A clause in a law or an agreement that permits the continuation of some use or practice that was permissible when established but is now no longer permissible. Such clauses ensure that property owners will not be penalized by retroactive laws. For instance, if a property owner, at great expense, has created a brick wall around her or his house for privacy purposes, and a new law dictates that such fences must be made of metal, a grandfather clause in the new law may allow the owner to keep her or his brick fence.

gross area The total floor space of a building, usually stated in terms of square feet and including nonusable space, measured from the outside walls.

gross income The total of a person's earnings from his or her job plus any other income (e.g., interest income or dividends on stock) in a given period, before that person's expenses are deducted.

growing-equity mortgage (GEM) A mortgage in which the payments increase at stated intervals but the interest rate remains the same. The increased portion of the payments is applied directly to the outstanding principal on the mortgage, thereby reducing the outstanding principal more quickly.

guaranty fee Fannie Mae's fee for insuring a mortgage.

H
.....

habitable A dwelling or property that is acceptable for human occupancy; that is, it is not derelict and meets standards of decency.

handyman's special A property that requires substantial work to bring it up to normal standards. Such a property is often sold at a lower price than it would be if it were in excellent repair.

heterogeneous An appraisal term describing an area comprised of buildings of varying styles or uses. Not as desirable as homogenous property.

hidden amenities Qualities that may not be immediately (or visually) apparent but that add to the value of a particular property, such as the fact that a building has been constructed of high-quality materials.

high-rise A tall apartment or commercial building that meets one or both of two criteria: 1.) it is taller than six stories; and/or 2.) it is tall enough to make an elevator a necessity rather than a convenience.

historic district A classification (from a zoning, heritage or other agency) of a particular area of a community, usually within a city, denoting that the buildings within that area have historical value or significance. Such districts include Greenwich Village in New York City, Old Town in Chicago, the French Quarter in New Orleans and Beacon Hill in Boston. The historic district designation usually enhances the value of individual properties in the district because buyers know that the area will be preserved, maintaining its current charm. Such designations may also involve very strict rules regarding the ways in which buildings may be renovated or changed; in a commercial area, this may be resisted by property owners.

hold-harmless clause A clause in a contract in which one party releases another from legal liability for a stated risk. For example, a person who wishes to rent an apartment from a landlord may agree to sign a lease only if that lease includes a hold-harmless clause absolving the tenant from having to make any repairs that become necessary during the tenancy. Also known as a save-harmless clause.

home inspection report The official statement provided by a professional home inspector detailing the results of her or his examination of a specific property. This report may show problems (or potential problems) not obvious to a potential buyer, such as problems with the structure of a building. Many buyers, especially those who are considering the purchase of an older building, make their offer conditional on obtaining a satisfactory home inspection report.

home inspector Someone who offers his or her services as an examiner of the physical condition of property. Qualifications for this profession differ between jurisdictions.

homeowners' association A group of property owners in a particular area who band together in an informal cooperative so that they may have a stronger voice in combating specific ills in their neighborhood. One purpose of such an association could be to achieve a more powerful political voice than each property owner would have separately.

homeowner's/homestead tax exemption A tax break or reduction for property owners, offered in some jurisdictions, that reduces property tax assessments when the taxpayer actually resides in the property that he or she owns and on which the exemption is being claimed. Such exceptions often require periodic (usually annual) evidence that the owner continues to reside in the property.

homeowner's warranty (HOW) program A guarantee that is offered through certain builders by the National Association of Home Builders. The program sets standards for construction and requires warranties ranging from one to 10 years in duration on a range of things from minor defects in workmanship to major structural problems. Anyone who contemplates building a home should inquire whether the builders that they consider for the job participate in this program.

Housing and Urban Development (HUD) see Department of Housing and Urban Development.

Housing Assistance Council (HAC) A federal agency, funded by the U.S. Department of Housing and Urban Development, that supports the development of low-income housing in rural areas.

housing code The rules of a particular municipality that set out the minimum standards for dwellings in that area..

HUD see Department of Housing and Urban Development.

HUD median income A figure that is used by the U.S. Department of Housing and Urban Department (HUD) in determining eligibility for various HUD programs; it is the average income for a family in a specific area of the United States.

HUD-I settlement statement see closing statement.

I

improvements Any permanent structure or other development (usually buildings, but also streets, sewers and utilities) that enhances the value of what was formerly vacant land.

independent appraisal An estimate of the value of a property in which the appraiser has no interest in the property (e.g., is not a representative of the potential lender).

independent contractor A person who is hired to do building or renovation work for another person but is neither an employee nor an agent of that other person, such as a contractor who works for a fee.

infrastructure The improvements, not including buildings, that are made to a particular property or area (e.g., roads, sewers, utility installations).

inner city The older, central residential area of a metropolis that, often, has deteriorated. In the last 20 years, many inner-city neighborhoods in American cities have been renovated and restored and are once again considered desirable places to live.

institutional lender An accredited financial organization or company (e.g., a bank, a trust company, savings and loan, credit union) that offers loans or mortgages.

institutional mortgage A loan offered by an institutional lender that is secured against real estate.

interest There are two meanings for this term: 1.) a person's legal right to property; and 2.) the cost of borrowing money for any purpose, such as to buy property, charged as a percentage of the outstanding balanced that is owed.

involuntary lien A claim that is registered against a property without the consent (and sometimes the knowledge) of the owner, such as a claim by the government for unpaid property taxes. Conversely, a mortgage is a voluntary lien in which the borrower agrees that the lender may register a lien against the property until the loan covered by the mortgage is paid in full.

irrevocability date The time and date specified in a purchase offer for property. The buyer may not retract the offer until that date, and the seller has until that date to accept or reject the offer.

J

joint ownership agreement A contract between two or more people who have an interest in the same property. It sets out their rights and obligations and may also set out the way in which the parties agree to manage the property.

judgment lien A lien that applies to all the property that is owned by the loser in a court action and is located in the county in which the judgment is recorded.

K
....

kicker A form of added incentive; additional compensation for a property lender or investor, usually a share in the income from that property in addition to principal and interest on the loan for it. Also known as equity kicker or lender participation.

L
...

land A general term that usually refers to the ground and those natural objects that are more or less permanent on it. This includes trees, crops, and mineral deposits, unless they are specifically excepted in a contract.

land surveyor A professional who is trained to establish, measure and verify the boundaries of properties and the buildings constructed on those properties.

landlocked A property that does not border any public road; it is surrounded entirely by privately owned land.

landmark Any object that is fixed to the ground and may serve as a guide for a survey or boundary, such as an extended row of stones that serves as a fence. Also known as a monument.

landscaping The act of modifying a landscape, as well as the components used in such modification, such as changes in grade, trees and shrubs, lawns, flowers, and other plantings. The object of landscaping is to create a more pleasing appearance for the property, and one of its incidental goals is to enhance the value of that property. Landscaping may accomplish that goal, particularly if it is extensive, professional, and pleasing to a potential buyer.

latent defect A hidden or concealed defect in a property that, even assuming reasonable care, could not be found in an inspection. A seller must declare to the buyer any latent defect of which she or he is aware.

legal description A description of property that is acceptable in a court of law (i.e., meets legal requirements).

legal residence There are two meanings for this term, depending on location: 1.) for an American who is in the United States, it usually means street address, city, state, and zip code; 2.) for a person abroad, it can mean country of residence.

legal title The rights of ownership that are conferred on a person when he or she purchases a piece of property. These rights may be defended against any other, competing interests.

lender A general term referring to any individual or company that provides money to a borrower in return for periodic payments of principal and interest over time. In real estate, the term most often refers to a person (or institution) who offers a borrower a mortgage (i.e., loans the borrower the money to buy property) and places a lien on that property until the outstanding loan (i.e., the principal) and all the outstanding interest on that loan are paid.

letter of intent A formal letter stating that a prospective buyer is interested in a property. This is not a firm offer and it creates no legal obligation. A potential buyer could issue such a letter to a seller of a particular property, indicating that the buyer intends to make an offer for that property.

lien An encumbrance, or legal claim, against a property as security for payment of a debt, such as the lien involved in a mortgage.

lien holder The person or institution who issues a lien; that is, who has a claim against property (e.g., a mortgage) that must be satisfied (e.g., the mortgage must be fully paid) before that claim can be released.

like-kind property Two or more properties that are similar.

list/listing An agreement between an owner of a property and a real estate agent or agent in which the agent agrees to find a buyer or tenant in return for either a fee (in the case of rental property) or a commission (in the case of property to be sold). Also, the act of announcing that the property is for rent or for sale.

listing agent/broker The real estate professional who acts for the seller in marketing a property. This is not the same as the selling agent, who represents potential buyers. One agent may act in both capacities for a client (e.g., be responsible for selling a person's current residence, then help them to find a new residence).

loan-to-value ratio The difference between the appraised value of a property and the amount being loaned on a mortgage.

location The factor that is often cited as the primary factor in determining the worth of a property—as in the expression location, location, location! It refers to the following phenomenon: if two very similar properties are located in two different areas within the same city or town, and one of those areas is more convenient to the area's most popular amenities (e.g., shopping, entertainment) than the other, the property in the more desirable area will almost certainly be more expensive.

lot In general, any portion or parcel of real estate (i.e., a measured section of land). Often refers to a portion of a subdivision.

lot line The legal boundaries of a property, shown on a survey of that property.

low-ball offer A slang term meaning to offer a purchase price that is much lower than the asking price. Such offers, which are often lower than the appraised market value, are frequently made when a property has been on the market for a long time and potential buyers try to take advantage of pressure on the seller to sell.

M

market price The amount actually paid for a property. At the moment of sale, that amount is imagined to be its current valuation; subsequently, the market price, depending on economic factors, either appreciates or depreciates.

market segmentation Submarkets within a larger market, such as neighborhoods within a city.

market value An estimation of the price at which a property would sell in the current real estate market.

market-value approach An appraisal technique in which the value of a property is estimated by comparing it with similar properties (i.e., "comparables") that have recently been sold.

marketability The probability of selling a particular property within a specified period and price range.

marketable title Ownership of a particular property that can be sold without complications because there are no competing claims to that property (i.e., no liens or encumbrances).

marketing plan A description (usually written) of how a real estate agent or agent intends to market a particular property in order to obtain the best possible price. A good agent should offer his or her clients such plans and solicit their comments on them.

minimum down payment The smallest amount of money that a purchaser is allowed to provide toward the purchase price of a house under a lender's guidelines for a mortgage. Down payments on residential property in the United States, for many years, have typically been 20 percent of the purchase price. However, down payments of 10 percent or even five percent recently have become more common. With down payments of less than 20 percent, lenders usually require additional insurance on the mortgage. The borrower may cancel this insurance when the principal on the loan reaches 20 percent.

mortgage A loan that is usually granted for the purpose of allowing a borrower to purchase property. The loan is secured (i.e., guaranteed) by that property; in other words, the mortgage is registered on the title (i.e., the ownership record) as a claim on that property.

mortgagee In a mortgage transaction, this is the lender; that is, the bank, other institution (private or government) or person making the loan for property.

mortgagee in possession A lender that has taken over control of a property because the borrower has defaulted. This is a first step in foreclosure.

most probable selling price An estimate of the amount a property will bring in a sale in a given market at a given time.

Multiple Listing Service (MLS) A local service that is created and staffed by real estate professionals. It brings together all property listed for sale in a given area (e.g., a town and its surrounding area or a city and its suburbs) so that real estate agents and agents can review all available properties on behalf of their clients. The MLS also governs commission splitting and other relations between agents. Licensed real estate professionals have access to the service.

municipal address The designation (i.e., the street address, city, state, and zip code) by which a property is known.

muniments of title Any written or printed documents that may be used to prove property ownership.

N
.....

National Association of Independent Fee Appraisers (NAIFA) An organization of real estate appraisers; it offers professional licensure to qualified persons.

National Association of Real Estate Brokers (NAREB) A national trade association whose members include not just real estate agents but also appraisers, property managers and other interested real estate professionals.

National Association of Realtors® (NAR) An organization of people engaged in the real estate business. NAR is dedicated to the betterment of the industry through education and legislation. It also sets high ethical and professional standards for its members. Founded in 1908, it currently comprises more than three-quarters of a million members.

negotiable A term that commonly refers to something that is assignable or transferable (i.e., something that is capable of being negotiated). In real estate, the term refers to the fact that the price of a property is often the result of a negotiation between the buyer and seller, and that many of the charges on a home loan are also subject to negotiation.

neighborhood A term that usually refers to an area of a city that can be defined by common properties, common use, atmosphere, and the presence of a business center (i.e., a main street or streets). Often, neighborhoods in large cities have names–Chelsea in New York, Edgewater in Chicago, Pacific Heights in San Francisco–as if they were small towns within the larger city.

neighborhood life cycle The pattern of development and change that occurs in a neighborhood over a given period.

net listing An agreement between a real estate agent and a seller in regard to a sale price (i.e., the net price). In such an agreement, the seller is guaranteed to receive the agreed sale price and the agent to receive as commission the amount that exceeds that price when the property is sold. This kind of arrangement is illegal in some American states.

no money down A slang term for the strategy of purchasing real estate using as little of the buyer's own money as possible. Can also refer to an uncommon kind of mortgage that requires very little or no down payment.

nonassumption clause A clause in a mortgage contract forbidding the borrower from transferring the mortgage to another person without the consent of the lender.

nonconforming loan/mortgage A loan that is not eligible for backing by Fannie Mae or Freddie Mac because it does not adhere to their requirements.

nonexclusive listing A kind of property agreement. The seller lists a property with a real estate agent, who has the exclusive right to sell that property. However, if the owner sells the property without any help from the agent, the owner is not liable to pay a commission to the agent. Sometimes also called an agency agreement.

normal wear-and-tear Damage to a property that is the result of neither carelessness nor maliciousness but simply reasonable use and the passage of time.

null and void Unenforceable; no longer legally binding.

O

objection A buyer's concern about a property being purchased and his or her requirement that the seller correct the problem before closing (e.g., something that is wrong with the heating system and must be fixed before the sale is concluded). Also known as requisition.

occupancy The physical possession of a building or property.

offer A statement (either spoken or written) that informs one party of another's willingness to buy or sell a specific property on the terms set out in that statement. Once made, an offer usually must be accepted within a specific period (i.e., it is usually not open-ended). Once accepted, the offer by the one party and the acceptance by the other both are regarded as binding.

offer and acceptance see offer.

offeree The person who receives an offer.

Office of Interstate Land Sales Registration An agency of the U.S. Department of Housing and Urban Development (HUD) that has the responsibility of enforcing the Interstate Land Sales Full Disclosure Act.

off-street parking Spaces for cars that are located on private property rather than on public streets. Local bylaws, particularly in big cities, increasingly require that any new commercial, retail or residential development provide a certain number of parking spaces as part of the development in order to reduce street congestion.

on-site improvements Any work performed on a property that adds to its utility, value or attractiveness.

open house A property that is available for public viewing during a set period. Potential buyers who wish to view the property do not need an appointment and the real estate agent usually is present to conduct tours of the property and answer questions.

open listing A written authorization from a property owner to a real estate agent stipulating that the owner will pay the agent a commission if the agent presents an offer of specified price and terms. The agent does not, however, have an exclusive right to sell; in fact, the owner may have made the same arrangement with several agents and only the successful agent will be paid the commission.

open mortgage Any mortgage that may be paid in full (or in part) at any time during the life of the mortgage without a penalty being charged to the borrower.

ordinary repairs Repairs that are necessary to keep a property in good condition, as opposed to ordinary wear-and-tear.

original cost The purchase price of a property; the amount that was paid by the current owner.

original face value The principal owed on a mortgage on the day that the mortgage came into effect.

outbuilding A structure that is not part of the main building, such as a garage.

owner One who has rights of ownership in a property.

owner-occupied Any property in which the owner occupies all or part of the property.

owner's title insurance A policy that protects a property owner from any defects in title that were not apparent at the time of purchase.

P
....

parcel A general term meaning any piece of land.

party wall A shared wall, usually on the property line, such as exists between row houses, townhouses, or semidetached houses.

personal residence A person's home; the place from which that person votes, pays taxes, etc.

pipestem lot see flagpole lot.

PITI An acronym for principal, interest, taxes and insurance, which are the most common components of a monthly mortgage payment.

planning commission A city or county board that must approve all proposed building projects. Also known as planning board or zoning board.

plat or platte A map dividing a parcel of land into lots, as in a subdivision.

plat book A public record of street maps, plans, etc.

plot plan A survey or diagram of a property that shows current or planned improvements and uses of the land.

possession The state of being in control of property, regardless of ownership. Thus, possession may be either legal or wrongful.

preapproved mortgage A commitment from a lender to provide a mortgage loan to a borrower on stated terms before the borrower has found a property to buy. Most real estate agents recommend that their clients who are potential buyers secure this kind of commitment because it allows them to make a firm offer when they find a desirable property; that is, they do not have to ask a seller to wait several weeks while they attempt to obtain financing. Sometimes sellers are unwilling to wait and potential buyers may lose property.

preclosing A meeting of the parties to a mortgage loan transaction before the actual closing date. This allows any complicated issues to be settled before closing; in addition, some of the documents can be signed in advance.

premises A descriptive and general term for the land or (more often) the building involved in a real estate transaction.

prequalification Completion of the mortgage application process before the borrower has found a property to buy as a way of establishing how much money the borrower is qualified to obtain in a mortgage.

prescriptive easement The legal right to make use of all or part of the property of another person as a result of the continuous use of that property for a stated period. Such easements vary according to local statutes.

principal broker The head of a real estate brokerage (also licensed as a broker), who is responsible for all the actions of that firm.

principal residence The dwelling in which someone resides most of the time.

private mortgage insurance (PMI) Insurance that is required by a lender (and obtained from a nongovernment insurer) if the down payment on a property is less than 20 percent of its value.

property In real estate, any land or building on that land that is owned by someone.

property line The boundary of a parcel of land.

property tax A tax that is levied on real property. The amount of tax is dependent on the assessed valuation of the property. Sometimes called realty tax.

prospect A potential tenant, buyer or seller, rather than someone who is in the process of leasing, buying or selling.

prospectus A brochure that serves to advertise and market a particular property. It is usually printed in color and contains pictures of the interior and exterior of the property, as well as a written description of the property.

public auction A real estate auction that is open to the public at which properties are sold to pay mortgages that are in default. Such auctions are popular with potential buyers because properties being sold at a public auction often bring less than their market value.

purchase agreement see agreement of sale.

purchaser A person who buys a property.

purchase price The amount paid by the buyer to the seller in the acquisition of a property.

R
....

ratified sales contract A firm and binding agreement for the purchase or sale of land or property.

ready, willing and able A term describing an individual who is in a position to complete a property contract. An agent providing an offer from a ready, willing and able buyer, which meets the price and terms of the listing, is entitled to a commission, regardless of whether the seller actually accepts the offer.

real estate The term for land and all fixtures to land, including buildings and improvements. Personal property is not usually considered real estate. A house is real estate, but the furniture in the house is not.

real estate agent Someone who works for a real estate agency and is involved in the buying and selling of property. The listing agent acts for the seller; the selling agent acts for the buyer.

real estate commission The amount that is paid to a real estate agent or agent on the sale of property.

real estate license A state license that grants an individual status as either an agent or an agent after she or he passes an examination. Some state examinations are very stringent.

real estate market The real estate activity (i.e., purchases and sales) in a particular area at a particular time.

Real Estate Settlement Procedures Act (RESPA) A statute adopted in 1975 that requires federally insured lenders to provide advance notice to borrowers of all the fees to be charged at closing.

real property see real estate.

reassessment Re-estimating the value of all property in a given area for tax assessment purposes. In most municipalities, these re-estimates happen with some regularity.

recorder's office The county office where title instruments are kept on file. Sometimes called the county recorder's office.

recording The act of entering a title (or titles) into the public records.

recording fees The fee paid for recording a mortgage or other transaction.

referral The act of a past client in recommending a real estate agent or agent to someone who currently wishes to buy or sell property. There are also other kinds of referrals, such as the recommendation of one agent by another or the recommendation of a good property lawyer, potential mortgage lender or appraiser by an agent to a client.

registration Submitting instruments relating to title in (i.e., ownership of) land or property to the public record. Different U.S. jurisdictions have different rules of submission. Once registered, documents are given a registration number, then recorded on a title abstract index.

rehabilitation tax credit An income tax credit that is equal to as much as 20 percent of a person's costs for the refurbishing of historic properties.

release of lien A document that, when it is registered, removes a claim against the title to (i.e., ownership of) a property.

relocation clause A condition in a lease that allows a landlord to move a tenant to a new unit, within the same building or elsewhere. The clause usually specifies that the new premises must be of the same standard and quality as the old premises from which the tenant is being moved.

relocation network As association of real estate professionals in different geographic areas whose purpose is to share information about their respective areas, making it easier for clients to move from one of the areas to another.

relocation service A firm that helps clients who have been transferred to a new area make an easy transition. The firm may provide information about moving services, new homes, schools and other amenities in the new area.

remodel/remodeling To refurbish and redecorate a property or premises (and sometimes to make minor structural changes), often as a preliminary to a sale, so as to make the property more attractive and appealing to potential buyers or tenants.

renegotiation An attempt to agree on new terms to an existing contract. In real estate, there are two common examples of renegotiation: 1.) when the necessary repairs to a property, as established by a home inspection, are more extensive than the seller had announced or the buyer had expected; and 2.) when the appraisal of a property establishes a value or market price considerably below the price on which the parties to the contract had agreed. In both cases, the buyer will wish to renegotiate the price of sale.

renovate Another word for remodel, though it implies a much more extensive upgrade to the property.

rescind/rescission To treat a property contract as ended or void; that is, to withdraw one's offer or acceptance of a contract. Rescission normally happens as a result of a breach of the contract by the other party to that contract.

reserve fund The fund that is maintained by a condominium corporation (or a cooperative) for future contingencies, such as unforeseen major structural repairs to the condominium building that are very expensive. A reserve fund is usually created by charging unit owners a monthly assessment that is slightly more than what is needed to cover the basic maintenance expenses of the building and placing the extra amount in the reserve fund.

reserve price The base price set before an auction that must be met in order for a particular property to sell during the auction process. For example, a house that is being auctioned with a set price (i.e., a reserve price) of $200,000 may bring $225,000 but would not be sold for $195,000.

residence A place, or dwelling, where someone lives. May also refer to the country in which a person lives, or to the state or province in that country.

residential broker A real estate professional who deals exclusively with the buying and selling of homes (i.e., does not deal with commercial properties).

residential property A property intended for human occupation.

restore To refurbish or renovate a property to its original condition. The term is most often used with regard to properties of historic interest, such as a house built in the 19th century that has become run-down or has been remodeled with substandard or inappropriate materials and is restored to its initial appearance.

right of first refusal Allowing someone to make an offer on a property that is for sale before it is offered to others or to the public in general.

right-of-way The legal right to use a portion of another person's property, usually for the purpose of accessing one's own property.

riparian rights The rights of the owner of land that borders water (e.g., a river, a lake, a creek) to use or control that body of water.

row house A dwelling that is attached to its neighbors (on both sides unless it is a corner house) by common walls.

run/running with the land A rule, right or restriction that forms part of the land and is transferred to each new owner, such as an easement that allows a landlocked property owner right-of-way over the subject property.

rural Located in the country, as opposed to the city.

S

sale price The amount of money that is paid by the buyer to the seller for a particular property. Also known as purchase price.

sales-assessment ratio The ratio of the assessed value of a property to its actual selling price, which is assumed to be the market value. For example, if a house were assessed at $160,000 and then sold for $200,000, it would have sold at 125 percent of its assessed value and the market value of the house would then be $200,000 rather than $160,000.

sales associate/salesperson A real estate professional who is employed by and works under a real estate agent.

sales-comparison approach In appraisal, estimating the value of a property by comparing it with similar properties that have recently been sold.

sales contract see agreement of sale.

satisfaction/satisfaction of mortgage Written verification from a lender that a property loan (i.e., a mortgage) has been paid in full and the borrower is released from any further obligation to the lender.

savings and loan association (S&L) An association that is chartered to hold savings and make real estate loans. These institutions are federally insured, and are a common and important source of mortgage loans in the United States.

scenic easement A right to the use of land that is given to ensure that the land is never developed and that the natural beauty of a specific area is preserved.

second mortgage A mortgage that ranks after a first mortgage in priority. A single property may have more than one mortgage; each is ranked by number to indicate the order in which it must be paid. In the event of a default and therefore sale of the property, second and subsequent mortgages are paid, in order, only if there are funds left after payment of the first mortgage.

security Real or personal property that is pledged by a borrower as a guarantee or protection for the lender. With a mortgage, the borrower pledges the property that the borrower is actually buying; this security is registered on the title to the property and the lender may claim the property if the borrower defaults on (i.e., fails to pay) the loan.

seller financing An arrangement in which a seller agrees to receive payment of part or all of the purchase price over an extended period. The debt is registered on the title as a mortgage, and the seller acts as the lender, accepting monthly payments of principal and accumulated interest.

seller's market The situation that exists when demand for property exceeds the availability of property. In such situations, a seller may set a price for her or his property that is higher than its real market value.

septic system A sewage system in which waste is drained through pipes and a tile field into a septic tank. Such systems are used in areas where city or county sewers have not yet been installed, such as rural areas and newly incorporated and newly developed parts of metropolitan areas.

septic tank An underground tank into which a sanitary sewer drains from a building. The sewage is held until bacterial action changes the solids into liquids and/or gases, which are then released into the surrounding ground.

setback ordinance A municipal government bylaw that decrees the minimum distance a building must be set back from property lines.

settlement costs see closing costs.

settlement sheet At closing, the information sheet that sets out the allocation of the various funds necessary to effect the transfer of the property.

sever/severance To divide one property from another so that each may be sold or used separately.

severalty Ownership of land by an individual.

single-family home/residence/unit A house or condominium unit that is designed for just a single family.

site A plot of land that is set aside for a specific use, such as for the construction of a new factory.

soft market The situation that exists when there is more property for sale than there are buyers to buy it; as a result, prices decrease. Also known as buyer's market.

stamp tax Charges that are levied by governments (usually the local municipality) on the transfer of ownership of property.

standard mortgage The general description of a mortgage that involves equal periodic (usually monthly) payments and is paid in full at the end of its term.

standards of practice A professional code of behavior devised by the National Association of Realtors® to guide the business practices of real estate professionals.

starter home/condominium A small house or condominium unit that is usually inexpensive and is suitable for a first-time buyer. The assumption is that the buyer will build up equity in the property and then use the equity as a down payment on a larger dwelling.

state stamps Property transfer taxes that are levied by the state.

suburb/suburban The small communities that have grown up around a central city and, despite being outside the official boundaries of the city, are dependent on it economically, socially and culturally. Most suburbs originally were extra residential areas for workers from the city. However, in recent years, some suburbs have themselves become greater economic forces, with "mini-downtowns" of their own. In addition, an increasing number of Americans commute from one suburb to work in another.

survey Usually a pictorial depiction of land, showing its boundaries and the improvements that have been made to it.

surveyor A professional who is trained to prepare accurate surveys.

sweat equity A slang term for the improvements an owner makes to property through his or her own manual labor. Such improvements are expected to add to the value of the property.

sweetener A slang term for an inducement to enter a property agreement. For example, a seller may offer to include some of her or his furniture in the purchase price of a house as a way to persuade a wavering potential purchaser to conclude the deal.

T
....

tax A government levy against real property. If taxes are unpaid, the government may attach a lien to the property. Such liens are regarded as preeminent (i.e., they are given priority over mortgages).

tax base The assessed valuation of a piece of real property. This value is multiplied by the government's tax rate to determine the amount of property tax due.

tax district The area in which a particular government body has the authority to levy taxes, such as a city or county.

tax lien A registered claim for the nonpayment of property taxes.

tax rate The assessment that is in effect; it is traditionally expressed as the number of dollars per thousand dollars of evaluation.

tax search That part of a title search that determines whether there are any outstanding taxes that would constitute a lien, registered or not, on that property.

termite clause A term in a sale agreement that allows the buyer to inspect for termites. If any are found, the buyer may require the seller to fix the problem; otherwise, the buyer has the right to cancel the sale agreement. Termite infestation can be a serious problem, especially in the southern United States, where the climate can be subtropical.

terms The various clauses in a lease or a purchase or sale agreement.

title The evidence an owner has of his or her right of possession of property.

title company A corporation that sells insurance policies that guarantee the ownership of (and quality of title to) property. Also known as a title insurance company.

title covenants Clauses (i.e., promises) in an instrument of conveyance that give the purchaser assurances that the title to property is good and valid.

title defect A claim against property, such as a tax lien, that affects the owner's title in that property.

title insurance policy An insurance policy that protects an owner (or lender) against loss from defective title.

title report A document that sets out the current state of the title to a specific property.

title search A review of all the recorded documents that affect a particular property. The purpose of this review is to determine the current state of title and usually also to establish whether the current owner has clear title (i.e., without liens, competing claims, mortgages, etc.).

Torrens system A system of registration of ownership of property in which all documents that relate to ownership are closely monitored by the recording agency to make sure that they are correct and that title can be transferred without difficulty.

townhouse A house that is not freestanding; it shares at least one wall with a neighboring house (or houses).

tract A parcel of land. In some areas of the United States, the term also means subdivision.

transfer tax A state tax on the transfer of real property. In some areas of the United States, it is referred to as documentary transfer tax.

trustee Someone who is appointed by a court to execute any kind of trust arrangement. In real estate, a trustee may hold title to property under specific conditions and for a designated period.

U
.....

unencumbered property Property that is free of any liens, claims or mortgages registered against it.

unenforceable contract An agreement that is not legal, for one of many different reasons (e.g., one of the parties to the contract was legally incapacitated, the contract was signed as a result of a threat, some of the terms of the contract are illegal).

Uniform Vendor and Purchaser Risk Act A law that says that both buyer and seller of a property are responsible for any fire damage that occurs between the signing of the agreement of sale and the closing.

uninsurable title Ownership of land that is some way flawed, to the extent that a title company refuses to insure it.

unit A single dwelling in a larger complex. The term is most often used with regard to a condominium project. It refers to a unit (or, in a rental building, an apartment) that is reserved for the exclusive use of the owner, as opposed to the common areas (e.g., lobby, sun deck, laundry room) that are intended for the use of all the owners.

unmarketable title A property that is not saleable because of serious defects in the public record of its ownership. Similar to uninsurable title.

upland Property that borders a body of water.

upset price An amount, set by a court, that creates a base price for an auction of property; the property may not be sold for less than the upset price.

Urban Development Action Grant (UDAG) A loan from the U.S. Department of Housing and Urban Development (HUD) for the revitalization and refurbishment of commercial areas.

urea-formaldehyde form insulation (UFFI) A residential and commercial insulation that was used extensively in buildings during the 1970s. It subsequently was found to emit toxic gases.

Because of health fears, UFFI-insulated buildings now sell for much less than similar properties without such insulation. In many U.S. jurisdictions, the seller of residential property must inform any potential buyer of the presence or absence of UFFI.

use A term mainly used in zoning bylaws or ordinances to indicate the purpose for which a property is occupied. The usual types of use include residential, industrial, commercial and retail.

utilities Services that are needed in any premises or dwelling (e.g., gas, electricity, sewers, water) and that the owner pays for separately from any payments on a loan. In some jurisdictions, arrears in payment of bills for utilities may create a lien on the property.

V

VA see Department of Veterans' Affairs.

VA loan A home loan, offered to a military veteran, that is guaranteed by the U.S. Department of Veterans' Affairs. It allows the veteran to buy a home with no money down.

vacate To move out of premises.

valuation The estimation of the worth, or likely sale price, of land or property. Also known as appraisal.

variance An indulgence that is granted by a local government authority to allow an unconventional use of property. This could be an exception granted to a homeowner that allows him or her to create a basement apartment for a sick relative in an area in which zoning bylaws ordinarily allow for only single-family homes.

vendor Another word for a seller that is commonly used in some kinds of property contracts.

void/void contract A contract that is not legally enforceable (i.e., is canceled).

voluntary lien A claim against property that is registered with the consent of the owner. The most common example is a mortgage. The lender has an enforceable claim against that property until the mortgage loan is paid.

W

walk-through inspection An examination, by the buyer, of the property she or he is purchasing. The walk-through inspection usually takes place immediately before closing and is intended to assure the buyer that no changes have taken place (and no damage has been done) to the property since the buyer agreed to buy. It also reassures the buyer that fixtures and chattels included in the sale actually remain on the property.

warm-air heating system A heating system in which air is heated in a furnace and then circulated through ducts. One of its advantages is that it usually allows for the addition of central air conditioning.

warrant A legally binding assurance that title in any transfer of ownership of property is good.

warranty A legally binding promise that is usually given at the time of sale in which the seller gives the buyer certain assurances as to the condition of the property being sold.

water rights The legal right to use water on a property.

water table There are two meanings for this term: 1.) the accumulation of water below ground or the natural underground water often used for wells; and 2.) the distance from the surface of the ground to this underground water.

wear-and-tear The loss in value of a property that is caused by normal and reasonable use of that property. Usually, in a lease, a tenant is not responsible for normal wear-and-tear in the premises that tenant leases.

weathering The deterioration of the exterior of a building caused by nature (i.e., weather).

without recourse A situation where the lender may look only to the property as security for the loan; the lender may not touch any of the borrower's other assets in the event of a default.

wood-frame construction Buildings in which the internal elements (e.g., walls, floors) are all constructed of wood. This does not refer to the exterior of the building, which may be constructed of other materials, such as brick.

Z

zero lot line The construction of a building on the boundary lines of a lot. This usually is the front line (e.g., a store built directly to the sidewalk). In the older neighborhoods of some American cities, it is also common for residences to be built up to the sidewalk.

Index

· · · · · ·

FREE

Get over $100 in forms online at:

www.socrates.com/books/ForSaleByOwner.aspx

To claim your forms, register your purchase using the registration code provided on the enclosed CD.

FREE FORMS INCLUDE:

- Agreement to Sell Real Estate
- Agreement to Amend Real Estate Purchase Contract
- Lead-Based Paint Disclosure
- Real Estate Sales Disclosure
- Limited Power of Attorney
- Homeowner's Association Disclosure Summary
- Condominium Association Disclosure Statement
- Seller's Acceptance of Purchase Offer
- Checklist for Selling Your Home
- Holding an Open House Getting Ready Checklist
- Prepare Your Home for Sale Checklist
- Sample Sales Contract
- Seller's Checklist – What to Take to closing

Your registration also provides you with a 15% discount on the purchase of other Socrates products for your Personal, Business and Real Estate needs.

For Sale By Owner: Sell Your House, Condo or Townhouse and Save

SPECIAL OFFER FOR BOOK BUYERS—SAVE 15% ON THESE ESSENTIAL LANDLORDING PRODUCTS AT

Socrates.com/books/forsalebyowner.aspx

Socrates.com offers essential business, personal and real estate do-it-yourself products that can help you:

- Sell or lease a property
- Write a will or trust
- Start a business
- Get a divorce
- Hire a contractor
- Manage employees
- And much more

Real Estate Forms Library Software (SS502)

CONTAINS REAL ESTATE DICTIONARY AND MORE THAN 100 LEGAL FORMS

Simplify the process of purchasing or selling real estate and streamline your operations as a landlord. The forms in this comprehensive software will help you hire a real estate agent, make an offer on property, perform a home inspection, evaluate the best mortgage options, write a purchase contract and more. If you are leasing property, these comprehensive forms help you with screening tenants, writing lease agreements, collecting rent and, in extreme cases, starting eviction proceedings.

Personal Legal Forms & Agreements Software (SS4322)

INCLUDES MORE THAN 140 FORMS FOR NEARLY EVERY LEGAL ASPECT OF YOUR LIFE.

There are many occasions in your life—probably more than you think—when you need a legal document to protect yourself or your family and to manage your life more efficiently. With this comprehensive collection of forms and agreements, you'll have the documents you need, when you need them, so you can easily generate legal agreements, manage your credit, create binding contracts and protect yourself against legal action—all without costly legal fees.

FORMS FOR SITUATIONS INCLUDING:

- Basic agreements & contracts
- Loans and borrowing
- Employment
- Credit and collection
- Receipts
- Warranties
- Demands and notices
- Buying and selling
- Leases and tenancies
- Transfers and assignments
- Personal and family issues
- Powers of attorney
- Purchase offers

Last Will & Testament Kit (K307)

INCLUDES INSTRUCTION MANUAL AND 17 FORMS.

Protect your loved ones, make your wishes known and award your assets as you desire. This kit contains the forms and instructions you need to plan your estate responsibly and affordably.

TOPICS COVERED INCLUDE:

- Learning how to prepare your own will
- Determining who will inherit your assets
- Designating a child guardian and executor

Buying & Selling Your Home Kit (K311)

INCLUDES INSTRUCTION MANUAL, 23 FORMS AND LEAD PAINT DISCLOSURE INFORMATION ON CD.

Purchasing or selling a home without a real estate agent can save you money, but it can be a difficult process if you don't have the know-how to do it right. Before you get started, learn how to save time, maximize your profits, reduce legal fees and make the process go smoothly from beginning to end.

TOPICS COVERED INCLUDE:

- Cleaning up your credit & financing
- Pre-qualification vs. preapproval
- Open houses & avoiding discrimination
- Negotiating a sale and sales contracts
- Pre-settlement walk-through
- Tax breaks and more

Living Will & Power of Attorney for Health Care Kit (K306)

INCLUDES INSTRUCTION MANUAL AND 12 FORMS. STATE-SPECIFIC LIVING WILL FORMS AVAILABLE FREE AT SOCRATES.COM WHEN YOU REGISTER YOUR PURCHASE.

No one wants to think about the possibility of being permanently incapacitated and unable to communicate his or her health care preferences. With a living will, you can express, while still in good health, your choice of when to discontinue treatment and life support—and who should have the power to make that decision for you.

TOPICS COVERED INCLUDE:

- Durable power of attorney for health care
- Revoking a power of attorney
- Completing your living will
- Creating your living will
- Revoking your living will

Credit Repair Kit (K303)

INCLUDES INSTRUCTION MANUAL AND 14 FORMS AND LETTERS.

A bad credit report can have a negative effect on your buying power and your life. It can make buying a car or home, obtaining a credit card, entering into leases and other agreements and building the financial future of you and your family difficult, or even impossible. You can take control and turn your credit around with this easy-to-use Credit Repair Kit. It provides everything you need to determine your credit status and repair your credit rating.

TOPICS COVERED INCLUDE:

- Understanding credit ratings and reports
- Common reasons for credit denial
- How to get a copy of your credit report
- Your legal rights
- 10-step strategy to repairing your credit
- Tax liens
- Bankruptcy